Sweet Seasons

Sweet Seasons

FABULOUS RESTAURANT

DESSERTS MADE SIMPLE

Richard Leach

PHOTOGRAPHY BY BOYD HAGEN

WILEY

John Wiley & Sons, Inc.

Earlier versions of recipes appeared as follows:

Pages 5–7, 23–24, 103–104, and 143–144 in *Art Culinaire* (issue numbers 19 [pages 5–7] and 45).

Pages 49, 161–162, 167–169 in *Chocolatier* (March 1990, March 1994, September 1997, respectively).

Pages 15–18 in *Food Arts* (April 1991).

Pages 161–162 in *Great Chefs of the East* (January 1995).

Pages 167–169 in *Pastry Art & Design* (Summer 1997).

This book is printed on acid-free paper. ∞

Published by John Wiley & Sons, Inc.

Published simultaneously in Canada.

This publication is designed to provide accurate and authoritative information in regard to the subject matter covered. It is sold with the understanding that the publisher is not engaged in rendering professional services. If professional advice or other expert assistance is required, the services of a competent professional person should be sought.

LIBRARY OF CONGRESS CATALOGING-IN-PUBLICATION DATA

Leach, Richard, 1965–

      Sweet seasons : fabulous restaurant desserts made simple / Richard Leach ; photography by Boyd Hagen.

          p. cm.   Includes index.

       ISBN-13: 978-0-471-38738-1 (cloth : alk. paper)

       1. Desserts. I. Title.

TX773.L37 2001   641.8'6—dc21   2001017668

PRINTED IN THE UNITED STATES OF AMERICA

Book design by Richard Oriolo

10 9 8 7 6 5

Dedicated to my wife, Diane,

and my sons, Richard and Henry

BASIC RECIPES | 243

In writing this book, much to my surprise, I found that I could utilize some of my skills as a chef. Instead of creating and transferring ideas of my desserts onto plates as I usually do, I placed them on paper. Although the tools and equipment used in writing a book are quite different from those used in a kitchen, my basic organizational skills came in handy. The intense focus and attention to detail were critical as well. As in a kitchen, a dedicated and strong staff of supporters is a must in producing a quality product. Some of the people who have helped me with this book, I have known and relied on for a long time. Others, whom I have

ACKNOWLEDGMENTS

recently met while working on this book, have amazed me with their dedication. ■ **I would like to thank** my wife, Diane—without her dedication, patience, and hard work this book would have been impossible; Boyd Hagen, who shared the same visualization of the desserts and captured them perfectly on film; Karen Gantz Zahler, for selling and pitching the idea behind this book to the right people; JoAnna Turtletaub, for believing in this book and bringing it to life, and Eileen Chetti, of John Wiley & Sons, Inc., as well as designer Richard Oriolo; Fred Miller, my sous chef, who watched over the restaurant as I worked on this book; my father and my sister Carol, for their help on the impressive book proposal; the management and staff of Park Avenue Cafe, for their cooperation with the making of this book; and Bernardaud China, for supplying their beautiful china for some of the photographs. ■ **If ever any of you** are willing to put on some whites and sweat it out, you are always welcome in my kitchen.

I wasn't born with a sweet tooth, and you will not find me craving pints of ice cream or raw cookie dough. In fact, I am not sure whether there is any sugar in my house. I was not born to bake. For me, making desserts is a profession and a craft, not a deliberate move to supply some craving for sweets. ■ **My looks are deceiving. I** am tall and thin, which seems to surprise a lot of people when I tell them what I do for a living. I am not quite sure what people expect: the fat, jolly little chef dipping his finger in the frosting? I have a reputation for being demanding. This is a characteristic, I feel, that is necessary in organizing and motivating a team of cooks.

INTRODUCTION

Assembling my desserts calls for quickness, efficient moves, cleanliness, exact timing, and organized, repetitive steps. These characteristics ensure consistent quality and perfect presentations. ■ **I base my desserts on** my past cooking experiences and schooling. Except for three weeks of pastry classes at the Culinary Institute of America, I am self-taught. I was always very lucky to be among inspiring people, not only the chefs I have worked for but the line cooks as well. When I started as a line cook at the River Café, it was a terrific experience, in a demanding and disciplined environment. Not only did I feel pressure to do my best from the chef and sous chefs but from the other cooks as well. This type of environment ensured a great work ethic from everyone and a strong camaraderie among the cooks. This attitude was carried over and adapted to Aureole when it opened in 1988. With the opening of Aureole, I had asked if I could work in the pastry department. At that point, I was a cook who wanted to learn more about pastry so that some day I would be a more well-rounded chef. I was given the job of assistant pastry chef under the helm of Gerry Hayden, the opening pastry chef. Gerry was a great inspiration and also a former line cook who stepped into pastry to help open the restaurant. A couple of months later, when Gerry decided that he wanted to return to cooking, Charlie Palmer offered me a once-in-a-lifetime opportunity to give pastry my best shot. By experimenting, reading, and putting in too many hours to count, that's what I did. I began to read everything. I reviewed my old school notes and picked up a few basic pastry books. These books were good for the basics, but only so much of the information could be applied to a restaurant situation. I liked the style of cooking I had done in the past and decided to look at cooking as an influence. For inspiration, I would watch the cooking presentations at Aureole and started reading more cookbooks than pastry books. At the time, new American cuisine was the cutting edge and getting a great deal of attention. I thought I would try to adapt this style to pastry and push it a little further. ■ **My style grew out of** a combination of cooking skill and lack of classical pastry training. The vertical and architectural presentations blend imagination with practicality and reflect the geometric shapes of the equipment I use. To me, visually, some classical pastry never made sense. I do not agree with deliberately representing animals or anything else. I always thought that cuteness in food should be reserved for the children's menu. In the restaurants that I have worked in, people expect top-quality food, excellent service, and beautiful ambience, and in my mind, dessert should be a memorable ending to a great meal. Nature and food are made up of geometric shapes and clean lines of design. I wanted a new look based on these shapes—a look that respects dessert as food, giving it the same stature as appetizers or entrees. I always thought that desserts should be much more serious and less playful but at the same time be visually striking. Customers watch the desserts as they move across a dining room. In a restaurant, a dessert can sell itself by looking great and attracting attention. I started by standing components on end to give them some height and an off-balance look that will catch someone's eye. I like to add contrast to dessert by stacking or layering different components of temperature and texture, so that when my desserts are eaten, some elements are hot and cold, or smooth and crunchy. I do not alter my recipes or make items extra-thick or strong to make a look happen. If the initial look and concept of a dessert go as planned, great; if not, I change it. ■ **When I create a dessert,** I always begin with a flavor or combination of flavors that are going to be in season. I try to prepare ahead and think of ideas slightly before a season begins. The time of year, fruits, and seasonal ingredients determine whether the components will be hot, cold, soft, or crunchy. Sometimes I like them to be a little of each. Once I know the components, I look at the cooking preparation and limitations. This determines the shapes and sizes that I can use. I sketch some ideas for the look of a dish and follow with a few trial-and-error tests. The dessert then goes on the menu and stands the trial of service, where the kinks are worked out. ■ **Because my roots in the** food industry are from cooking and not baking, I approach my desserts from a cook's view and build it from its simple natural state. I may start out thinking strawberries, then think of accompaniments, flavor combinations, or presentations that I have done in the past. Over the years, I built up and stored away ideas of dishes and combinations that have been successful. Of course there is always space for something new. It is my past line-cooking experience that makes me combine and finish desserts to order as you would with hot food. Not only can it give your desserts a fresher appeal, but it allows you to combine different textures and temperatures at the last second before the plate is presented. I like to use fresh real products, as opposed to prepackaged products, and to start from scratch. I do not buy premade garnishes, frozen fruit purees, or shortcut items. I enjoy the skill and results of cooking and creating desserts from simple ingredients. Nothing compares to starting a dessert with a great raw product, especially fruit. Whenever possible, I add sliced or diced fruit to a plate; this can add contrast and texture to a dish. ■ **In this book, the desserts** are real. They all have been listed on my menus and served at the restaurants in which I have worked over the years. When you place an order for dessert, this is what you will get. ■ **Organization of your work, yourself,** and your staff is the key to making it all happen. I could never do all of this work alone and I would never claim to. I have always been fortunate to have a strong staff of cooks. One of the most enjoyable parts of the restaurant business is the diversity of the staff. People come from all over the world to work in New York City. It's a great combination of talented chefs, freaks, beginners, and people who should never be cooking. Add a few languages, stressful situations at a fast pace, and sharp knives, and you have a restaurant kitchen. There are times when the combinations of personalities click and the motivation of the crew can end up pushing you more than you know. If everyone shares the same enthusiasm, it can be a great working experience. ■ **That is my world at** the restaurant. If you are a professional, you are familiar with this environment. If you are a home cook, you will find some guidance for organizing and preparing these desserts helpful. I have tried to provide a time line for producing different components, instructions on how to store them, and methods for reheating them when necessary. Most of the ingredients are fairly common and easily found. For some unique items I have provided an ingredients listing for substitutions or sources. ■ **I don't expect all readers** to put in the time required to create some of the desserts in this book. The dishes here are my suggestion and my arrangement and design. Feel free to rearrange and disassemble them as you wish. All of the recipes and components have been separated so that they can be combined easily to create a dessert or used alone. You can simply serve some goat cheese fritters with your favorite ice cream or feel adventurous and use my suggestion of pear soup. The visual impact of a dessert is my impression and design, but is your option. You may even use one of the looks to improve a presentation of your own. Ultimately, by looking at these dishes, you will develop a style of your own. Books have always been a great inspiration for me, and I do hope this book gives you some inspiration to try recipes and create your own desserts.

Fall's arrival seems, to me, to be a fresh start. The cool and crisp morning air wakes me up and makes me feel alive. What a great relief it is from New York City's summer heat and humidity. Summer's work conditions are a pastry chef's worst nightmare and the cool fall weather means smooth sailing until May, when the heat returns. For city restaurants, this is the start of the busiest time of the year, as local people return home from their vacations and the holiday season begins. ▪ **With the onset of cooler** weather, summer fruits seem to vanish abruptly. In their place, many varieties of apples, pears, pumpkins, figs, and grapes become readily available. Dried fruits, seeds, chocolate, nuts, and spices are seasonal dessert components that I consider. To me, all of these ingredients symbolize fall holidays and family traditions: apple picking, cider drinking, and pumpkin carving. ▪ **Which variety of apples do** I use? These are my simple rules: Tart apples, such as Granny Smiths or Jonathans, have a firmer, crunchier flesh that is best used raw, sliced, baked for tarts, or poached. Naturally sweet apples, like Rome or Golden or Red Delicious, have a softer flesh and are naturally higher in sugar content. These types of apple do not hold up well to the heat of baking or poaching, so I like to use them for purees, sorbets, and fillings. Last is the category of apples that fall in between. These apples, such as Ida Red and Empire, are crunchy, sweet with a touch of tartness, and work well cooked or raw. They are great all-purpose apples and usually the ones that I use. ▪ **In deciding on pears, texture** and the cooking process determine which variety I choose. Bartlett pears are juicy, soft, and sweet and work well in baking, and are also the best for sorbets and purees. Firmer-textured pears, such as Anjou, are better for baking and poaching. ▪ **In autumn, my desserts and** the fall ingredients that I use tend to be naturally richer and denser, as opposed to the lighter and more refreshing feel of my spring and summer desserts. Customers seem to look for richer desserts when it gets cooler outdoors, and mine tend to have a comforting, warm tone that offsets the chill in the air. When the weather is brisk, my recipes are more likely to incorporate brandies and liqueurs, which I rarely use in the warmer seasons. ▪ **The following recipes are some** of my fall favorites. I have included a few recipes with certain ingredients such as apples and pears because so many varieties of each are available in abundance this time of the year. Several desserts are based on fall traditions and flavors, to which I look forward every year.

Chilled Pear Soup with Goat Cheese Fritters

CHILLED PEAR SOUP

6 very ripe Bartlett pears

2 vanilla beans, split in half and seeds scraped

1 cup / 236 ml granulated sugar

Peel, core, and dice the pears. Place in a saucepan and add the scraped pods and seeds of vanilla beans, and sugar. Add enough water to just cover the pears. Place over medium heat and simmer until pears are tender. Take out the vanilla pods. Remove mixture from heat and puree until fine. Pass through a chinois and cool in an ice bath. Keep cold.

GOAT CHEESE FRITTERS

Vegetable oil, for deep-frying

1 cup / 236 ml fresh goat cheese

1 cup / 236 ml ricotta cheese

2 egg whites

1 cup / 236 ml semolina flour

½ cup / 118 ml cake flour

¾ cup / 177 ml granulated sugar

1½ tablespoons / 22 ml baking powder

½ teaspoon / 2 ml salt

½ cup / 118 ml confectioners' sugar

Heat the oil in a deep fryer to 325 degrees. Combine all ingredients in a mixing bowl and mix until well blended. To deep-fry, carefully spoon 1 teaspoon of mixture into the oil at a time. Allow fritters to fry until golden brown, about 3 minutes, then remove from the fryer and drain on towel. Dust with the confectioners' sugar.

GOAT CHEESE TIMBALES

2 cups / 473 ml fresh goat cheese

Cream the goat cheese until smooth and pack into 1-inch timbales.

ASSEMBLY

Goat Cheese Timbales

2 Bartlett pears, peeled, cored, and julienned

Chilled Pear Soup

Goat Cheese Fritters

Honey Tuiles (page 247)

Unmold the goat cheese timbales into eight small glass dessert bowls. Carefully place the julienned pears on top of the timbales. Pour the pear soup around the timbales. Place five goat cheese fritters next to each soup bowl and garnish the bowls with the tuiles.

SERVES 8

The key to this soup is to use very soft, very ripe pears. Pears in this condition will provide the smooth texture and potent flavor that makes the dish light and refreshing. The warm fritters should be crisp on the outside and moist on the inside. I feel that the two components complement each other extremely well. The pear soup can be prepared a day in advance, but the fritters should be made as you need them.

Pear and Pistachio Torte with Pear Fritters and Roasted Pear Puree

PEAR AND PISTACHIO TORTE

Pistachio Genoise

6 eggs

1½ cups / 354 ml granulated sugar

½ cup / 118 ml sifted cake flour

3 tablespoons / 45 ml sifted cornstarch

½ cup / 118 ml pistachio flour

2 tablespoons / 30 g unsalted butter, melted

Roasted Pear and Mascarpone Filling

½ cup / 118 ml Roasted Pear Puree

½ cup / 118 ml mascarpone cheese

½ cup / 118 ml heavy cream

2 tablespoons / 29 ml granulated sugar

Roasted Pear Puree

5 Bartlett pears

2 tablespoons / 30 ml clarified butter

½ cup / 118 ml honey

4 tablespoons / 58 ml Pear Williams liqueur

Preheat oven to 325 degrees. Generously butter two 8-inch round cake pans.

Combine eggs and sugar in a mixing bowl and whisk over hot water until slightly warm. With an electric mixer, whisk until fluffy and pale yellow, 8 to 10 minutes. Gently fold in the dry ingredients and then the butter. Pour batter into cake pans and bake until light golden in color and firm to the touch, about 30 minutes. Allow cakes to cool slightly, then remove from pan to a wire rack to cool. Refrigerate overnight. Cold cakes will slice more easily.

Combine all ingredients for the filling in an electric mixer bowl and whisk until stiff. Refrigerate until ready to use.

Cut the genoise into three ¼-inch slices. Place a disk of parchment paper on the bottom of an 8-inch cake pan. Put a layer of cake in the pan and then pipe a ¼-inch layer of filling. Continue to alternate layers until you have three layers of cake and two layers of filling in between. Chill for at least 4 hours, then cut into eight equal wedges. Trim the round end of the cake wedge flat so that it will stand on end.

Preheat oven to 450 degrees.

Peel, core, and quarter pears. Place a heavy roasting pan in hot oven and heat pan for 10 minutes. Quickly and carefully add the butter and pears. Stir and then roast until nicely browned and tender, 10–15 minutes. Add honey and roast until honey begins to caramelize, an additional 5 minutes. Remove from the oven and deglaze pan with liqueur. Once cooled, puree pears in a food processor until smooth. Set aside.

SERVES 8

This balancing act was always a surprise for customers and a challenge for the waitstaff. The cool weather brings out the city street vendors selling roasted nuts, offering a smell that seems to match the fall season. A variety of pears are available—ripe, juicy Bartletts are my choice. They have a terrific flavor, a smooth texture, and a great fragrance. All the components of this recipe should be prepared one day in advance.

CHEF'S NOTE

Pistachio flour (for the pistachio genoise) is nothing more than pistachios ground very fine. It can be purchased commercially, but I have yet to see it available at retail stores.

PEAR FRITTERS

Vegetable oil, for deep-frying

2 halves Poached Pears ∎

2½ cups / 591 ml all-purpose flour

1 cup / 236 ml granulated sugar

2 tablespoons / 29 ml baking powder

2 cups / 473 ml cold water

2 cups / 473 ml Panko bread crumbs (available in Japanese markets)

¼ cup / 58 ml confectioners' sugar, for dusting

∎ Poached Pears

4 Bartlett pears

2 cups / 473 ml granulated sugar

2 cups / 473 ml water

Juice of 1 lemon

1 cinnamon stick

½ vanilla bean

Heat the oil to 350 degrees.

Slice each pear half into eight wedges. Pat the pears dry with a towel. Combine flour, sugar, and baking powder in a mixing bowl and whisk in the cold water until smooth. Dip the pears in the batter, coating lightly. Roll in bread crumbs and deep-fry until golden brown, about 4 to 6 minutes. Drain on paper and dust with confectioners' sugar.

Peel, core, and halve the pears. Combine pears with remaining ingredients in a saucepan and place over high heat, bringing to a boil. Reduce the heat and simmer until the pears are tender, about 10–15 minutes. Cool pears in the liquid.

STRUDEL DOUGH TUBES

4 sheets strudel dough

½ cup / 118 ml clarified butter

Preheat oven to 350 degrees.

Carefully spread a sheet of strudel dough out on a flat surface. Lightly brush with melted butter and place another sheet of dough on top. Continue until there are four sheets of dough. Cut into 3-inch-wide strips. Roll dough strips onto metal pipes that measure 4 inches long and 1 inch in diameter. Bake until golden brown, about 10–15 minutes. Allow to cool and slide off the pipe. Store in an airtight container.

SPICED GRAPES

24 red seedless grapes

1 cup / 236 ml water

½ cup / 118 ml granulated sugar

1 tablespoon / 15 ml mustard seeds, toasted

1 cardamom pod, toasted

10 white peppercorns

1 cinnamon stick

1 whole clove

1 teaspoon / 5 ml lemon juice

Place grapes in a large bowl. In a saucepan, combine the rest of the ingredients and bring to a boil. Pour the hot liquid over the grapes. Allow to cool, then refrigerate overnight. Store grapes in the liquid.

PEAR SORBET

6 ripe or overripe Bartlett pears

1 cup / 236 ml granulated sugar

2 cups / 473 ml water

1 tablespoon / 15 ml lemon juice

Peel, core, and quarter pears. Combine all ingredients in a saucepan, bring to a boil, reduce heat, and simmer until tender, about 20 minutes. Remove from the stove and place in an ice bath to cool. Once cooled, puree until smooth and pass through a fine sieve. Process in an ice cream machine according to the manufacturer's instructions.

ASSEMBLY

Pear and Pistachio Torte

Strudel Dough Tubes

Pear Fritters

2 cups Pear Sabayon Sauce (page 250)

½ cup Pistachio Oil (page 259)

Spiced Grapes

Roasted Pear Puree

Strudel Crisps (page 252)

Pear Sorbet

Sugar Garnish (page 253)

Serve on eight long or oval plates. On each plate, stand a wedge of the torte off center toward one end of the plate. Stand a strudel tube off center toward the opposite side of the plate. Leave a 2-inch space in between. Place the pear fritters between the two. Pipe two pools of sabayon sauce, one in front of the torte and the other in front of the strudel tube. Drizzle pistachio oil around the plate. Slice grapes in half and place around the plate. Fill the strudel tube halfway with pear puree. Carefully balance the strudel crisp on top of the torte and strudel tube, creating a bridge. Gently place a small scoop of sorbet on the center of the strudel crisp. Lean a sugar stick against the sorbet.

Roasted Pears on Brioche with Frozen Pear Pops

ROASTED PEARS

5 Anjou pears

2 tablespoons / 30 ml clarified butter

½ cup / 118 ml honey

1 4- to 5-inch sprig fresh rosemary

4 tablespoons / 58 ml Pear Williams liqueur

Preheat oven to 450 degrees.

Place a heavy roasting pan in oven and heat for 10 minutes. Peel, core, and halve the pears. Carefully add the butter and pears to pan, stir, and roast until pears are nicely brown and tender, about 10–15 minutes. Add honey and rosemary, and continue to roast until the honey begins to caramelize, about 5 minutes more. Remove from oven and deglaze pan with the liqueur. Once cooled, remove from the pan, and cut each pear half into four slices. Discard liqueur.

BRIOCHE DISKS

¼ cup / 59 ml milk

*2 tablespoons fresh yeast or
1 tablespoon dry active yeast*

2¼ cups / 53 g all-purpose flour

4 eggs

2 tablespoons / 30 ml granulated sugar

1 teaspoon / 5 ml salt

1 cup / 225 g unsalted butter, at room temperature, in pieces

In a small mixing bowl, warm the milk to body temperature, then add the yeast and ¼ cup of the flour. Whisk until smooth, cover with plastic wrap, and leave to rise in a warm place until doubled in size, about 10–15 minutes. Transfer yeast mixture to a larger mixing bowl and add the eggs, remaining flour, the sugar, and salt. Using a dough hook attachment, mix the ingredients until smooth and elastic, approximately 10 minutes. On medium speed, slowly incorporate the butter a little at a time, allowing it to incorporate each time. Mix the ingredients for 1 to 2 minutes, and then remove from the machine. Cover the dough with a damp towel and allow to rise until doubled in size, about 30 minutes. Punch dough down and refrigerate for 4 to 6 hours before using.

The brioche is baked in four metal ring molds 3 inches in diameter and 1½ inches high. Once the dough is ready, remove from refrigerator and roll into small balls about one-third the size of the ring molds. Place balls in molds, cover, and allow to rise in a warm place for 20–30 minutes, or until balls double in size.

Preheat oven to 300 degrees. Cover molds and dough with a sheet of parchment paper and a flat

SERVES 8

You just cannot beat the combination of smooth warm pears, crunchy phyllo, crispy kataifi, and a chewy brioche all joined together with a touch of cream and the fragrance of rosemary. As for the pops, what's better than food on a stick? With the exception of the roasted pears, everything can be prepared one day in advance.

sheet pan. Place in oven and bake until golden brown, about 15–25 minutes. Cool the brioche, remove from the rings, and trim the ends. Cut brioche in half, making two flat, round disks.

STRUDEL BALLS

2 sheets strudel dough

¼ cup / 59 ml clarified butter

Preheat oven to 350 degrees.

Carefully spread a sheet of strudel dough on a flat surface and lightly brush with butter. Place the second sheet on stop. Use a 5-inch round cutter to cut the strudel dough into eight disks. Fold and twist each disk into a ball shape. Place each ball in a 3-inch-diameter ring mold and bake until golden brown, about 10–15 minutes. Allow to cool and remove from the rings.

KATAIFI DISKS

¼ package kataifi dough

¼ cup / 59 ml clarified butter

1 tablespoon / 15 ml confectioners' sugar

Preheat oven to 350 degrees.

Carefully separate the strands of kataifi dough and gently toss with butter and sugar to lightly coat. Fill 4-inch tartlet pans with enough dough to cover the bottom. Place another pan on top to sandwich the dough. Bake until the dough is golden brown, about 10–20 minutes. Store in an airtight container.

PEAR SYRUP

4 Anjou pears

1 vanilla bean, split in half

6 cups / 1419 ml water

3 cups / 709 ml granulated sugar

Juice of ½ lemon

Cut the pears into large dice and place in a large saucepan. Add the rest of the ingredients and cook over a medium heat until mixture is reduced by half, about 30 minutes. Strain and cool.

FROZEN PEAR POPS

16 Seckel pears

6 cups / 1419 ml water

3 cups / 709 ml granulated sugar

1 vanilla bean, split in half

Zest of 1 orange

Juice of 1 lemon

1½ cups / 354 ml vanilla ice cream, softened

Peel the pears and trim the stems with a knife. Using a small Parisian scoop, remove the seeds from the bottom of each pear. In a small saucepan, combine remaining ingredients. Add pears and bring the mixture to a simmer and cook until tender, about 10–15 minutes. Remove the pot and place in an ice bath to cool. Once the pears are cooled, remove from poaching liquid and place on a towel to drain.

Place the vanilla ice cream in a small piping bag and

carefully pipe some ice cream into the bottom of each pear. Immediately place the pears in the freezer. Once pears are firm, put a cocktail stirrer into the stem end of each pear. Keep frozen.

VANILLA PASTRY CREAM

1 cup / 236 ml milk

¼ cup / 55 ml granulated sugar

½ vanilla bean, split in half

1 tablespoon / 15 ml cornstarch

1½ tablespoons / 22 ml cold milk

4 egg yolks

2 tablespoons / 30 g unsalted butter

In a small saucepan, combine milk, sugar, and vanilla bean. Bring the mixture to a simmer and then cool.

In a small mixing bowl, combine the cornstarch and cold milk, whisking until smooth and dissolved. Add the egg yolks and cooled milk to the cornstarch. Strain the mixture into a clean bowl and place in a double boiler. Whisk mixture over hot water until thick, approximately 10 minutes. Remove from heat and whisk in the butter. Transfer the mixture to a clean pan and refrigerate until cool.

ASSEMBLY

Brioche Disks, toasted

Vanilla Pastry Cream

Kataifi Disks

Roasted Pears

Strudel Balls

Pear Syrup

2 cups Rosemary Sabayon Sauce (page 250)

Frozen Pear Pops

1 cup Meringue Crumbs (page 248)

Honey Tuiles (page 247)

Sugar Garnish (page 253)

Place a toasted brioche disk toward the front of each of eight plates. Pipe a small amount of pastry cream on top of the brioche. Place a kataifi disk on top of the cream. Arrange the roasted pear slices on top of the kataifi disk and carefully place the strudel ball on top of the pears. Pipe some pear syrup around the base of the brioche. Place some dots of sabayon sauce around the syrup. Dip two frozen pear pops, bottoms only, into the meringue crumbs to coat. Place the pear pops toward the back of the plate. On the handle of each pop, carefully place a honey tuile. Place a sugar stick through the strudel ball.

Pear Gratin with Frozen Pear Dacquoise

SERVES 8

This is certainly not an authentic dacquoise. The crunchy layers of meringue are still there, but the buttery filling has been replaced with a light layer of pear sorbet. The glazed pear and cheese gratin provides a warm and creamy contrast to the chilled dacquoise. All components of this dish except for the sautéed pears can be prepared a day in advance, especially the dacquoise. Prepare the sautéed pears at the last minute so they can be served warm.

PEAR GRATIN

Ricotta Cheese Custard

1½ cups / 354 ml cream cheese

¾ cup / 177 ml ricotta cheese

½ cup / 118 ml granulated sugar

½ vanilla bean, split open and seeds scraped

2 whole eggs

1 egg white

¾ cup / 177 ml heavy cream

Slow-Baked Pears

6 Bartlett pears

1 cup / 236 ml granulated sugar

FROZEN DACQUOISE

1½ cups / 348 ml granulated sugar

½ cup / 118 ml almonds, sliced and blanched

½ cup / 118 ml confectioners' sugar

5 egg whites

3 cups Pear Sorbet (page 7)

Preheat oven to 275 degrees.

In an electric mixer bowl, combine the cream cheese, ricotta, sugar, and vanilla seeds. Cream until smooth, then add the whole eggs and egg white, and cream until smooth. Add the cream and mix until incorporated. Pour the mixture into eight 3-inch-diameter gratin dishes and bake in a water bath until set and firm, about 30 minutes. Remove and allow to cool.

Preheat oven to 250 degrees.

Peel the pears and cut 1 inch off the neck of each pear. Cut each pear around the core into four pieces. Slice each piece into very thin slices, using a knife or mandolin. Sprinkle a thin layer of sugar on a silicone baking sheet and spread the pear slices out on top of the sugar. Sprinkle more sugar on top of the pears and bake for 10 minutes. Once the pear slices have cooled, arrange them in a fan pattern around the top of the cheese custard.

Preheat oven to 250 degrees.

Create a stencil (page 252) that will be the width and length of the terrine or loaf pan, about 3½ inches by 9 inches, that you are using to mold the dacquoise.

In a food processor, combine 1 cup of the granulated sugar, the almonds, and confectioners' sugar, and puree until smooth. In an electric mixer bowl, whisk the egg whites until soft peaks are formed and add the remaining ½ cup sugar. Continue to whisk until firm peaks are formed. Fold in the dry ingredients.

On parchment-lined sheet trays, using the stencil that you have created, spread the meringue on the stencil to create five long rectangles. Remove the stencil. Bake until light golden brown, 20 to 30 minutes. Remove from oven and allow to cool.

Line terrine mold with parchment paper. Place a sheet of meringue on the bottom and spread a layer of equal thickness of pear sorbet. Continue alternating the meringue and sorbet until you have five layers of meringue and four layers of sorbet. Place in the freezer and freeze overnight. Once frozen, slice into 1-inch-thick slices.

SAUTÉED PEARS

3 Bartlett pears

½ cup / 118 ml granulated sugar

½ vanilla bean, split open and seeds scraped

⅛ teaspoon / .62 ml grated orange rind

¼ cup / 59 ml Pear Williams liqueur

Peel and dice the pears. Preheat a large sauté pan and add the granulated sugar. Slowly allow the sugar to caramelize to a light, amber color. Sauté the diced pears with the vanilla seeds for about 2 minutes. Add the orange rind and liqueur. Flame the liqueur, which eliminates some of the alcohol, and remove from the heat. Set aside.

ASSEMBLY

Pear Gratin

1 cup Brûlée Sugar (page 244)

Honey Tuiles (page 247)

Sautéed Pears

Vanilla Ice Cream (page 254)

Frozen Dacquoise

2 cups Vanilla Sabayon Sauce (page 250)

1 cup Clear Caramel Sauce (page 246)

Sugar Garnish (page 253)

Sprinkle each gratin with brûlée sugar and glaze lightly with a blowtorch. Place each gratin in the center of an oval plate. On one side of the gratin place a honey tuile and fill with the sautéed pears. Place a small scoop of the vanilla ice cream on top of the pears. On the opposite side of the gratin, place a slice of the frozen dacquoise. Pipe sabayon sauce and caramel sauce around the plates and decorate with a sugar garnish.

Warm Apple Tart with Sour Cream Ice Cream and Date Puree

APPLE TART

4 Empire apples

8 disks puff pastry, in 5-inch rounds (page 249)

1 cup / 236 ml Roasted Apple Puree

3 tablespoons / 44 ml clarified butter

½ cup / 118 ml Brûlée Sugar (page 244)

Preheat oven to 325 degrees.

Peel and core apples; cut each apple into 24 slices. Place each disk of pastry in a 4-inch flan ring. The edge of the dough should form a rim halfway up the inside of the flan ring. Spread ¼-inch layer of apple puree on the bottom of each shell. Fan out apple slices in a circular pattern on top of the puree. Brush the apples lightly with clarified butter and sprinkle with brûlée sugar. Bake for 40 minutes or until the bottom of the dough is golden brown. Allow to cool. When ready to serve, reheat the tart in a 325-degree oven for five minutes.

Roasted Apple Puree

6 Empire apples

½ cup / 118 ml granulated sugar

Preheat oven to 275 degrees.

Peel, core, and quarter apples. Place apples on a papered sheet pan and sprinkle with sugar. Roast until soft and light brown, about 1 hour. Remove from oven and allow to cool. Place into a food processor and puree until smooth. Refrigerate.

DATE PUREE BARRELS

3 cups / 709 ml pitted dates

1 cup / 236 ml Panko bread crumbs (available in Japanese groceries)

2 cups / 473 ml sliced, blanched almonds, toasted

Place dates in a saucepan and cover with water; bring to a boil, and drain. Place softened, warm dates in a food mill and pass through to remove skins. Mix date paste well with the bread crumbs and refrigerate until cold. Roll date paste into ½-inch barrel-shaped balls, then roll in almonds. Set aside. Refrigerate to store overnight.

SOUR CREAM ICE CREAM

4 cups / 946 ml heavy cream

1½ cups / 354 ml granulated sugar

12 egg yolks

2 cups / 473 ml sour cream

Combine cream and sugar in a saucepan and bring to a boil. Place the egg yolks in a large bowl. In one motion, whisk the hot cream into the yolks. Stir in sour cream. Pass mixture through a fine sieve. Chill, then process in an ice cream machine according to the manufacturer's instructions. Allow to freeze at least 4 hours.

SERVES 8

This adaptation of a classic apple tart is enriched by the roasted apple puree and the smooth, tangy sour cream ice cream. The date puree is an easy way to prepare and eat dried fruit. With the exception of the apple tart, all the components can be prepared up to two days in advance.

APPLE CHIPS

1 cup / 236 ml Roasted Apple Puree
(page 15)

Create and cut a stencil (page 252) out of plastic. Spread the puree on a nonstick silicone baking sheet. Bake at 200 degrees until dry and crisp, about 2 hours. Remove while warm and bend chips around a 3-inch jar or can to create curved shapes. Store in an airtight container.

MERINGUE CUPS

1 cup / 236 ml sliced, blanched almonds

1 cup / 236 ml granulated sugar

½ cup / 118 ml confectioners' sugar

5 egg whites

Preheat oven to 225 degrees.

Combine almonds, ½ cup granulated sugar, and confectioners' sugar in a food processor and puree until fine. Whip egg whites into soft peaks. Slowly add remaining ½ cup granulated sugar and continue to whisk until stiff peaks form. Fold dry ingredients into egg whites. Fill a pastry bag with meringue and pipe mixture into well-greased mini muffin pans. Bake for 10 minutes, then remove and gently press meringues with a stick or knife end to create a cup shape. Place back in the oven and bake until dry and light golden brown, about 1 hour. Allow to cool. Store in an air-tight container.

ASSEMBLY

2 cups Vanilla Sabayon Sauce (page 250)

½ cup Clear Caramel Sauce (page 246)

Apple Tart

2 fresh Empire apples, cut into 1-inch batons

Date Puree Barrels

Sour Cream Ice Cream

Meringue Cups

Apple Chips

Sugar Garnish (page 253)

Pipe a 5-inch circle of vanilla sabayon in the center of each dessert plate. Pipe a thin border of caramel sauce along the outside of the sabayon. Place a tart in the center of the sauce. Placing off center on the apple tart, crisscross and stack four apple batons. Place a date barrel on top of the batons. Scoop a small ball of ice cream onto a meringue cup and place cup opposite the batons on the apple tart. Stick two apple chips into the ice cream ball and lean against the date barrel. Run a sugar stick through the date barrel into the tart.

Apple Terrine with Pistachios and Apple Strudel

APPLE TERRINE WITH PISTACHIOS

Vanilla Crepes

¾ cup / 177 ml all-purpose flour

2 egg yolks

2 whole eggs

1 cup / 236 ml milk

¼ cup / 55 g unsalted butter

½ vanilla bean, split in half

Roasted Pistachio Paste

2 cups / 473 ml shelled pistachios

1 cup / 236 ml granulated sugar

Pistachio Mascarpone Filling

1½ cups / 354 ml mascarpone cheese

½ cup / 118 ml heavy cream

Caramelized Apples

4 Ida Red apples

1½ cups / 354 ml granulated sugar

Place flour in a medium mixing bowl. In a separate small bowl, combine and whisk together yolks, whole eggs, and milk. Slowly whisk wet ingredients into flour until smooth. Melt butter with vanilla bean and whisk together. Add melted butter to the batter. Using an 8-inch nonstick sauté pan, make the crepes (page 247). You will need ten crepes in total. Set aside.

In a 350-degree oven, toast the pistachios for the paste on a sheet tray for 15 minutes. Combine the pistachios with the sugar and puree in a food processor until smooth. Measure out ¾ cup for the filling and set the rest aside.

Combine mascarpone cheese, cream, and ¾ cup pistachio paste in a mixing bowl and whisk until stiff. Keep refrigerated until ready to use.

Peel and core the apples to be caramelized. Cut into ¼-inch-thick wedges. Sprinkle the bottom of a sauté pan with the sugar and place over high heat. Once the sugar starts to caramelize, place the apple wedges in the pan and caramelize on both sides. Remove from the pan and allow to cool.

To assemble, line a 4-inch by 10-inch terrine with plastic wrap. Place two crepes in the pan to cover the bottom. Pipe a thin layer of filling on top. Follow with another layer of two crepes, then some pistachio paste. Add a layer of caramelized apples and repeat layers of filling, paste, crepes, and caramelized apples until terrine is full. Refrigerate overnight.

SERVES 8

As if the many layers and textures of the terrine were not enough, I threw in the bonus of a crisp, warm strudel. With the exception of the strudel, everything in this recipe can be made a day in advance.

CHEF'S NOTE

For the caramelized apples, sauté small amounts of apples at a time. Put in just enough apples to almost cover the bottom of the pan, and repeat the process until the apples are done. Do not overfill your pan.

APPLE STRUDEL

2 Ida Red apples

¼ cup / 59 ml granulated sugar

4 sheets strudel dough

½ cup / 118 ml clarified butter

Peel and core apples for the filling. Cut apples into medium dice. In a sauté pan, sprinkle bottom of pan with sugar and place over high heat. Once sugar starts to caramelize, add the apples and sauté until tender.

Preheat oven to 350 degrees.

Carefully spread a sheet of strudel dough on a flat surface. Lightly brush with butter and place another sheet of strudel dough on top. Continue until there are four sheets of strudel dough.

Cut dough into eight 5-inch disks. Place a small amount of apple filling in center of each disk and fold sides over to create a pouch. Place pouches on a parchment-lined sheet tray with the seam side down. Bake for 20 to 30 minutes, until golden brown.

ASSEMBLY

Apple Terrine with Pistachios

2 cups Applejack Sabayon Sauce (page 250)

½ cup Clear Caramel Sauce (page 246)

Apple Strudel

Honey Tuiles (page 247)

Vanilla Ice Cream (page 254)

Whipped crème fraîche

Finely chopped pistachios

Sugar Garnish (page 253)

Cut the apple terrine into ½-inch-thick slices and place each slice in the center of eight oval or rectangular plates. Pipe two small pools of sabayon sauce, one on each side of each terrine slice. Pipe a thin line of caramel sauce above and below the terrine slice. Place the strudel on one of the pools of sauce. On the opposite sauce pool, place a small, round tuile and put a small ball of ice cream on top. Carefully place a small quenelle of whipped crème fraîche next to the strudel. Sprinkle with chopped pistachios. Lay two sugar sticks across the plate, resting on top of the ice cream and crème fraîche.

Roasted Apple Tartlet with Beignet and Cider Parfait

SERVES 8

The three components of this dessert provide something for everyone. Warmth is provided by the moist apple tartlet, chewiness by the fresh yeast beignet, and a tart sensation by the parfait. Prepare the cider parfaits and sauces a day in advance.

APPLE-DATE BEIGNETS

2 tablespoons fresh yeast or 1 tablespoon dry active yeast

2 tablespoons / 30 g milk

1 egg

2 cups / 500 ml all-purpose flour

½ cup / 118 ml granulated sugar

¾ teaspoon / 3 ml salt

½ cup / 118 ml water

2 tablespoons / 30 g unsalted butter

½ pound / 225 g pitted dates

3 Empire apples

Vegetable oil, for deep-frying

1 cup / 236 ml Brûlée Sugar (page 244)

Combine yeast and milk in a large mixing bowl and whisk until the yeast is dissolved. Add egg, flour, ¼ cup of the sugar, and salt. In a small saucepan, combine water and butter and heat until butter melts. Pour butter-water mixture into mixing bowl and mix until fully incorporated. Refrigerate for at least 2 hours.

Place dates in a small saucepan and cover with water. Bring to a boil and then drain. Place softened, warm dates in a food mill and pass through to remove the skins.

Preheat oven to 275 degrees.

Peel, core, and quarter apples. Place apples on a prepared sheet pan and sprinkle with remaining ¼ cup sugar. Bake until soft and light brown, approximately 1 hour. Remove from oven and allow to cool. Place apples in a food processor and puree until smooth.

Combine the apple and date purees and mix until smooth. Place in a piping bag and reserve for the beignets.

Roll out beignet dough on a floured surface to a long rectangular shape. On half of the dough, pipe out the apple and date puree mix in small balls about the size of a nickel, placing them about 3 inches apart. Carefully fold the other half of the dough over the filling, creating a sandwhich with the puree in the center. Using a 2-inch round cutter, cut out the beignets carefully and transfer to a floured sheet pan.

When ready to fry the beignets, heat oil to 325 degrees and deep-fry beignets 5 minutes, until golden brown, a few at a time. Remove from the oil and immediately coat with the brûlée sugar.

Knead the dough until smooth.

Roll the dough into a long rectangle ½ inch thick.

Brush lightly with a damp brush.

Pipe the apple and date puree into small balls.

Carefully slide the back of your hands under the dough, and lift the dough.

Fold half of the dough completely over.

Cut out the beignets, making sure that the puree is in the center of each.

Place on a floured sheet pan.

After deep-frying, roll in brûlée sugar.

Dust with confectioners' sugar and serve warm.

FROZEN CIDER PARFAITS

Cider Sorbet

3 cups / 709 ml fresh apple cider

1½ cups / 354 ml granulated sugar

Frozen Vanilla Soufflé

4 eggs, separated

¾ cup / 177 ml granulated sugar

1 vanilla bean, split in half

2 cups / 473 ml heavy cream

Combine cider and sugar for sorbet in a pot. Heat until warm, then cool in an ice bath and chill. Process in an ice cream machine according to the manufacturer's instructions. Keep frozen.

Combine egg yolks, ¼ cup granulated sugar, and seeds from the vanilla bean for the soufflé in an electric mixer bowl and whisk until pale and fluffy, 5 to 6 minutes. In a separate mixing bowl, beat egg whites until firm peaks are formed. Add the remaining ½ cup sugar and whisk for 1 minute. Remove from electric mixer and fold whites into yolks. Whip heavy cream and fold into the egg mixture.

Using metal molds 1 inch in diameter and 2½ inches tall, pipe mixture until molds are half filled, and harden in the freezer. Once the soufflé is frozen, pipe on the sorbet until the mold is full, and smooth the top. Keep frozen.

APPLE TARTLETS

8 disks Sucre Dough (page 253),
5 inches in diameter

4 Granny Smith apples

6 cups / 1419 ml water

3 cups / 709 ml granulated sugar

1 vanilla bean

1 cinnamon stick

1 orange peel

2 lemons, juiced

½ cup / 118 ml clarified butter

1 cup / 236 ml Roasted Apple Puree ▪

Preheat oven to 300 degrees.

Line eight 4-inch metal tartlet pans with dough and blind bake until golden brown, about 20 minutes.

Peel and core apples, trimming the ends. Cut the remaining pieces in half down the center, creating two doughnut shapes for eight equal, round shapes.

In a saucepan, combine the water, sugar, vanilla bean, cinnamon, orange peel, and lemon juice. Bring to a quick boil and reduce heat. Add the apples and simmer for 4 to 5 minutes, until tender. Immediately remove, drain, pat dry, and allow to cool.

In a sauté pan, heat the clarified butter, add the poached apples, and cook on one side until golden brown, about 5 to 7 minutes. Remove apples and allow to cool.

Preheat oven to 300 degrees.

Pipe a thin layer of apple puree on the bottom of each tart shell. Carefully place the sautéed apples, browned side up, on top of the puree. Place tarts in oven for 10 to 15 minutes to lightly brown, then remove from oven and allow to cool. Reheat tartlets in oven for 5 minutes before serving.

▪ Roasted Apple Puree

3 Empire apples

¼ cup / 59 ml granulated sugar

Preheat oven to 275 degrees.

Peel, core, and quarter apples. Place apples on a papered sheet pan and sprinkle with sugar. Roast until soft and light brown, about 1 hour. Remove from oven and allow to cool. Place into a food processor and puree until smooth. Refrigerate.

CIDER SAUCE

4 cups / 946 ml fresh apple cider

1 cup / 236 ml granulated sugar

Combine the cider and sugar in a saucepan and bring to a boil. Reduce to a simmer and cook until only 2 cups remain. Set aside.

ASSEMBLY

2 cups Vanilla Sabayon Sauce (page 250)

Cider Sauce

Apple Tartlets

Frozen Cider Parfaits

Apple-Date Beignets

Apple Chips (page 16)

Honey Tuiles (page 247)

Sugar Garnish (page 253)

Pipe two pools of sauce—one of sabayon and the other of cider—next to each other in the centers of each of eight plates. Place the tartlets on the sabayon sauce. Unmold the parfaits onto the cider sauce. Place the warm beignets on top of the tartlets. Garnish each parfait with an apple chip, honey tuile, and sugar garnish.

Warm Apple Crepe with Cinnamon Ice Cream and Spiced Carrot Syrup

WARM APPLE CREPES

Crepes

3/4 cup / 177 ml all-purpose flour

1/4 teaspoon / 1 ml ground cinnamon

2 egg yolks

2 whole eggs

1 cup / 236 ml milk

1/4 cup / 55 g unsalted butter, melted

1/2 vanilla bean, split in half

Apple Filling

4 Rome apples

1/2 cup / 118 ml granulated sugar

2 teaspoons / 10 ml lemon juice

1/4 cup / 59 ml Calvados brandy

1/2 cup / 118 ml light brown sugar

1/2 cup / 115 g unsalted butter, melted

Place flour and cinnamon in a medium mixing bowl. In a separate small bowl, combine and whisk together yolks, whole eggs, and milk. Slowly whisk the wet ingredients into the dry until smooth. Combine butter and vanilla bean in a saucepan; melt butter and whisk together. Add melted butter to crepe batter. Using an 8-inch nonstick sauté pan, make crepes (page 247). Stack the crepes on top of each other and cover with a damp cloth until ready for use.

The filling must be sautéed quickly. If the sauté pan you are using is too small, it may be best to divide the recipe and make two half-batches. Peel, core, and cut the apples into large 1/4-inch dice.

Preheat a large sauté pan. When it is very hot, add the sugar and allow to melt and caramelize until amber in color. Add the diced apples and lemon juice. Sauté quickly, then add the brandy. The brandy will flame up, so be careful. Remove from stove and pour the diced apples into a large bowl.

In a food processor, place one-third of the sautéed apples, all of the brown sugar, and the melted butter. Puree until smooth. Stir back into the remaining sautéed apples and allow the filling to cool.

Place 3 tablespoons of filling in the center of a cinnamon crepe. Fold over the edges to create a round puck shape. Fill remaining crepes and cover with a damp towel until ready to serve.

SERVES 8

I never cared for carrot cake, but I liked the idea behind it. Combining spices and sweet carrot juice was my way of presenting the flavors in a lighter, more appealing form. The sauce is a nice complement to the warm baked apple crepe. Prepare the ice cream, sauce, and chips up to two days in advance. The crepes can be prepared and assembled two to three hours before serving.

CINNAMON ICE CREAM

4 cups / 946 ml heavy cream

2 cups / 473 ml milk

1½ cups / 354 ml granulated sugar

6 cinnamon sticks

2 teaspoons / 10 ml ground cinnamon

12 egg yolks

In a large saucepan, combine the cream, milk, sugar, and cinnamon sticks. Bring to a simmer and then steep for 30 minutes.

In one motion, pour and whisk the hot cream into the yolks. Pass the mixture through a fine sieve, chill, and then process in an ice cream machine according to the manufacturer's instructions. Keep frozen.

SPICED CARROT SYRUP

4 cups / 946 ml Apple Stock (page 243)

2 cups / 473 ml fresh carrot juice

½ teaspoon / 2 ml ground cinnamon

⅛ teaspoon / .62 ml ground cardamom

⅛ teaspoon / .62 ml ground nutmeg

⅛ teaspoon / .62 ml ground white pepper

1 cup / 236 ml granulated sugar

Place the apple stock in a saucepan and reduce until 2 cups remain. Combine the reduced stock with the remaining ingredients, bring to a boil, and place in an ice bath to cool.

CARROT CHIPS

6 medium carrots

¼ cup / 59 ml confectioners' sugar

1 tablespoon / 15 ml light corn syrup

Peel and cut carrots into 1-inch lengths. Cover with water and cook until tender, about 5 minutes. Remove from water and allow to cool. Puree carrots with confectioners' sugar and corn syrup. Spread the mixture on a nonstick silicone baking sheet. Use a stencil to create a shape. Bake at 200 degrees until crisp, about 1 hour. Store in an airtight container.

ASSEMBLY

Warm Apple Crepes

Strudel Crisps (page 252)

Cinnamon Ice Cream

Carrot Chips

Spiced Carrot Syrup

1 cup Vanilla Sabayon Sauce (page 250)

Sugar Garnish (page 253)

Warm the apple crepes in a 325° oven for five minutes, then place one in the center of each of eight plates. Lay a strudel crisp on each crepe. Place a scoop of ice cream on the crisp, then put another strudel crisp into the ice cream so it stands tall. Stick a carrot chip in the ice cream. Pipe the carrot syrup around the plate and finish with dots of sabayon sauce. Lean a sugar stick against each crepe.

Warm Chocolate Cake with Spiced Poached Pears and Crème Caramel

WARM CHOCOLATE CAKE

1½ cups / 354 ml semisweet chocolate, finely chopped

3 tablespoons / 40 g unsalted butter

2½ egg yolks

3 tablespoons / 40 g water

¼ cup / 59 ml almond flour

1 tablespoon / 15 ml cornstarch

1 tablespoon / 15 ml cocoa powder

7 / 225 g egg whites

½ cup / 118 ml granulated sugar

Preheat oven to 350 degrees. Butter eight 4-inch ramekins.

Combine chocolate and butter in a double boiler and melt over hot water. In an electric mixer bowl, whisk egg yolks and water until pale and foamy. Fold into chocolate. Fold in almond flour, cornstarch, and cocoa powder. Whisk egg whites until soft peaks form, then add sugar and continue to whisk for 1 minute. Fold whites into batter. Pour batter into ramekins and bake until set and firm, about 15 minutes. The cakes should rise during the baking and fall once out of the oven. Remove from oven and allow to cool slightly; then carefully tip out of the ramekins onto parchment paper.

CRÈME CARAMEL

Caramelized Sugar

2 cups / 473 ml granulated sugar

1 cup / 236 ml water

Custard

2 cups / 473 ml milk

½ vanilla bean

1 cinnamon stick

½ cardamom pod

½ cup / 118 ml granulated sugar

3 whole eggs

2 egg yolks

In a heavy saucepan, combine sugar and water. Boil until a deep amber color, then pour into and coat a 5-inch by 9-inch loaf pan with the hot caramel. Allow to cool.

Combine milk, vanilla, cinnamon, cardamom, and sugar in a saucepan and bring to a simmer. Remove from heat and let the liquid steep for 20 minutes, then cool in an ice bath.

Preheat oven to 300 degrees.

Once milk is cooled, add eggs and yolks. Pass through a fine sieve and pour custard into the loaf pan. Set loaf pan in a water bath and bake until firm and set, about 45 minutes. Refrigerate overnight. Carefully unmold custard and cut into 1-inch-thick slices.

SERVES 8

The cake is nothing more than a fallen soufflé. When baked just right, it develops a nice crust and retains a moist interior. The flan's cool creaminess cuts the richness of the deep chocolate cake, and the caramel is enough to sweeten them both. The crème caramel must be made the day prior to serving. The chocolate curls and pears can also be prepared in advance. The cake should be baked as needed.

SPICED POACHED PEARS

4 Anjou pears

1 cup / 236 ml granulated sugar

2 cups / 473 ml water

Juice of 1 lemon

Juice of 1 orange

1 cardamom pod

$\frac{1}{2}$ vanilla bean, split in half

1 cinnamon stick

$\frac{1}{2}$ fresh bay leaf

10 white peppercorns

Peel, core, and halve pears. Combine pears with remaining ingredients in a saucepan. Bring to a low boil, reduce heat, and simmer until tender, about 15 minutes. Place pears and liquid in an ice bath to cool.

CHOCOLATE CURLS

$1\frac{1}{2}$ cups / 354 ml semisweet chocolate, melted

Spread melted chocolate on the back of a warm sheet pan. Refrigerate until solid, then remove and let sit at room temperature until the chocolate is pliable with a knife. Using a paring knife, carefully peel curls of chocolate off of the pan. Keep chocolate curls refrigerated until ready to use.

Warm the pan slightly in an oven.

Spread the chocolate, covering the surface of the sheet pan.

Correct the spreading to make sure it is even. After refrigeration, allow the chocolate to sit at room temperature until pliable.

Trim the edge.

Cut into strips.

Angle the blade of a paring knife and drag it under the strip.

Continue to drag and let the chocolate curl around itself.

Cut the curl with the knife.

Refrigerate the curls as soon as they are formed.

ASSEMBLY

2 cups Vanilla Sabayon Sauce (page 250)

Warm Chocolate Cake

Crème Caramel

Spiced Poached Pears

2 cups Chocolate Sauce (page 246)

Sugar Garnish (page 253)

Chocolate Curls

Use eight rectangular or oval serving plates for this dessert. Pour a small pool of sabayon sauce toward one end of each plate. Place a warm chocolate cake on top. Place a slice of crème caramel on the opposite side of the plate. Slice and fan out a pear half on each serving and garnish with chocolate sauce, caramel sauce from the custard, caramel sugar garnish, and chocolate curls.

Bittersweet Chocolate Mousse Torte with Chocolate Bourbon Ice Cream

BITTERSWEET CHOCOLATE MOUSSE TORTE

Chocolate Cake

1 cup / 225 g unsalted butter

2¼ cups / 528 ml granulated sugar

1 cup / 236 ml black cocoa powder

2¾ cups / 646 ml all-purpose flour

2 teaspoons / 10 ml baking powder

½ tablespoon / 7 ml baking soda

3 eggs

2 cups / 473 ml warm water

Chocolate Mousse

1½ cups / 354 ml bittersweet chocolate, finely chopped

½ cup / 118 ml milk

½ cup / 118 ml unsalted butter

2 egg yolks

1½ tablespoons / 22 ml granulated sugar

2 cups / 473 ml heavy cream

Chocolate cake crumbs

Preheat oven to 325 degrees. Butter two 8-inch round cake pans.

Cream butter, sugar, and cocoa. Add flour, baking powder, and baking soda and mix until smooth. Add eggs and slowly add water. Pour mixture into pans and bake for 30 to 40 minutes, until firm and springy to the touch. Remove from pan and allow to cool on rack. Refrigerate overnight for easier slicing.

Combine chocolate, milk, and butter in a double boiler over hot water to melt. In a mixing bowl, whisk yolks and sugar until pale ribbons form. Fold yolks into the melted chocolate. Whip cream until medium peaks form, and fold into the chocolate mixture. Refrigerate the mousse until firm.

Slice cake into three ¼-inch-thick slices. To assemble the torte, use an 8-inch cake pan. Line the pan with parchment paper. Place a layer of cake in first. Follow with the mousse; alternate layers. There should be three layers of cake and two layers of mousse. Refrigerate for 4 hours. Cut into eight pieces, trimming the ends to form triangles. Coat each piece with cake crumbs.

SERVES 8

At first sight, the chocolate cake is a little shocking—it's jet black! People wonder if I have purposely burned it. Well, not quite. I use a very dark black cocoa. While unfamiliar to most pastry shops and restaurants, it is used in some popular commercial products. The bourbon ice cream provides a cool contrast to the chocolate. Bake the cakes and prepare the ice cream a day in advance. The tortes can be assembled in advance on the day they are to be served.

CHEF'S NOTE

Cake crumbs (for the chocolate mousse) are easy to make. Dry any trimmings left over from the cake in a 200-degree oven overnight and process until smooth in a food processor. Store dry.

CHOCOLATE BOURBON ICE CREAM

4 cups / 946 ml heavy cream

2 cups / 473 ml milk

1½ cups / 354 ml granulated sugar

12 egg yolks

1½ cups / 354 ml extra-bitter chocolate, finely chopped

1 cup / 236 ml bourbon

Place the cream in a large, heavy saucepan with the milk and 1 cup of sugar. Set over medium heat. Place the egg yolks and remaining ½ cup sugar in a medium bowl and stir to combine. Bring milk mixture to a full boil and quickly whisk the boiling liquid into the yolks and sugar. Immediately add the chocolate, stirring until smooth. Strain through a fine-meshed sieve into a clean mixing bowl. Place in an ice bath to cool, and add the bourbon to the mixture. When the mixture is cold, transfer it to an ice cream maker and freeze according to the manufacturer's instructions.

ASSEMBLY

2 cups Chocolate Sauce (page 246)

1 cup Clear Caramel Sauce (page 246)

Chocolate Bourbon Ice Cream

Bittersweet Chocolate Mousse Torte

Chocolate Tuiles (page 247)

Chocolate Garnishes (page 245)

Pipe thin lines of chocolate sauce and dots of clear caramel sauce on each of eight serving plates. Stand a wedge of the torte on end in the center of each plate. Place a scoop of ice cream against the torte. Gently stick tuiles and chocolate garnishes into the cake and ice cream.

Pumpkin Praline Pie with Spice Cake and Praline Ice Cream

PUMPKIN PRALINE PIE

8 5-inch rounds of Sucre Dough (page 253)

1½ cups / 354 ml pumpkin puree

¼ cup / 55 ml praline paste

½ cup / 118 ml granulated sugar

1 teaspoon / 5 ml ground cinnamon

½ cup / 115 g milk

Pinch of salt

¾ cup / 170 g heavy cream

3 eggs

1 cup / 236 ml crème fraîche

Preheat oven to 300 degrees.

Line eight 4-inch metal tart pans or pie plates with dough and blind bake until golden brown, about 20 minutes.

In an electric mixer, cream pumpkin puree, praline paste, and sugar until smooth. Slowly add cinnamon, milk, salt, cream, and eggs. Mix until smooth. Fill each pre-baked tart shell with the pumpkin mix and bake at 300 degrees until set and firm to the touch, about 30 minutes. Allow to cool, then unmold.

Whip the crème fraîche until stiff. With a hot spoon, shape two quenelles of whipped crème fraîche on the top of each pie.

PRALINE ICE CREAM

4 cups / 946 ml heavy cream

2 cups / 473 ml milk

1½ cups / 354 ml granulated sugar

1½ cups / 354 ml praline paste

½ cup / 118 ml pumpkin puree

1 teaspoon / 5 ml ground cinnamon

⅛ teaspoon / .62 ml ground cardamom

⅛ teaspoon / .62 ml ground cloves

⅛ teaspoon / .62 ml ground nutmeg

12 egg yolks

Combine all ingredients except the yolks in a large saucepan and bring to a boil. Place the yolks in a large bowl. In one motion, pour and whisk the hot cream into the yolks. Pass the mixture through a fine sieve. Chill and process in an ice cream machine according to the manufacturer's instructions.

PUMPKIN CHIPS

2 cups / 473 ml pumpkin puree

2 tablespoons / 29 ml confectioners' sugar

1 tablespoon / 15 ml light corn syrup

Preheat oven to 200 degrees.

Puree ingredients until smooth. Use a cut-out stencil (page 252) to create a shape. Spread the mixture over the stencil on a nonstick silicone baking sheet. Bake until crisp, about 1 hour. While the pumpkin chips are hot and flexible, roll them around a 1-inch-wide pipe to form a tube. Store in an airtight container.

SERVES 8

This visually spectacular version of the standard dessert is guaranteed to turn heads and stop conversations when served. It combines symbols of two fall holidays: the traditional pumpkin pie of Thanksgiving and the glowing jack-o'-lantern of Halloween. A few nontraditional components are added to balance the plate. The ice cream, chips, and spice cake should be prepared one to two days in advance. The pies should be prepared the day that you need them, but they can be stored at room temperature for a couple of hours.

SPICE CAKE

3 cups / 709 ml all-purpose flour

9 tablespoons / 133 ml ground cinnamon

3 tablespoons / 44 ml ground cardamom

3 tablespoons / 44 ml baking soda

½ cup / 118 ml brown sugar

6 egg yolks

½ cup / 118 ml molasses

1 cup / 236 ml maple syrup

7 tablespoons / 103 ml crème fraîche

1 cup / 236 ml unsalted butter, melted

12 egg whites

½ cup / 118 ml granulated sugar

Preheat oven to 325 degrees. Butter two 8-inch round cake pans.

Combine flour, spices, baking soda, brown sugar, yolks, molasses and syrup, and crème fraîche. Cream until smooth. Fold in the butter. Whip the egg whites until soft peaks are formed, and add the sugar. Whisk for 1 minute, then fold the beaten whites into the batter. Pour into cake pans and bake until firm to the touch, about 30 minutes. Allow to cool on rack. Cut into 12 wedges.

ASSEMBLY

Pumpkin Praline Pie

Spice Cake

Praline Ice Cream

Honey Tuiles (page 247)

Pumpkin Chips

2 cups Praline Sauce (page 249)

1 cup Spice Syrup (page 251)

Sugar Garnish (page 253)

Place pumpkin pie toward the front of each of eight serving plates. On one side stand a wedge of spice cake. On the other side, place a round scoop of praline ice cream on a round honey tuile. Stick a candle in the ice cream, light it, and cover with a pumpkin chip. Pipe praline sauce and spice syrup around the plate. Garnish the plate with a honey tuile and caramelized sugar sticks.

Ricotta Brûlée with Toasted Walnuts and Sage

RICOTTA BRÛLÉE

Walnut Base

4 cups / 946 ml toasted walnut pieces

1 cup / 236 ml dark corn syrup

2 teaspoons / 10 ml finely chopped fresh sage

½ cup / 118 ml water

Ricotta Cheese Layer

1½ cups / 354 ml cream cheese

¾ cup / 177 ml ricotta

½ cup / 118 ml granulated sugar

½ teaspoon / 2 ml finely chopped, fresh sage

½ vanilla bean, split in half

2 whole eggs

1 egg white

¾ cup / 170 g heavy cream

ASSEMBLY

Ricotta Brûlée

2 cups Brûlée Sugar (page 244)

Spun Sugar (page 253)

Honey Tuiles (page 247)

Fresh sage leaves

Combine the walnut base ingredients in a saucepan and bring to a boil. Allow to cool. Spread a layer of the base on the bottom of each of eight brûlée dishes or ramekins. Use just enough to cover the bottom evenly—do not fill more than halfway. Place dishes in freezer overnight.

Preheat oven to 300 degrees.

In an electric mixer bowl, place the cream cheese, ricotta, sugar, sage, and vanilla bean. Cream until smooth, then add the whole eggs, egg white, and cream. Mix until smooth. Pass through a sieve. Pour the cheese mixture over the frozen walnut base, enough to fill the dish. Bake in a water bath until set and cheese mix is firm to the touch, about 40 minutes. Allow to cool, then refrigerate.

Sprinkle and evenly coat the top of each custard with brûlée sugar. Using a blowtorch, glaze to a golden amber caramel. Allow to cool for a minute, then garnish each with spun sugar, tuile, and fresh sage.

SERVES 8

This dessert was always one of my favorite flavor combinations. It certainly is not on the best-seller list, but those who have tried it seem to enjoy it. People tell me that they still remember eating it years ago. The great thing about a bi-level custard is that you can savor all the components in one spoonful. Caramelizing the sugar on top warms the ricotta cheese custard, creating a smooth opposition to the sweet, chewy walnuts below. Set the walnut base one to two days in advance.

Roasted Pecan Napoleon with Chilled Pecan Terrine

PECAN STRUDEL DISKS

12 sheets strudel dough

1 cup / 236 ml clarified butter

2 cups / 473 ml pecans, finely ground

Preheat oven to 350 degrees.

Carefully place a sheet of strudel dough on a flat surface and lightly brush with clarified butter. Lightly sprinkle the ground pecans on the dough. Place another sheet of dough on top. Repeat the above until six sheets are used. Using a 3-inch round cutter, cut the dough into disks. A total of forty disks are needed, as five are used per serving. Place the disks on parchment paper on a sheet pan and bake until golden brown. Let cool and set aside.

PECAN PASTRY CREAM

3 cups / 709 ml milk

1 cup / 236 ml toasted crushed pecans

3 tablespoons / 45 ml cornstarch

4 tablespoons / 59 ml cold milk

8 egg yolks

¼ cup / 55 ml granulated sugar

2 tablespoons / 30 ml honey

¼ cup / 55 g unsalted butter

In a small saucepan, combine milk and toasted pecans. Bring to a simmer, then steep for 20 to 30 minutes. Strain the liquid and reserve 2 cups pecan milk.

In a small mixing bowl, combine constarch with cold milk. Whisk until smooth. Add egg yolks, pecan milk, granulated sugar, and honey and mix well. Strain into a new bowl and place in a double boiler. Cook the mixture over hot water until thick, 10 to 12 minutes. Remove from heat, whisk in butter, transfer to a clean pan, cover, and refrigerate until ready to use.

CANDIED PECANS

3 cups / 709 ml pecan halves

¼ cup / 59 ml molasses

Preheat oven to 250 degrees.

Place pecans in a small saucepan and cover with water. Bring to a boil and drain. Allow to cool, place on a sheet tray, and dry in oven for 10 minutes. Remove the pecans from the oven and coat with molasses. Return the pecans to the sheet tray and bake at 250 degrees until dry, not sticky, approximately 30 minutes.

SERVES 8

A deceptive dessert—people always compliment me on the lightness of the napoleon. The crisp, airy texture of the strudel dough takes your mind off the rich ingredients. A touch of rum in the chilled pecan terrine makes it seem smoother than you thought possible. All components except the strudel disks should be prepared one day in advance.

CHEF'S NOTE

Strudel dough dries out quickly. When you're making the pecan strudel disks, butter each sheet as soon as you lay it out and keep a lightly damp towel over the rest of the dough.

CHILLED PECAN TERRINE

Frozen Vanilla Soufflé

4 eggs, separated

$3/4$ cup / 177 ml granulated sugar

$1/2$ vanilla bean, split and seeds scraped

2 cups / 473 ml heavy cream

Pecan Terrine Filling

$1^1/2$ cups / 354 ml pecans, chopped

2 eggs

1 cup / 236 ml dark brown sugar

$1/2$ cup / 118 ml dark corn syrup

Pinch of salt

2 tablespoons / 29 ml dark rum

2 tablespoons / 30 g unsalted butter, melted

ASSEMBLY

Pecan Strudel Disks

Pecan Pastry Cream

Sugar Garnish (page 253)

Chilled Pecan Terrine

3 cups Meringue Crumbs (page 248)

Honey Tuiles (page 247)

Spice Syrup (page 251)

2 cups Vanilla Sabayon Sauce (page 250)

Candied Pecans

Using an electric mixer, combine egg yolks, $1/4$ cup of the sugar, and the vanilla seeds, and whisk until pale and thick. Remove from the machine. In a separate mixing bowl, mix egg whites into soft peaks. Add remaining $1/2$ cup sugar and continue to whisk until firm peaks are formed. Fold whites into egg yolk mixture. In another bowl, whip cream until firm peaks are formed and add to egg mixture. Refrigerate until ready to assemble.

Preheat oven to 275 degrees.

In a mixing bowl, combine all ingredients for filling except butter. Mix until smooth and then add butter. Pour mixture into a 9-inch by 9-inch ceramic dish and bake until set and firm, about 40 minutes. Allow to cool, then transfer mixture to a pastry bag.

The terrine consists of three layers. The bottom and top layers are the vanilla soufflé; the middle is the pecan filling. Line a 4-inch by 10-inch terrine mold with plastic wrap. Pipe the soufflé mixture into the terrine until one-third is full. Place the mold in the freezer to set firm, about 20 minutes. Remove from freezer and carefully pipe on a layer of filling—the terrine should now be two-thirds full. Carefully pipe on the remaining soufflé mixture and smooth the top. Return terrine to freezer and chill overnight. Once it is firmly frozen, carefully remove the terrine and slice into $1/2$-inch-thick slices.

Place a strudel disk on each of eight plates and carefully pipe the pecan pastry cream on top. Alternate strudel disks and pastry cream until all five disks are used for each serving. Place a sugar stick through the napoleon to hold its shape. Carefully coat a slice of the terrine in the meringue crumbs and place next to the napoleon. Place the two honey tuiles on the pecan terrine. Place dots of spice syrup and sabayon sauce around the plate. Garnish with candied pecans.

Chilled Pumpkin Parfait in Shell

CHILLED PUMPKIN PARFAIT

8 mini pumpkins

Cashew Nougat

¾ cup / 177 ml granulated sugar

6 tablespoons / 85 g unsalted butter

1 cup / 236 ml cashews

Pinch of salt

Frozen Pumpkin Soufflé

4 egg yolks

½ cup / 118 ml granulated sugar

1 cup / 236 ml dark corn syrup

1 cup / 236 ml pumpkin puree

½ tablespoon / 7 ml ground cinnamon

⅛ teaspoon / .62 ml ground cloves

⅛ teaspoon / .62 ml ground nutmeg

4 egg whites

1 cup / 236 ml heavy cream

1 cup / 236 ml crème fraîche

CANDIED CASHEWS

2 cups / 473 ml raw cashews

¼ cup / 59 ml molasses

Carefully cut off the tops of pumpkins. Using a paring knife, core pumpkins. Scrape out the seeds using a teaspoon or tablespoon. Place pumpkins in a freezer and allow to chill.

Place sugar for the nougat in a heavy pot and cook over medium heat until sugar begins to melt, then stir and cook until sugar is deep amber. Add butter and continue to stir. Add cashews and salt. Pour mixture onto an oiled sheet pan and allow to cool. Once it has cooled, crush and chop with a fine knife.

In an electric mixer bowl, combine the egg yolks and ¼ cup of sugar. Whisk until pale and fluffy, about 5 minutes. In a separate mixing bowl, combine the corn syrup, pumpkin puree, cinnamon, cloves, and nutmeg. Mix until smooth. Fold the whipped yolk mixture into the pumpkin puree mixture.

In a separate, clean bowl, whisk egg whites until firm peaks are formed. Add the remaining ¼ cup sugar and continue to whisk for 1 minute. Remove from mixer and fold into the puree-yolk mixture.

Combine cream and crème fraîche and whip until firm peaks are formed. Fold cream into egg mixture, then fold in 2 cups of reserved cashew nougat. Pipe mixture into frozen pumpkin shells, filling them slightly above the rim. Freeze overnight.

Put the cashews in a saucepan and cover with cold water. Bring to a boil, drain, and allow to dry.

Preheat oven to 250 degrees.

Spread cashews on a sheet pan and bake until dry, about 10 minutes. Coat cashews with molasses and continue to bake until dry, not sticky, approximately 1 hour.

SERVES 8

This is a great-looking dessert that can be made in advance. It is perfect for capturing the holiday spirit at a small party or family gathering. The best part is that all of the components can be prepared a day or two in advance and assembly takes just a few minutes.

ASSEMBLY

Chilled Pumpkin Parfait

Strudel Crisps (page 252)

Candied Cashews

Sugar Garnish (page 253)

Place the parfaits in the center of each of eight plates. Arrange the strudel crisps around the pumpkin parfaits. Place the candied cashews around the base of each parfait. Top the parfaits with a sugar garnish.

Warm Black Mission Fig and Goat Cheese Cake

WARM FIG AND GOAT CHEESE CAKE

1 cup / 236 ml all-purpose flour

1 cup / 236 ml semolina flour

1 cup / 236 ml granulated sugar

1¼ tablespoons / 18 ml baking powder

½ teaspoon / 2 ml grated, orange zest

½ teaspoon / 2 ml salt

4 egg whites

½ cup / 118 ml milk

1 cup / 236 ml fresh goat cheese

1 cup / 225 g unsalted butter, melted

6 to 8 Black Mission figs, sliced

FIG SORBET

3 cups / 709 ml coarsely diced Black Mission figs

1 cup / 236 ml dried apricot halves

1 cup / 236 ml Ruby Port wine

2 cups / 473 ml water

2 cups / 473 ml granulated sugar

Preheat oven to 300 degrees.

Using in an electric mixer with a paddle attachment, combine flours, sugar, baking powder, orange zest, and salt. In a small bowl, combine egg whites, milk, and ½ cup of goat cheese. Whisk until smooth, then add to the dry mixture. Mix until smooth, then add the melted butter. Pour the batter into eight small, buttered 3½-inch metal tart pans. Crumble the remaining goat cheese on top of the batter and bake until firm and a light golden color, about 15 minutes. Allow to cool, remove from the pans, and cover with fig slices.

Combine ingredients in a saucepan and bring to a boil. Remove from heat, cover, and allow to cool. Puree in a blender and pass through a fine sieve. Chill, then process in an ice cream machine according to the manufacturer's instructions.

SERVES 8

This is a light, warm cake dotted with bits of goat cheese and fresh, ripe figs. The mild goat cheese does not overpower the dessert. Instead it is a nice balance for the rich taste of the figs and the intensity of the port sauce. The fig and goat cheese cakes should be baked when needed, but the other components can be made a day in advance.

CHEF'S NOTE

Some varieties of figs can have tough, thick skins. I prefer Black Mission figs for this cake; when ripe they have a thin and tender skin.

FIG BRÛLÉE

6 to 8 fresh figs, thinly sliced

¼ cup / 59 ml Port Sauce ∎

1¼ cups / 291 ml cream cheese

½ cup / 118 ml ricotta cheese

¼ cup / 55 ml fresh goat cheese

½ cup / 118 ml granulated sugar

½ teaspoon / 2 ml grated orange zest

½ vanilla bean, split in half

2 whole eggs

1 egg white

¾ cup / 170 g heavy cream

∎ **Port Sauce**

2 cups / 473 ml Ruby Port wine

4 fresh figs, diced

½ cup / 118 ml granulated sugar

On the bottom of each of eight 4-ounce ramekins or dishes, place a layer of fig slices—enough to fill one-third of the dish. Pour port sauce over the figs to cover halfway. Place dishes in freezer for at least 4 hours.

Preheat oven to 300 degrees.

Place the cream cheese, ricotta cheese, goat cheese, sugar, orange zest, and vanilla bean in an electric mixer. Cream until smooth. Add the whole eggs, egg whites, and cream. Mix until smooth, then pass through a sieve. Pour cheese mixture over the frozen sliced figs and sauce—enough to fill the dish. Bake in a water bath until set and cheese mix is firm to the touch, about 40 minutes. Allow to cool, then refrigerate.

Combine all ingredients in a saucepan and reduce over medium heat until 1 cup remains. Puree and cool.

WHIPPED GOAT CHEESE CREAM

½ cup / 118 ml mascarpone cheese

½ cup / 118 ml fresh goat cheese

¾ cup / 177 ml heavy cream

½ cup / 118 ml granulated sugar

¾ cup / 59 ml grated orange zest

Combine all ingredients and whisk until stiff. Place in a pastry bag.

ASSEMBLY

Fig Sorbet

Snap Cookies (page 251)

Whipped Goat Cheese Cream

Sucre Dough (page 253)

Warm Fig and Goat Cheese Cake

Honey Tuiles (page 247)

Port Sauce

1 cup Brûlée Sugar (page 244)

Fig Brûlée

Sugar Garnishes (page 253)

Place a small scoop of fig sorbet on each of eight dessert plates. Fill a round snap cookie with whipped goat cheese cream and place an inch from the sorbet. Lay a long triangular piece of sucre dough on top of the sorbet and snap cookie. Carefully place the warm fig and goat cheese cake on the sucre triangle. Stick two tuiles into the sorbet. Pipe dots of port sauce around the border of each plate. Place fig brûlée on second plate. Sprinkle a thin layer of brûlée sugar on the fig brûlée and glaze with a blowtorch until a light amber color. Garnish both plates with sugar decorations.

Frozen Banana Glacé with Walnut Nougat

FROZEN BANANA GLACÉ

4 eggs, separated

¾ cup / 177 ml granulated sugar

2 bananas

1 cup / 236 ml mascarpone cheese

2 cups / 473 ml heavy cream, whipped

2 cups / 473 ml Walnut Nougat ▪

▪ Walnut Nougat

¾ cup / 177 ml granulated sugar

6 tablespoons / 85 g unsalted butter

1 cup / 236 ml walnuts, toasted

Pinch of salt

ASSEMBLY

2 cups Chocolate Sauce (page 246)

1 cup Clear Caramel Sauce (page 246)

Frozen Banana Glacé

Chocolate Garnish (page 245)

Snap Cookie cup (page 251)

Whipped cream

In an electric mixer bowl, combine the egg yolks and ¼ cup sugar. Whisk until pale and fluffy. Puree bananas and stir together with mascarpone cheese until smooth. Fold the banana mixture into yolk mixture. Whisk egg whites to stiff peaks, add remaining ½ cup sugar, and continue to whisk for 1 minute. Fold the whites into the banana-yolk mixture. Fold the whipped cream and walnut nougat into the mixture. Pour into a paper-lined 8-inch round cake pan and freeze overnight. The next day, unmold the glacé and cut it into eight equal wedges. Trim the round end off of each wedge so that it will stand on end. Keep frozen.

Place sugar in a heavy saucepan. Cook over medium heat until the sugar starts to melt, then cook longer, stirring, until it is a deep amber color. Add butter and stir in, then add walnuts and salt. Pour onto an oiled sheet pan to cool. Crush or chop fine with a knife.

Pipe chocolate sauce and caramel sauce onto eight dessert plates. Place a slice of the frozen banana glacé, standing on end like an upright triangle, in the center of each plate. Place a chocolate garnish on the side of the glacé wedge. Place a snap cookie cup in front of the banana glacé and fill with whipped cream.

SERVES 8

This was one of my first desserts—simple, traditional ice cream sundae flavors stepped up with a refined look. The frozen mascarpone has a lighter texture than ice cream. The walnuts are given a caramelized crunch of nougat, and the chocolate sauce adds a simple, pure accent. All components can be prepared one to two days in advance.

CHEF'S NOTE

All nougats can be made well in advance. Once the nougat cools, chop it quickly and store it in an airtight container at room temperature.

Chilled Concord Grape and Sesame Parfait

FROZEN ORANGE-SESAME MOUSSE

4 egg yolks

¼ cup / 59 ml honey

3 tablespoons / 44 ml tahini paste

Zest and juice of 1 orange

4 egg whites

½ cup / 118 ml granulated sugar

2 cups / 473 ml heavy cream

1 cup / 236 ml toasted sesame seeds

1 cup / 236 ml meringue crumbs (page 248)

Using an electric mixer, combine and whisk egg yolks, honey, tahini paste, and orange zest and juice. Whisk mixture until pale and foamy, then remove from machine. Whisk egg whites into soft peaks, add sugar, and whisk until stiff peaks form. Remove and fold into yolk mixture. Whip cream into soft peaks and fold into egg mixture. Pipe into eight plastic cone-shaped molds and freeze. Once all are frozen, unmold and roll in toasted sesame seeds and meringue crumbs. Keep frozen.

CONCORD GRAPE SORBET AND SAUCE

2 quarts / 1892 ml Concord grapes, no stems

1 quart / 946 ml water

Juice of 1 lemon

3 cups / 709 ml granulated sugar

Combine all ingredients in a saucepan and simmer until the grapes are soft, about 10 minutes. Puree and pass through a fine sieve, then cool mixture in an ice bath. Freeze half of the mixture in an ice cream machine for the sorbet according to the manufacturer's instructions. Reserve the remaining mixture for the sauce.

ORANGE MERINGUE DISKS

½ cup / 118 ml confectioners' sugar

1 cup / 236 ml sliced, blanched almonds

2 teaspoons / 10 ml grated orange zest

1 cup / 236 ml granulated sugar

5 egg whites

Preheat oven to 225 degrees.

Combine confectioners' sugar, almonds, orange zest, and ½ cup of granulated sugar in a food processor and puree until smooth. In an electric mixer, whisk egg whites until firm peaks form and then add the remaining ½ cup sugar. Whisk until smooth and remove from the machine. Fold the dry ingredients into the egg whites. Using a 2½-inch round stencil, spread the meringue mixture on a nonstick silicone sheet and bake until dry and light golden brown, approximately 30 minutes.

SERVES 8

This parfait is a sophisticated twist on the theme of peanut butter and jelly. The toasted sesame seeds and tahini paste have a peanut-buttery quality. When sweetened with honey and a hint of orange, the sesame flavor blends nicely with the tart grape. The sauce is simple to prepare and tastes best when served well chilled, on ice cold plates. All these components can be prepared one to two days in advance.

ASSEMBLY

Concord Grape Sorbet

Orange Meringue Disks

Frozen Orange-Sesame Mousse

Sesame Snap Cookies (page 251)

Sugar Garnish (page 253)

Orange segments

Candied Orange Rinds (page 244)

Concord Grape Sauce

On each dessert plate, place a scoop of grape sorbet between two orange meringue disks to create a sandwich, positioning in the center of each plate. Place a cone-shaped orange-sesame mousse on top of the meringue disk so that it points straight up. Carefully place a sesame snap cookie on the point of the cone. Stick a sugar garnish down through the cookie hole into the frozen mousse. Garnish the plate with orange segments and candied rinds. In a blender, puree the grape sauce until frothy and light. Pour around each plate. Serve immediately.

Fresh Figs with Crisp Corn Pudding and Frozen Fig Torte

CORN PUDDING

2 cups / 473 ml milk

½ vanilla bean, split in half

¾ cup / 177 ml granulated sugar

½ cup / 118 ml yellow cornmeal

1 cup / 236 ml heavy cream

3 whole eggs

2 egg yolks

Vegetable oil, for deep-frying

½ cup / 118 ml all-purpose flour

3 egg whites, lightly beaten

2 cups / 473 ml Panko bread crumbs
(available in Japanese groceries)

In a small saucepan, combine milk, vanilla bean, and sugar. Bring to a boil and quickly whisk in the cornmeal. Continue to whisk and cook until the mixture is very thick, approximately 10 minutes. Remove from heat and allow to cool slightly.

Preheat oven to 300 degrees.

In a separate mixing bowl, combine the cream, whole eggs, and egg yolks. Whisk the mixture until smooth and gently temper into the cooked cornmeal base. Line a 10-inch cake pan with plastic wrap and fill until half full. Bake until set, about 40 minutes. Remove pan from the oven, allow to rest, then refrigerate overnight.

Heat oil to 325 degrees in a deep-fryer.

Cut the corn pudding into 2-inch disks. Place flour, egg whites, and bread crumbs in separate shallow bowls. Coat disks first with flour, then dip in egg white and coat with bread crumbs. Just before serving, deep-fry the disks until golden brown on both sides, about 5–7 minutes.

SERVES 8

Throughout the year, figs are the fruit that I look forward to working with the most. They have a natural richness that matches perfectly with a deep-flavored port. Here, the crisp and creamy corn pudding mellows the two. I find that very soft and ripe figs work best for the sauce and frozen torte. All the components can be prepared a day in advance, but fry the corn pudding just before you serve dessert.

FROZEN FIG TORTE

Frangipane

1 cup / 236 ml almond paste

1 cup / 236 ml granulated sugar

1 cup less 2 tablespoons / 200 g unsalted butter

4 eggs

½ cup / 118 ml cake flour

Preheat oven to 300 degrees.

In a mixing bowl, combine almond paste, sugar, and butter until smooth. Add eggs and flour, and continue to cream until all ingredients are fully incorporated. Pour the batter into a buttered 8-inch round cake pan and bake until set and golden brown, about 35 minutes. Remove from oven, allow to cool, and refrigerate overnight. Slice the frangipane into two ¼-inch-thick slices.

Filling

4 to 6 medium figs

1 cup / 236 ml Ruby Port wine

1¼ cups / 295 ml granulated sugar

2 eggs, separated

1 tablespoon / 15 ml honey

½ vanilla bean, split in half and seeds scraped

1 cup / 236 ml heavy cream

Trim stems of the figs and cut figs in half. In a small saucepan, combine the wine and 1 cup of the sugar. Bring mixture to a boil and pour over figs. Allow figs to sit for 20 to 30 minutes, then drain. Cut figs into small dice.

Using an electric mixer, combine egg yolks, honey, and vanilla seeds, whipping until light and fluffy. In another mixing bowl, whisk egg whites until firm peaks are formed. Add the remaining ¼ cup sugar and continue to whisk for 1 minute. Fold whites into the egg yolks. Whip cream and fold into egg mixture. Once the mixture is incorporated, fold in the diced, steeped figs.

Line an 8-inch round cake pan with paper and place a ¼-inch-thick slice of frangipane on the bottom. Fill with the fig filling until 1 inch thick. Smooth filling out and place another frangipane slice on top. Place the pan in the freezer until firm. Once it has frozen, use a hot knife to cut into 10 portions. Trim the top and bottom of each portion so that it will stand like a triangle.

PORT SYRUP

2 cups / 473 ml Ruby Port wine

½ cup / 118 ml diced figs

1 cup / 236 ml granulated sugar

Combine ingredients in a saucepan and simmer for 20 minutes. Remove from heat and puree.

ASSEMBLY

Corn Pudding

Diced fresh figs

Port Syrup

2 cups Vanilla Sabayon Sauce (page 250)

Frozen Fig Torte

Whipped crème fraîche

Honey Tuiles (page 247)

Sugar Garnish (page 253)

Place the fried corn pudding off center on each of eight dessert plates. Place a small 2-inch ring mold on top of each corn pudding and fill with diced fresh figs. Press down on the figs to make level and then remove the ring. Pipe the port syrup and sabayon sauce around the plates. Stand a wedge of the frozen torte on each plate behind the corn pudding. Place a quenelle of crème fraîche on top of the diced figs. Garnish the plates with honey tuiles and a sugar garnish.

Warm Cranberry Financiers

1³/₄ cups / 413 ml confectioners' sugar

¹/₄ cup / 55 ml all-purpose flour

¹/₂ cup / 118 ml natural almond flour

3 egg whites

¹/₄ cup / 55 g salted butter

3 tablespoons / 44 ml chopped dried cranberries

¹/₂ cup / 118 ml fresh whole cranberries

Preheat oven to 325 degrees.

In an electric mixer bowl, combine the sugar, flours, and egg whites. Whisk until smooth. In a small saucepan, brown the butter and add to batter. Add the dried cranberries and place mixture in a piping bag.

Lightly butter 24 petit four metal tartlet molds. Pipe the batter into the molds until each mold is three-quarters filled. Place one or two whole cranberries on top and bake until light golden brown and firm, 15 to 20 minutes.

YIELDS 24 FINANCIERS

These tart little cakes are best served warm. Virtually any dried or fresh fruit can be substituted for the cranberries.

Fresh Figs Stuffed with Sour Cream Ice Cream

12 Black Mission figs

12 small balls Sour Cream Ice Cream (page 15)

1 tablespoon / 15 ml granulated sugar

Trim the stem ends of the figs. Cut a thin slice off of the trimmed ends; reserve this slice for later use. Using a small scoop, partially hollow out the figs. Place an ice cream ball in each fig and place the thin slice on top. Sprinkle with granulated sugar. Serve.

YIELDS 12 FIGS

The key to this petit four is the ripeness of the figs. To me, a fresh fig can stand on its own, but the ice cream adds a surprising frozen element not regularly seen in petit fours.

CLOCKWISE FROM TOP LEFT:
*Chocolate Truffle Financier, Roasted
Seckel Pears with Manchego Cheese
and Black Pepper, Roasted Lady
Apples with Vanilla Mascarpone,
and Sweet Potato Tartlet*

Roasted Lady Apples with Vanilla Mascarpone

12 Lady apples

½ cup / 118 ml clarified butter

1½ cups / 354 ml Brûlée Sugar (page 244)

½ cup / 118 ml mascarpone cheese

¼ cup / 59 ml heavy cream

3 tablespoons / 44 ml granulated sugar

½ vanilla bean, split in half and seeds scraped

24 Apple Chips (page 16)

12 Meringue Cups (page 16)

Trim the top and bottom of each Lady apple and remove cores. Sauté whole apples in clarified butter until light golden brown on each side, about 5 minutes. Remove apples from pan and allow to cool slightly.

Preheat oven to 325 degrees.

Roll each apple in brûlée sugar to coat, place sugared apples in a new pan, and bake for 10 minutes. Remove from oven and coat apples in brûlée sugar once again. Return to oven and bake for 10 minutes more. Remove apples from pan and allow to cool.

In an electric mixer, combine mascarpone cheese, cream, sugar, and vanilla seeds, and whisk until stiff peaks are formed. Place mixture in a piping bag. Once apples are cooled, place apples on small meringue cups and pipe mascarpone mixture into the center core of each apple. Garnish with apple chips.

YIELDS 12 LADY APPLES

It wouldn't be fall without apples. Roasting the Lady apples is the best way, I find, to intensify the flavor. Vanilla mascarpone complements the tartness of the apple wonderfully.

Sweet Potato Tartlet

1 large sweet potato

1 cup / 236 ml Brûlée Sugar (page 244)

12 2-inch disks of Sucre Dough (page 253)

¼ cup / 59 ml crème fraîche, whipped

15 to 20 strands kataifi dough, toasted

Peel the sweet potato and cut into ½-inch slices. Using a 1-inch round cutter, cut the sweet potato into rounds. Place the rounds in a small saucepan and cover with cold water. Bring to a simmer and cook until almost tender, about 8 minutes. Drain and allow to steam cool on a rack.

Preheat oven to 325 degrees.

Toss sweet potato disks in the brûlée sugar until coated. Place on a clean pan and bake until tender, 20 to 30 minutes. Turn oven to 300 degrees. Create tartlet shells from the 12 sucre dough disks. Blind bake the shells until golden brown, 20 minutes. Remove and allow to cool. Place a disk of sweet potato in each tartlet shell. Using a small demitasse spoon, place a quenelle of crème fraîche on top of the sweet potato. Garnish with the kataifi dough. Serve.

YIELDS 12 TARTLETS

This is an adaptation of the traditional sweet potato pie, with the added tartness of crème fraîche and the crunch of kataifi dough.

Chocolate Truffle Financier *(photograph on page 56)*

YIELDS 24 FINANCIERS

It's a moist, rich chocolate cake in its own right. The melted truffle adds an extra jolt of chocolate that no one seems to mind.

1¾ cups / 413 ml confectioners' sugar

¼ cup / 55 ml all-purpose flour

½ cup / 118 ml natural almond flour

1 tablespoon / 30 ml cocoa powder

3 egg whites

¼ cup / 55 g salted butter

½ cup / 118 ml heavy cream

1½ cups / 354 ml Extra-bitter chocolate, finely chopped

1 tablespoon / 15 ml Grand Marnier liqueur

In an electric mixer bowl, combine the sugar, flours, cocoa , and egg whites. Whisk until smooth. In a small saucepan, brown the salted butter and add to the batter. Place batter in a piping bag.

In a small saucepan, bring cream to a boil and pour over the chopped chocolate. Whisk until smooth and then add the Grand Marnier. Refrigerate the truffle base until solid, about 1 hour.

Use a small #10 Parisian scoop to form truffle balls. Keep truffle balls refrigerated until ready to use.

Preheat oven to 325 degrees.

Lightly butter 24 petit four metal tartlet shells. Pipe the batter into the shells until each shell is three-fourths filled. Bake until firm, 15 to 20 minutes. Remove from the oven and allow to cool slightly. Press one truffle ball into the center of each financier. Return the financiers to the oven for 2 minutes, then let cool. Serve at room temperature and garnish with chocolate cigarettes.

Roasted Seckel Pears with Manchego Cheese and Black Pepper *(photograph on page 56)*

6 seckel pears

½ cup / 118 ml clarified butter

1 cup / 236 ml granulated sugar

¼ teaspoon / 1 ml coarsely ground black pepper

4 ounces / 115 g Manchego cheese

Trim both ends of each pear. Cut pears in half lengthwise and remove seeds with a small Parisian scoop. Sauté the pears flesh side down in the clarified butter until light golden brown, about 5 minutes. Remove from pan and allow to cool slightly.

Preheat oven to 325 degrees.

Toss and coat pears with sugar and place in a baking pan skin side down. Bake until tender, 20 to 30 minutes. Remove from oven and sprinkle lightly with black pepper. Allow to cool. Using a vegetable peeler or zester, slice thin shards of Manchego cheese. Arrange a small amount of cheese on each pear and serve.

YIELDS 12 PEAR SERVINGS

I like to use cheese whenever possible. This is a great way to combine a sharp cheese and sweet roasted pears with a touch of spice.

Date and Goat Cheese Strudel

2 sheets strudel dough

½ cup / 118 ml clarified butter

½ cup / 118 ml fresh goat cheese

½ cup / 118 ml Date Puree ▪

Preheat oven to 350 degrees.

Carefully spread a sheet of strudel dough on a flat surface. Brush lightly with butter and place a second sheet of dough on top. Brush again lightly with butter. Cut dough into long 1-inch-wide strips. At the end of each strudel dough strip, place a small amount of goat cheese. Place date puree in a pastry bag and pipe a small amount of date puree on top of the goat cheese, then fold the dough into a triangular shape. Brush with butter and bake until golden brown, about 20 minutes.

YIELDS 12 STRUDELS

These are best when served hot from the oven. The chewy strudel dough encases the intense flavor of the dates and goat cheese. Serve them simply with confectioners' sugar or a little Vanilla Sabayon Sauce for dipping.

▪ **Date Puree**

1 cup / 236 ml dates, pitted

Place the dates in a medium saucepan and cover with cold water. Bring to a quick boil and drain immediately. Pass dates through a food mill while still warm. Let puree cool.

While most of my favorite winter memories are of home, I cannot forget my first introduction to New York City. Although the city was dark and cold, it was decorated beautifully for the holiday season. My visits usually involved spending the day at work with my father and eating at some terrific ethnic restaurants. New York City has such a wide variety of foods from all over the world that eating lunch was always an adventure. I was surprised by the use of acidic accents in Mexican and Thai food. I still remember the Chinese sesame and honey candies and their strangely sweet and salty dried fruits. Memories of these great meals still spark my creativity to think of new and exciting dishes. 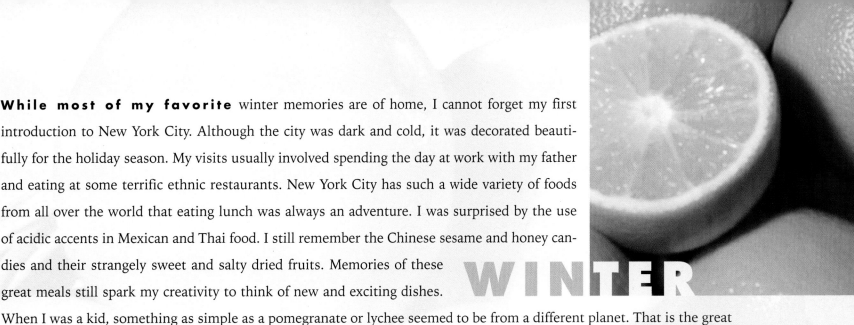 WINTER When I was a kid, something as simple as a pomegranate or lychee seemed to be from a different planet. That is the great thrill of the city. It is an endless resource: on every corner you turn, you learn something new. ■ **At home, winter was always** spent with family and centered in the kitchen, and this is still true today. I was fortunate that my mother was a great cook. The cooking was not extravagant, but the kitchen was a wonderful gathering place for great conversation and serious snacking. It seemed as if we were always snacking, whether it was on nuts, cheese, my sister's cookies, or citrus fruit sent by a relative. These memories still influence the flavors I use in my winter desserts. They will always contain nuts, chocolate, dried fruits, and perhaps some form of sweet wine or port. Though I live in the Northeast, where winter is cold and snowy, it always seems odd to me that it is the peak season for citrus. Because of the abundance of citrus at this time of year, I use these fruits to add some refreshing lighter touches to a winter menu. In a way, it is perfect timing. ■

Winter weather is a great advantage in the professional pastry kitchen. The cool, dry air makes this the ideal time for more elaborate sugar work, tuiles, and chocolate decorations because there is no heat and humidity to melt and ruin the work. Most pastry kitchens I have worked in are near the delivery door; this means that whatever the outside temperature, the kitchen is the same. It seems ideal to have a cold work space instead of a hot kitchen, but cold has its disadvantages. Chocolate sets too hard before you can cut it or bend it. Sugar presents a similar problem. As for getting yeast dough to rise, the room temperature is often closer to 60 degrees, rather than the 90 degrees that the dough needs. When this happens, I turn on every heat source in the kitchen or move temporarily to the main kitchen, where it is a bit warmer. Whether you are a chef, pastry chef, line cook, or home cook, being able to adapt and troubleshoot in any situation is the key to success. ■ **The winter brings customers in** droves. It is easily the most hectic time in a restaurant's year. It seems that everyone is celebrating holidays, throwing parties, or just taking a break from shopping. Just when my crew and I become used to the chaos, the season hits its peak with the holidays. After New Year's Eve, a steadier pace returns. ■ **Serving people at home during** the holidays can be stressful and challenging for some. At this time of year, organization is necessary not just for gift shopping but for planning and preparing a meal or party as well. For each dessert, I have provided timing tips for preparation as well as ways to properly store items. Whether you try to replicate the entire dessert or just a component or two, I hope this information helps you to plan the perfect holiday meal.

Citrus Panna Cotta with Warm Poppyseed Cake and Citrus Sorbet

CITRUS PANNA COTTA

2 cups / 473 ml milk

2 cups / 473 ml heavy cream

1 cup / 236 ml granulated sugar

Zest of 1 lemon

Zest of ½ orange

1 teabag chamomile tea

3 stalks lemongrass, finely chopped

4 teaspoons powdered gelatin or 4 sheets gelatin (If powdered gelatin is used, dissolve in 4 tablespoons water.)

Combine all ingredients, except for the gelatin, in a saucepan and bring to a quick boil. Remove from the heat and allow to steep for 20 to 30 minutes. Soften or bloom the gelatin and add to the warm milk base. Pass the mixture through a chinois and pour the panna cotta mix into eight small 2-ounce metal cups. Refrigerate and allow to set at least 3 hours. When ready to serve, quickly dip the outside of the metal cup in warm water and pop out.

POPPYSEED CAKE

1 cup / 236 ml semolina flour

1 cup / 236 ml all-purpose flour

1 cup / 236 ml granulated sugar

1¼ tablespoons / 6 ml baking powder

½ teaspoon / 2 ml salt

½ cup / 118 ml egg whites

1 cup / 236 ml milk

Grated zest of 1 lemon

1 tablespoon / 15 ml poppyseeds

½ cup / 115 g unsalted butter, melted

Preheat oven to 300 degrees.

In a mixing bowl, combine all the ingredients except the butter. Mix until smooth. Add the butter and mix only until incorporated. Pour batter into eight small buttered savarin molds or a 3-inch metal tart shell, and bake until firm and set, approximately 20 minutes. To reheat the cake, place in a 300-degree oven for 5 minutes.

SERVES 8

This dessert is a nice blend of temperatures. The cool panna cotta almost melts into the warm poppyseed cake. The sorbet is a clean, sharp accent to the warm sauce. The citrus cotton candy is a lighthearted option. All the components of this dessert except for the poppyseed cake can be prepared a day in advance.

CHEF'S NOTE

If you cannot find citric acid for the sour lemon meringues, substitute the juice of one lemon to add a little tartness.

SOUR LEMON MERINGUES

1 cup / 236 ml sliced, blanched almonds

1 cup / 236 ml granulated sugar

Zest of 1 lemon

1 tablespoon / 15 ml citric acid

¼ teaspoon / 1 ml turmeric

½ cup / 118 ml confectioners' sugar

5 egg whites

Preheat oven to 250 degrees.

Combine the almonds, ½ cup granulated sugar, lemon zest, citric acid, turmeric, and confectioners' sugar in a food processor and process until smooth. In an electric mixer, mix the egg whites until soft peaks are formed. Add the remaining ½ cup of sugar and continue to whisk until firm peaks are formed. Whisk for an additional minute and then remove from the machine. Fold the dry ingredients into the egg whites.

On a parchment-lined sheet tray, use a small round stencil (page 252) that you have created, and spread the meringue over the stencil. Make eight round disks. Bake until light golden brown in color, 20 to 30 minutes. Remove from the oven and allow to cool. Store in an airtight container.

CITRUS SORBET

1 cup / 236 ml granulated sugar

½ cup / 118 ml water

1 cup / 236 ml tangerine juice

1 cup / 236 ml grapefruit juice

1 cup / 236 ml lemon juice

In a saucepan, combine the sugar and water and bring to a boil. Allow to cool, then add to the fruit juices and process in an ice cream machine according to the manufacturer's instructions. Keep frozen.

CITRUS SAUCE

½ cup / 118 ml lemon juice

½ cup / 118 ml tangerine juice

½ cup / 118 ml water

⅓ cup / 88 ml granulated sugar

1 tablespoon / 15 ml poppyseeds

1 tablespoon /15 ml unsalted butter

Combine all the ingredients in a saucepan and bring to a rapid boil. Boil for 10 to 15 seconds, then remove from heat.

Note: This sauce is made at the end of the assembly of the dessert and added to the dessert while still hot.

ASSEMBLY

Poppyseed Cake

Lemon Curd (page 248)

Citrus Panna Cotta

Sour Lemon Meringues

Citrus Sorbet

Honey Tuiles (page 247)

Orange sections

Grapefruit sections

Citrus Sauce

Cotton Candy

Sugar Garnish (page 253)

Warm the poppyseed cakes and place one in each of eight dessert bowls. Place a small amount of lemon curd in the center of each cake. Unmold the panna cottas onto the sour lemon meringue disks and place one on top of each cake. Place a round scoop of citrus sorbet on a honey tuile and place next to the warm cake. Garnish the bowls with orange and grapefruit sections. Heat the citrus sauce and immediately pour around the fruit sections. Finish the dessert with cotton candy and a sugar garnish.

Lemon Papaya Millefeuille

LEMON STRUDEL DISKS

1 cup / 236 ml clarified butter

Zest of 2 lemons

12 sheets strudel dough

Combine the butter and lemon zest and simmer over a low flame for 2–3 minutes. Remove from heat and allow to steep for 20 minutes.

Preheat oven to 350 degrees.

Carefully place a sheet of strudel dough on a flat surface. Brush with lemon butter. Place another sheet of strudel dough on top. Repeat until six of the strudel sheets have been used. Using a 2-inch round cutter, cut through the dough, making 2-inch round disks. A total of 40 disks is needed, as 5 are used per serving. Place the disks on a parchment-lined sheet pan and bake until golden brown, about 15–20 minutes. Allow to cool. Store in an airtight container.

LEMON CURD SAUCE

1 cup / 236 ml Lemon Curd (page 248)

1 cup / 236 ml milk

1 tablespoon / 15 ml granulated sugar

Combine the ingredients and whisk until smooth. Refrigerate.

FROZEN CRÈME FRAÎCHE PARFAIT

Papaya Sorbet and Sauce

4 cups / 946 ml diced ripe papaya

1½ cups / 354 ml granulated sugar

Juice of 1 lemon

4 eggs, separated

¾ cup / 177 ml granulated sugar

2 cups / 473 ml crème fraîche, whipped

Combine the ingredients for the sorbet and sauce in a blender and puree until smooth. Pass through a chinois. Reserve 2 cups of the puree for the sauce. Run the remainder of the puree through an ice cream machine according to the manufacturer's instructions. Keep frozen.

Combine the egg yolks and ¼ cup sugar in a mixing bowl and whisk until pale and fluffy, 5 to 6 minutes. In a separate mixing bowl, whisk the egg whites until firm peaks are formed. Add the remaining ½ cup sugar and continue to whisk for 1 minute. Remove the whites from the mixer and fold into the egg yolks. Add the crème fraîche to the egg mixture.

Using eight metal ring molds measuring 2½ inches in diameter, pipe the crème fraîche mixture into the bottom half of each ring. Place in the freezer and allow

SERVES 8

Ripe papaya has a wonderful fragrance but needs an acidic touch. The light, crunchy elements of the millefeuille are a tangy contrast to the mellow crème fraîche and papaya parfait. Prepare this dessert one to two days in advance, and assemble the components just before serving.

CHEF'S NOTE

Frozen phyllo dough can be substituted for the strudel dough in the recipe for lemon strudel disks. Just be sure to defrost properly to keep the dough from cracking.

to set. Once the crème fraîche has set, fill the remainder of the mold with the papaya sorbet. Smooth the top of the mold. Keep frozen.

ASSEMBLY

Lemon Strudel Disks

Lemon Curd (page 248)

Sugar Garnish (page 253)

Frozen Crème Fraîche Parfait

Diced papaya

Lemon Curd Sauce

Papaya Sauce

Sour Lemon Meringues (page 64)

Honey Tuiles (page 247)

Place a strudel disk to one side of each of eight dessert plates and carefully pipe one tablespoon of lemon curd on top. Top with another disk and continue to alternate disks and lemon curd until all five disks are used for each serving. Palce a sugar stick through the millefeuille to hold its shape. Opposite the millefeuille, unmold and place the parfait. In between the two, place a small pile of diced papaya. Pipe small dots of the lemon curd and papaya sauces around the plates. Garnish the plates with a meringue crisp and a honey tuile.

Tangerine and Licorice Root Parfait

WINTER

Citrus

FROZEN TANGERINE SOUFFLÉ

Tangerine Sorbet

1 cup / 236 ml granulated sugar

½ cup / 118 ml water

3 cups / 709 ml tangerine juice

4 eggs, separated

¾ cup / 177 ml granulated sugar

Grated zest of 2 tangerines

Juice of ½ tangerine

1 cup / 236 ml crème fraîche

1 cup / 236 ml heavy cream

Combine the sugar for sorbet and water in a saucepan and bring to a boil. Allow the syrup to cool, then add the tangerine juice. Run through an ice cream machine according to the manufacturer's instructions. Keep frozen.

Combine the egg yolks, ¼ cup sugar, and tangerine zest and juice in a mixing bowl and whisk until pale and fluffy, 5 to 6 minutes. In a separate mixing bowl, whisk the egg whites until firm peaks are formed. Add the remaining ½ cup sugar and continue to mix for 1 minute. Remove from the machine and add the whites to the yolk mixture. In a separate bowl, whisk the crème fraîche and heavy cream; fold into the egg mixture.

On a parchment-lined sheet tray, spread the soufflé mixture until it is ½ inch thick. Freeze.

Using eight small triangular-shaped molds, cut out the soufflé base, allowing the bottom of the molds to be filled with soufflé base. Fill the remainder of each triangular mold with the tangerine sorbet, making sure to smooth out the top of each mold. Keep frozen. When ready to unmold, just rub the metal ring and the soufflé will slip out.

LICORICE ROOT MERINGUE DISKS

1 cup / 236 ml sliced, blanched almonds

1 cup / 236 ml granulated sugar

½ tablespoon / 7 ml citric acid

Grated zest of 2 tangerines

1 tablespoon / 15 ml licorice root powder

½ cup / 118 ml confectioners' sugar

5 egg whites

Preheat oven to 250 degrees.

In a food processor, combine almonds, ½ cup granulated sugar, the citric acid, tangerine zest, licorice root powder, and confectioners' sugar, and puree until smooth. In an electric mixer, whisk the egg whites until soft peaks are formed. Add the remaining ½ cup sugar and continue to whisk until firm peaks are formed. Whisk for an additional minute and then remove from the machine. Fold all of the dry ingredients into the egg mixture.

On a parchment-lined sheet tray, using a stencil (page 252) that you have created, 3½ inches round,

SERVES 8

Licorice root does not have the black licorice or anise flavor that you would expect. It is extremely strong, but when used correctly has an herbal tone about it. I first saw it used as an ingredient in Chinese dried and candied fruit. This adaptation with tangerine has become one of my favorite flavor combinations. Prepare this dessert one to two days in advance, but assemble just before serving.

CHEF'S NOTE

Licorice root powder for use in the licorice root meringue disks can be found in health food stores.

Tangerine and Licorice Root Parfait **69**

create eight 3½-inch disks. Bake until light golden brown, 20 to 30 minutes. Remove disks while still hot and, using a small ½-inch cutter, cut a hole out of each meringue disk. Set aside to cool. Store in an airtight container.

CITRUS LEMONGRASS SAUCE

Juice of 6 tangerines

Juice of 3 lemons

Juice of 3 limes

Juice of 1 blood orange

1 cup / 236 ml granulated sugar

2 lemongrass stalks

1 kafir lime leaf

Combine all the ingredients in a saucepan and bring to a simmer. Remove from the heat and allow to steep for 20 minutes. Strain through a fine sieve and place in the refrigerator.

ASSEMBLY

Frozen Tangerine Soufflé

Tangerine Sorbet

Honey Tuiles (page 247)

Licorice Root Meringue Disks

Tangerine sections

Citrus Lemongrass Sauce

Candied Tangerine Rinds (page 244)

Sugar Garnish (page 253)

In a bowl, unmold the frozen soufflé and place in the center of each of eight dessert dishes. Scoop eight small balls of tangerine sorbet and place on top of each. Place a long honey tuile into the side of the parfait. Carefully set the disks of licorice root meringue on top of the sorbets and through the tuiles. Scatter tangerine sections around the base of each dish. Pour in the lemongrass sauce and garnish with the candied rinds and sugar sticks.

Tangy Lemon Custard with Spiced Passion Fruit Sauce

LEMON CUSTARD BASE

1 cup / 236 ml lemon juice

½ cup / 118 ml granulated sugar

4 whole eggs

2 egg yolks

½ cup / 118 ml crème fraîche

Zest of 1 lemon

Preheat oven to 300 degrees.

Combine the lemon juice, sugar, whole eggs, and egg yolks and whisk until smooth. Pass through a fine sieve and then add the crème fraîche and lemon zest. Line eight 2½-inch tart shells with plastic wrap; make sure the plastic wrap is tight on the tart shells. Fill shells with the lemon custard until ½ inch deep. Place the shells in a water bath and bake until the custard base is set, 20 minutes. Allow to cool, and refrigerate. Once they are cold, remove the custards by gently pulling the plastic wrap out of the tart shells. Keep refrigerated.

LEMON POUND CAKE

1 cup / 225 g unsalted butter

¾ cup / 177 ml granulated sugar

¼ cup / 59 ml corn syrup

Grated zest of 2 lemons

1¼ cups / 295 ml all-purpose flour

3 tablespoons / 45 ml cornstarch

½ teaspoon / 2 ml baking powder

4 eggs

Preheat oven to 325 degrees.

Cream the butter, sugar, corn syrup, and lemon zest together until pale and smooth. Add the remaining ingredients and combine until incorporated. Pour the mixture into a buttered 8-inch round cake pan and bake until firm and set, about 30 minutes. Refrigerate overnight.

Cut the cake into slices ¼ inch thick. Using an oval cutter, make oval disks. Set aside. Keep refrigerated.

FROZEN PASSION FRUIT SOUFFLÉ

4 eggs, separated

¾ cup / 177 ml granulated sugar

½ cup / 118 ml Passion Fruit Puree ■

2 cups / 473 ml heavy cream

Combine the egg yolks and ¼ cup sugar in an electric mixer bowl and whisk until pale and fluffy. Remove from the machine and add the passion fruit puree. In a separate mixing bowl, whisk the egg whites until firm peaks are formed. Add the remaining ½ cup sugar and continue to mix for 1 minute. Remove from the machine and fold into the puree. Whip the heavy cream and fold into the egg mixture. Using metal tubes 1 inch in diameter and 3 inches in length, pipe the soufflé mixture into the tubes and freeze until set.

Keep frozen. To unmold, gently rub with your hands and slip the soufflé out of the tube.

Passion Fruit Puree

3 passion fruits, pulp and seeds only

2 tablespoons / 30 ml granulated sugar

3 tablespoons / 45 ml water

Combine all ingredients in a saucepan. Heat to a simmer. Puree with a small hand blender until smooth. Pass through a fine sieve and allow to cool.

SPICED PASSION FRUIT SAUCE

5 passion fruits, pulp and seeds only

¼ cup / 59 ml water

¼ cup / 59 ml granulated sugar

½ cinnamon stick

½ cardamom pod (i.e., ½ husk and ½ the seeds)

½ star anise pod

4 coriander seeds

Combine the passion fruit pulp, water, and sugar in a saucepan and bring to a simmer. Turn off heat and puree with a small hand blender until smooth. Add the spices and allow to steep for 20 minutes. Pass through a fine strainer and allow to cool. Set aside. Refrigerate to store.

ASSEMBLY

Lemon Custard Base

Sucre Dough (page 253), cut into eight 2¾-inch disks

Lemon Pound Cake

Honey Tuiles (page 247)

Lemon Curd (page 248)

Whipped crème fraîche

Spiced Passion Fruit Sauce

Lemon Curd Sauce (page 67)

Frozen Passion Fruit Soufflé

Meringue Crumbs (page 248)

Sugar Garnish (page 253)

Carefully place each custard base on a baked sucre disk on a flat work surface. Place a thin, oval slice of pound cake on top of the lemon custards. Place a small round honey tuile in the pound cakes and fill with lemon curd. Using a demitasse spoon, make a small quenelle of whipped crème fraîche and place next to the honey tuile. On each dessert plate, pour a small round pool of the passion fruit sauce in the center and place small dots of lemon curd sauce around the border. Unmold the passion fruit soufflés and roll each in the meringue crumbs. Cut each in half and place on the passion fruit sauce. Lift and place each entire lemon custard assembly on top of a frozen soufflé. Garnish with honey tuiles and a sugar garnish.

Glazed Coconut Custard with Warm Macaroon and Caramel Sauce

COCONUT CUSTARD

8 Sucre Dough disks, 3½ inches round (page 253)

2¼ cups / 532 ml milk

2 cups / 473 ml heavy cream

½ cup / 118 ml granulated sugar

1½ cups / 354 ml fine-grated unsweetened coconut

9 egg yolks

Preheat oven to 300 degrees.

Place the disks on a sheet tray lined with parchment paper. Carefully place 3-inch metal rings on top of the disks and press slightly to indent into the dough. Bake the rings on the disks until light golden brown, 15 minutes. Remove from the oven and allow to cool.

In a saucepan, combine the milk, cream, sugar, and ½ cup coconut. Bring to a simmer, turn off heat, and allow to steep for 20 minutes. Pass through a fine sieve and allow to cool.

Preheat oven to 250 degrees.

Add the egg yolks and remaining 1 cup coconut to the milk mixture. Pour the custard base into the metal rings until 1 inch deep. Bake until the custard is set, 30 minutes. Allow to cool. Using a paring knife, remove the rings. Keep custards refrigerated.

COCONUT MACAROONS

3½ cups / 827 ml fine-grated unsweetened coconut

¾ cup / 177 ml light corn syrup

¾ cup / 177 ml granulated sugar

3 egg whites

½ cup / 118 ml all-purpose flour

Preheat oven to 325 degrees.

Combine all the ingredients in a mixing bowl. Lightly butter eight 4-inch metal tart shells and pack the macaroon mix into the shells approximately ½ inch thick. Bake until light golden brown, 15 to 20 minutes. Remove from the oven, allow to cool slightly, and remove the tart shells. Set aside.

COCONUT SORBET

1 cup / 236 ml granulated sugar

½ cup / 118 ml water

2 cups / 473 ml frozen coconut milk

Combine the sugar and water in a saucepan and bring to a boil. Turn off heat and allow syrup to cool, then add to the coconut milk. Process in an ice cream machine according to the manufacturer's instructions. Keep frozen.

SERVES 8

Combining toasted coconut and caramel seems almost natural—it is a combination that we have seen since childhood. I like the warm, chewy macaroon, which makes the custard seem even creamier. With the exception of the coconut custard, the components can be prepared one day in advance. The coconut custard should be prepared the same day that you serve it.

CHEF'S NOTE

Coconut milk in cans (for use in the coconut sorbet) can be found in most supermarkets. Just avoid the sweetened variety. Frozen coconut milk can be found in most Asian markets.

COCONUT CARAMEL SAUCE

½ cup / 118 ml granulated sugar

½ cup / 118 ml coconut milk

½ cup / 118 ml heavy cream

ASSEMBLY

Coconut Macaroons

Coconut Custard

1 cup Brûlée Sugar (page 244)

2 cups Coconut Caramel Sauce

Honey Tuiles (page 247)

Coconut Sorbet

Sugar Garnish (page 253)

Toasted grated coconut

In a small saucepan, combine sugar with enough water to dissolve it. Heat the sugar over high heat until deep amber in color. Quickly whisk in the coconut milk and cream. Remove from heat and pass through a fine sieve. Chill in an ice bath.

Place the warm coconut macaroons in the center of each of eight dessert bowls. Using a blowtorch, lightly glaze the custard with brûlée sugar. Place the glazed custards on top of the macaroons. Pour coconut caramel sauce around the plates. Place a crisscrossed honey tuile over each custard. Carefully place a small scoop of coconut sorbet on top of the tuiles. Garnish with sugar sticks and shaved toasted coconut.

Pecan Crème Caramel

PECAN CRÈME CARAMEL BASE

2½ cups / 590 ml granulated sugar

1 cup / 236 ml water

3 cups / 709 ml milk

1 cup / 236 ml toasted and finely chopped pecans

4 whole eggs

2 egg yolks

In a small saucepan, combine 2 cups of the sugar and the water and bring to a boil. Continue to cook until golden amber in color. Carefully pour the caramel into eight 4-inch ramekins, enough to coat the bottoms.

In another small saucepan, combine the milk and chopped pecans. Bring to a simmer. Remove from the heat and allow to steep for 20 minutes. Strain the milk and reserve 2 cups. Allow to cool.

Combine the pecan milk with the whole eggs, egg yolks, and remaining ½ cup sugar. Whisk together until smooth and pass through a fine sieve.

Preheat oven to 300 degrees.

Once the coating of caramel has hardened on the bottom of the ramekins, pour milk mixture into the bases to measure 1 inch high in the ramekins. Place the ramekins in a water bath and bake until firm and set, 30 minutes. Remove and allow to cool. Refrigerate overnight.

Note: When removing the crème caramels, use a paring knife to carefully cut around the edges.

SERVES 8

Caramelized or candied nuts are always delicious. Infusing the nuts into the crème caramel successfully adds the great flavor of pecans, but also keeps the smooth texture of the custard. A touch of rum and a little date puree complete the dessert. A crème caramel should always be prepared a day in advance so the caramelized sugar completely liquifies. The candied pecans can be prepared a few days in advance, the other components just one day ahead.

PECAN AND BROWN-SUGAR ROUNDS

9 tablespoons / 130 g unsalted butter

1 cup / 236 ml light brown sugar

1 cup / 236 ml granulated sugar

2 eggs

½ cup / 118 ml all-purpose flour

2 teaspoons / 10 ml baking powder

¼ teaspoon / 1 ml salt

2 cups / 473 ml chopped pecans

Preheat oven to 300 degrees.

In an electric mixer bowl, combine the butter, brown sugar, and granulated sugar and cream until pale and fluffy. Stop the machine, add the remaining ingredients, and mix until incorporated.

Lightly butter a baking sheet and spread the dough on the sheet until ½ inch thick. Bake until firm and golden brown, 20–30 minutes. Remove from the oven and allow to cool. Using a 1-inch round cutter, cut eight circles/rounds out of the baked dough.

ASSEMBLY

Pecan Crème Caramel Base

Honey Tuiles (page 247)

Whipped cream

Date Puree (page 15)

Pecan and Brown-Sugar Rounds

Candied Pecans (page 41)

2 cups Rum Sabayon Sauce (page 250)

Sugar Garnish (page 253)

Unmold the crème caramels and place one in the center of each of eight dessert plates. Place two honey tuiles in each crème caramel. Carefully pipe the whipped cream into the honey tuiles. Pipe the date puree onto the brown-sugar rounds. Place two candied pecans on each round. Place the rounds around the border of each plate. Pipe the sabayon sauce on the plates and garnish each with a sugar ring.

Walnut Tartlet with Chilled Spiced Cream and Golden Raisins

WALNUT TARTLET BASE

1½ cups / 354 ml chopped walnuts

2 eggs

1 cup / 236 ml dark brown sugar

½ cup / 118 ml dark corn syrup

Pinch of salt

2 tablespoons / 29 ml Frangelica liqueur

2 tablespoons / 30 g unsalted butter, melted

Preheat oven to 275 degrees.

Combine all the ingredients, except the butter, in a mixing bowl. Mix until smooth and add the butter. Line eight 2½-inch tartlet shells with parchment paper and pour the mixture into the shells. Bake until set and firm, 30 minutes. Allow to cool. Using a paring knife to free the edges, carefully unmold. Set aside. Refrigerate to store.

WALNUT DOUGH

1 cup plus 2 tablespoons / 266 ml granulated sugar

2 cups / 472 ml chopped walnuts

1¼ cups / 340 g unsalted butter

2 eggs

2½ cups / 590 ml cake flour

2 teaspoons / 10 ml ground cinnamon

2 teaspoons / 10 ml baking powder

Preheat oven to 300 degrees.

In a food processor, combine the sugar and walnuts and puree until smooth. Transfer to an electric mixing bowl and add the butter. Cream the butter, sugar, and walnuts until smooth. Add the eggs, flour, cinnamon, and baking powder. Roll out the dough until ⅛ inch thick. Cut into eight 3-inch disks and bake until light golden brown, 15 minutes. Allow to cool on tray.

CHILLED SPICE CREAM

4 eggs, separated

¾ cup / 236 ml granulated sugar

¼ teaspoon / 1 ml ground cinnamon

⅛ teaspoon / .62 ml ground cardamon

Pinch of ground nutmeg

½ vanilla bean, split in half and seeds scraped out

2 cups / 473 ml heavy cream

In an electric mixer bowl, combine the egg yolks, ¼ cup of the sugar, spices, and vanilla seeds and whisk until pale and thick. Remove from the machine. In a separate mixing bowl, whisk the egg whites until firm peaks are formed. Add the remaining ½ cup sugar and continue to whisk for 1 minute. Fold the whites into the yolk mixture. In a third bowl, whip the cream and fold into the egg mixture. Spread the mixture on a parchment-lined sheet tray until ½ inch thick. Freeze. Cut the frozen cream into 2-inch-wide strips, then cut each strip into triangles. Keep frozen.

SERVES 8

A lot of chefs tend to sweeten nuts too much. I like to use nuts and spices bound into a tart or cake and sweeten them naturally with a golden raisin sauce. All components can be prepared one to two days in advance.

WALNUT CAKE

1 cup / 236 ml granulated sugar

1 cup / 236 ml chopped walnuts

1 cup / 225 g unsalted butter

2 tablespoons / 30 ml dark corn syrup

1 tablespoon / 15 ml walnut oil

1¼ cups / 295 ml all-purpose flour

3 tablespoons / 45 ml cornstarch

1 teaspoon / 5 ml baking powder

4 eggs

Preheat oven to 325 degrees.

In a food processor, combine the sugar and walnuts and puree until smooth. Transfer to an electric mixing bowl and add the butter, corn syrup, and walnut oil. Cream until smooth. Add the flour, cornstarch, baking powder, and eggs; cream until smooth. Transfer the mixture to a parchment-lined 4-inch by 10-inch loaf pan and bake until firm and set, 40 minutes. Allow to cool. Cut into 16 bars ½ inch thick and 3 inches in length. Set aside. Store in an airtight container overnight.

GOLDEN RAISIN SAUCE

1 cup / 236 ml golden raisins

3 cups / 709 ml water

1 cinnamon stick

Peel of ½ orange, removed with vegetable peeler

¼ cup / 59 ml granulated sugar

Place all ingredients in a small saucepan and bring to a simmer. Remove from heat and allow to steep for 20 minutes. Remove the cinnamon stick and orange peel. Puree in a blender until smooth and pass through a fine sieve. Set aside.

ASSEMBLY

Golden Raisin Sauce

Walnut Cake

Walnut Tartlet Base

Walnut Dough Disks

Chilled Spice Cream

2 cups Vanilla Sabayon Sauce (page 250)

Honey Tuiles (page 247)

Sugar Garnish (page 253)

Pour a small pool of raisin sauce into the center of each of eight dessert plates. Place two bars of the walnut cake on each sauce pool. Carefully place a walnut tartlet on top of each walnut dough disk. Place a triangle of the chilled spice cream on top of each tartlet. Place entire assembly on top of the two bars of walnut cake. Place dots of sabayon sauce around each plate. Garnish with honey tuiles and a sugar garnish.

Terrine of Almonds and Preserved Figs with Toasted Almond Ice Cream

SERVES 8

Dried figs are completely different from fresh and have a distinct flavor of their own—the natural sugars of the dried are more intense. The dried seeds crunch and develop a flavor and fragrance similar to that of fortified wine. I bring this element out further with a touch of sherry and match it with the rich almond flavor of the frangipane. The terrine and ice cream need to be prepared one to two days in advance. The sherry sauce can be prepared at the same time.

ALMOND AND FIG TERRINE

Poached Figs

3 cups / 709 ml medium-dry sherry

1 cup / 236 ml granulated sugar

4 cups / 946 ml stemmed and quartered dried figs

Frangipane Cake

2 cups / 472 ml almond paste

1½ cups plus 2 tablespoons / 400 g unsalted butter

2 cups / 472 ml granulated sugar

8 eggs

1 cup / 236 ml cake flour

Vanilla Mascarpone Filling

1 cup / 236 ml mascarpone cheese

½ cup / 118 ml heavy cream

¼ cup / 118 ml granulated sugar

1 vanilla bean, split in half and seeds scraped

In a small saucepan, combine the sherry and sugar for poached figs and bring to a boil. Pour the mixture over the figs. Cover and allow to cool to room temperature. Set aside.

Preheat oven to 325 degrees.

In an electric mixer bowl, cream almond paste, butter, and sugar until smooth. Add the eggs and flour and continue to mix until well blended. Spread ¼ inch thick on a buttered half sheet tray and bake until light golden brown and firm, 20 minutes. Allow to cool. Cut into strips that are 3 inches wide and 10 inches long. Set aside.

In an electric mixer bowl, combine all the ingredients for the filling and whisk until stiff. Place in a pastry bag and store in the refrigerator until ready to use.

Drain the figs, reserving the liquid for later use (see Sherry Sauce, below). Line a 4-inch by 10-inch terrine mold with plastic wrap. Place a layer of the frangipane cake on the bottom. Pipe a layer of the filling on top, then arrange a ½-inch layer of figs on top of the mascarpone filling. Place another layer of frangipane cake on top. Repeat the layers of filling and figs, ending with a third layer of frangipane on top. Refrigerate overnight. When ready to assemble, cut the terrine into 1-inch-thick slices. Refrigerate.

SHERRY SAUCE

2 cups / 473 ml sherry poaching liquid, from figs

Place the poaching liquid in a small saucepan and reduce slowly until only 1 cup remains. Cool.

TOASTED ALMOND ICE CREAM

4 cups / 946 ml heavy cream

3 cups / 708 ml milk

1½ cups / 354 ml granulated sugar

2 cups / 473 ml sliced, blanched, and toasted almonds

12 egg yolks

In a large saucepan, combine the cream, milk, and 1 cup of the sugar. Crush almonds with a rolling pin. Add almonds to the mixture and place pan over medium heat, and bring to a quick boil. Reduce the heat and simmer for 20 minutes.

Place egg yolks and remaining ½ cup sugar in a bowl and stir to combine. Quickly whisk the boiling mixture into the yolks, then strain through a fine chinois and place in an ice bath to cool. Process in an ice cream machine according to the manufacturer's instructions. Keep frozen.

ASSEMBLY

Almond and Fig Terrine

Honey Tuiles (page 247)

Toasted Almond Ice Cream

1 cup Vanilla Sabayon Sauce (page 250)

Sherry Sauce

Sugar Garnish (page 253)

Using eight oval dessert plates, place two slices of terrine in the center of each plate. The slices should be side by side with a 1-inch gap between the slices. Place a small round honey tuile between the slices. Place a scoop of the ice cream on top of the tuile. Place dots of the sabayon and sherry sauces around the plates. Garnish with a sugar garnish.

Chocolate Espresso Trio

CHOCOLATE ESPRESSO MOUSSE

Chocolate Espresso Meringue Disks

1 cup / 236 ml granulated sugar

4 ounces / 115 g sliced and blanched almonds

1/2 cup / 118 ml confectioners' sugar

1 teaspoon / 5 ml cocoa powder

1/2 teaspoon / 2 ml ground espresso beans

5 egg whites

Chocolate Espresso Mousse

1 1/2 cups / 354 ml bittersweet chocolate, finely chopped

1/2 cup / 118 ml unsalted butter

1/2 cup / 118 ml espresso

2 egg yolks

1 1/2 tablespoons / 22.5 ml granulated sugar

2 cups / 473 ml heavy cream

1/2 cup / 118 ml cocoa beans, crushed

Preheat oven to 250 degrees.

In a food processor, combine 1/2 cup of the sugar, the almonds, confectioners' sugar, cocoa powder, and espresso. Puree until smooth. In an electric mixer bowl, whisk the egg whites until soft peaks are formed. Add the remaining 1/2 cup granulated sugar and continue to whisk until firm peaks are formed. Whisk for an additional minute and remove from the machine. Fold the dry ingredients into the egg mixture. Create a stencil (page 252) for a 1 1/2-inch disk. Using parchment-lined sheet trays, spread the meringue mixture onto the stencil, creating disks. Bake until dry and a light golden color, 40 minutes. Remove from the oven and allow to cool. Set aside. Store in an airtight container.

Combine the chocolate, butter, and espresso in a double boiler and place over hot water, allowing the chocolate to melt. In an electric mixer bowl, whisk the egg yolks and sugar until pale ribbons form. Fold the yolks into the melted chocolate. In a separate bowl, whip cream until medium peaks form. Fold cream into the chocolate egg base.

Using metal rings that are 1 1/2 inches in diameter and 1 1/2 inches tall, place a 1 1/2-inch meringue disk in the bottom of each ring. Pipe the mousse into the rings until filled. Smooth the tops. Sprinkle crushed cocoa beans on the smooth surface. Place in the refrigerator and allow to set about 2 hours.

SERVES 8

Too much chocolate? Some say impossible! Too much espresso? Some still say impossible! Two evils join forces to bring most chocoholics and java junkies to their knees. The chocolate cake must be baked one to two days in advance. The other components can be prepared one day ahead or early the same day you plan to serve them.

CHOCOLATE ESPRESSO CUSTARD

2 cups / 473 ml milk

2 cups / 473 ml heavy cream

½ cup / 118 ml granulated sugar

½ cup / 118 ml espresso beans, crushed

1½ cups / 354 ml extra-bitter chocolate, chopped

9 egg yolks

In a saucepan, combine milk, cream, sugar, and espresso beans and bring to a simmer. Remove from heat and steep for 20 minutes. While still warm, whisk in chopped chocolate. Cool in an ice bath.

Preheat oven to 300 degrees.

Add egg yolks to mixture and pass through a fine chinois or strainer. Carefully pour into shot glasses, filling them 1 inch deep. Place shot glasses in a water bath and bake until the custard is set, 30 minutes. Remove from the oven and cool in the refrigerator. Keep cold.

FROZEN ESPRESSO MASCARPONE MOUSSE

1 cup / 236 ml mascarpone cheese

½ cup / 118 ml concentrated espresso (reduced from 1½ cups)

1¼ cups / 295 ml granulated sugar

3 egg whites

2 cups / 473 ml heavy cream

In a small bowl, combine the mascarpone cheese, reduced espresso, and ¼ cup of the sugar, and whisk until smooth. In an electric mixing bowl, whisk the egg whites until firm peaks are formed. Add the remaining 1 cup sugar and continue to whisk for 1 minute. Remove egg whites from the machine and fold into the mascarpone mixture. Whip the cream and fold into the egg-mascarpone cheese base. Pipe the mousse into 1-inch metal tubes and freeze. Keep frozen.

CHOCOLATE CAKE

1 cup / 236 ml unsalted butter

2¼ cups / 528 ml granulated sugar

1 cup / 236 ml black cocoa powder (see page 258)

2 teaspoons / 10 ml baking powder

½ tablespoon / 7 ml baking soda

1 tablespoon / 15 ml salt

2¾ cups / 649 ml all-purpose flour

3 eggs

2 cups warm water

Preheat oven to 325 degrees.

Cream butter, sugar, and cocoa until smooth. Add baking powder, baking soda, salt, and flour, and mix until smooth. Add the eggs and then slowly add water. Pour batter into a 4-inch by 10-inch loaf pan and bake for 30 to 40 minutes until firm and springy to the touch. Refrigerate overnight. When ready to assemble, cut into 2-inch-long bars ½ inch thick.

ASSEMBLY

Chocolate Espresso Mousse

Whipped crème fraîche

Chocolate Espresso Custard

2 cups Chocolate Sauce (page 246)

Steamed milk

Chocolate Cake

Frozen Espresso Mascarpone Mousse

Chocolate Tuiles (page 247)

2 cups Espresso Sabayon Sauce (page 250)

Chocolate Garnish (page 245)

Carefully unmold the chocolate mousse. Using a demi-tasse spoon, place a quenelle of whipped crème fraîche on top of each mousse. In a warm water bath, warm the shot glasses of chocolate custard. Carefully pipe a thin layer of chocolate sauce on top of the custards. Fill the rest of the glass with steamed milk. Place a mousse on each of eight dessert plates and off to one side. Place a shot glass next to the mousse in the center of each plate. Place two chocolate cake bars side by side next to the shot glass. Place the frozen mascarpone mousse on top of the cake bars. Garnish the desserts with chocolate tuiles and chocolate garnishes. Pipe the sabayon and chocolate sauces on the plates.

A Spiral of Chocolate Mousse with Chocolate Malted Ice Cream

CHOCOLATE MOUSSE SPIRALS

1½ cups / 354 ml bittersweet chocolate, finely chopped

½ cup / 118 ml milk

½ cup / 118 ml unsalted butter

Grated zest of 1 orange

2 egg yolks

½ tablespoon / 7.5 ml granulated sugar

2 cups / 473 ml crème fraîche

1½ cups / 354 ml bittersweet chocolate, melted

Combine the chopped chocolate, milk, butter, and orange zest in a double boiler and place over hot water to melt. In a mixing bowl, whisk the egg yolks and sugar until pale ribbons form. Fold the yolks into the melted chocolate. Whip the crème fraîche until medium peaks form, then carefully fold into the chocolate mixture. Pipe the mousse into metal tubes 1 inch in diameter and 3 inches in length (see page 256). Refrigerate overnight. To unmold the mousse, rub tube with your hands and the mousse with slip out.

Spread the melted chocolate on the back of a warmed sheet pan. Refrigerate the chocolate to harden again, then remove and allow the chocolate to sit out until pliable. Using a paring knife, cut long strips of chocolate. Carefully peel the strips off by placing a paring knife's blade flat against the pan and scraping under the chocolate (page 29). Remove the chocolate mousse from the tubes and carefully roll each mousse in the strips of chocolate, creating a spiral effect. Refrigerate immediately.

CHOCOLATE CAKE

Cake

1 cup / 236 ml unsalted butter

2¼ cups / 528 ml granulated sugar

1 cup / 236 ml black cocoa powder (see page 258)

2 teaspoons / 10 ml baking powder

½ tablespoon / 7 ml baking soda

2¾ cups / 649 ml all-purpose flour

1 tablespoon 15 ml salt

3 eggs

2 cups warm water

Preheat oven to 325 degrees.

Cream butter, sugar, and cocoa. Add baking powder, baking soda, flour, and salt and mix until smooth. Add eggs and slowly add water. Pour the mixture into 2 buttered 8-inch cake pans. Bake for 30 to 40 minutes, until firm and springy to the touch. Allow the cakes to cool. Refrigerate overnight, then carefully slice the cake into six ⅛-inch-thick layers.

Combine ingredients for filling in a mixing bowl and whisk until stiff. Carefully spread the filling onto 3 cake layers so that the filling is ⅛ inch thick. Place another layer of cake on top of each layer, making a sandwich of 2 cake layers and 1 filling layer. Flatten

SERVES 8

The malt flavor is a longtime favorite of mine. It is a nice complement to the chocolate and vanilla, but on its own the taste can be overwhelming and quite filling. I find that a small scoop of the malted ice cream and a few dots of the syrup are enough to accompany the other components. All the components should be prepared one to two days in advance for best results.

Vanilla Mascarpone Filling

2 cups / 473 ml mascarpone cheese

1 cup / 236 ml heavy cream

½ cup / 118 ml granulated sugar

1 vanilla bean

until smooth and freeze. Remove from the freezer and cut each sandwich with an oval cutter, creating three oval shapes per sandwich. You will have one spare oval. Keep frozen until ready to serve.

CHOCOLATE MALTED ICE CREAM

4 cups / 946 ml heavy cream

2 cups / 473 ml milk

1 cup / 236 ml malt syrup

12 egg yolks

½ cup / 118 ml granulated sugar

1 cup / 236 ml extra-bitter chocolate, finely chopped

2 cups / 473 ml chocolate cake crumbs

In a heavy saucepan, combine cream, milk, and syrup and place over medium heat. Put the yolks and sugar in a medium bowl and stir to combine. Bring cream mixture to a full boil, then quickly whisk into the yolks and sugar. Immediately add the chopped chocolate and stir until smooth. Pass through a fine sieve, then cool in an ice bath. Place in an ice cream machine and freeze according to the manufacturer's instructions. While ice cream is still soft, fold in cake crumbs and place in freezer.

ASSEMBLY

Chocolate Cake

Chocolate Mousse Spirals

Chocolate Malted Ice Cream

2 cups Chocolate Sauce (page 246)

Malt syrup

Chocolate Tuiles (page 247)

Chocolate Cigarettes

Cut a 1-inch hole in one end of each chocolate cake oval. Place each cake oval in the center of a dessert plate and stand a chocolate spiral in the hole. Place a small oval of ice cream next to each spiral. Pipe chocolate sauce and malt syrup onto the plates. Garnish the plates with chocolate tuiles and chocolate cigarettes.

Caramelized Banana and Milk Chocolate Custard with Banana-Praline Terrine and Banana Fritters

BANANA AND MILK CHOCOLATE CUSTARD

Base

¾ cup plus 2 tablespoons / 207 ml granulated sugar

½ cup / 118 ml chopped ripe bananas

4 cups / 946 ml milk

2 cups / 473 ml heavy cream

2¼ cups / 531 ml milk chocolate, finely chopped

11 egg yolks

2 whole eggs

6 bananas, thinly sliced

BANANA-PRALINE TERRINE

Caramel and Chocolate Genoise

¾ cup / 177 ml granulated sugar

5 eggs

½ cup / 118 ml cake flour, sifted

3 tablespoons / 45 ml cornstarch

1½ tablespoons / 22 ml cocoa powder

In a medium saucepan, combine ¾ cup of the sugar with just enough water to dissolve it. Place over high heat and boil until deep amber. Add the chopped bananas and stir. Immediately add the remaining 2 tablespoons sugar, the milk, and cream. Stir and bring to a simmer, remove from heat, and add chopped milk chocolate, stirring until smooth. Cool the mixture in an ice bath. Add the egg yolks and whole eggs and strain mixture through a fine chinois.

Preheat oven to 300 degrees.

Pour ⅓ cup of the mixture into each of eight small glasses or 4-ounce ramekins. Bake in a water bath until set, 30–40 minutes. Remove and allow to cool. Place in a refrigerator for 1 to 2 hours, then remove and add sliced bananas around the edge of the custard in a fan pattern. Refrigerate the custard until needed.

In a small saucepan, dissolve ¼ cup of the sugar in a little water. Place over medium heat and bring to a boil. Boil until caramelized. While the sugar is cooking, place the eggs and remaining ½ cup sugar in an electric mixer bowl and set over hot water. Whisk by hand until warm, then use electric mixer to whisk on high for 8 to 10 minutes. Carefully pour caramelized sugar into the whipping eggs. Stop machine and remove bowl. Carefully fold in flour, cornstarch, and cocoa.

Preheat oven to 300 degrees.

Spread batter on a parchment-lined sheet pan until ¼ inch thick. Bake until lightly golden brown and firm, 15 minutes. Let cool slightly.

Line a 3½-inch by 10-inch U-shaped plastic or metal terrine with parchment paper. Carefully cut long strips of the genoise and place in terrine to line pan. Place in freezer and allow to set until firm.

SERVES 8

Caramelized bananas seem the perfect addition to the milk chocolate custard. The warm banana cuts the sweetness of the milk chocolate. The praline-flavored terrine adds another touch of caramel that makes the dessert more flavorful and less sweet. The frozen terrine and sauces should be prepared a day in advance. The other components can be made the same day that you serve them.

Frozen Banana Praline Mousse

4 eggs, separated

5 tablespoons / 74 ml granulated sugar

½ cup / 118 ml praline paste

¼ cup / 59 ml pureed ripe banana

2¼ cups / 532 ml heavy cream

Combine egg yolks and 1 tablespoon of the sugar for the mousse in an electric mixer bowl and whisk until pale and fluffy. In a separate bowl, mixing by hand, combine the praline paste, banana puree, and ¼ cup of the cream until smooth. Fold the egg yolk mixture into the praline-banana mixture. In another mixing bowl, whisk the egg whites until firm peaks are formed. Add the remaining ¼ cup sugar and continue to whisk for 1 minute. Fold into the yolk-praline mixture. Whip the remaining 2 cups cream and fold that into the egg mixture. Fill the genoise-lined terrine with the mousse. Place the terrine back in the freezer and allow to set until firm, preferably overnight. Slice into ½-inch-thick slices, trimming the ends to make sure that they are clean and flat. Keep in freezer till ready to use.

BANANA FRITTERS

Vegetable oil, for deep-frying

4 ripe bananas

2½ cups / 591 ml all-purpose flour

1 cup / 236 ml granulated sugar

2 tablespoons / 29 ml baking powder

2 cups / 473 ml cold water

2 cups / 473 ml Panko bread crumbs (available in Japanese groceries)

Confectioners' sugar, for dusting

Heat the oil to 350 degrees.

Peel bananas and cut into 2-inch lengths. In a mixing bowl, combine flour, sugar, and baking powder. Whisk in the cold water until smooth. Dip bananas into fritter batter, coating lightly. Coat with the bread crumbs and deep-fry until golden brown, 3 minutes. Remove and place on towel. Dust with confectioners' sugar.

ASSEMBLY

Banana and Milk Chocolate Custard

1 cup Brûlée Sugar (page 244)

Banana Fritters

Banana-Praline Terrine Slices

2 cups Chocolate Sabayon Sauce (page 250)

2 cups Banana Caramel Sauce (page 246)

Milk Chocolate Garnish (page 245)

Chocolate Tuiles (page 247)

Sugar Garnish (page 253)

Sprinkle the custard with brûlée sugar and lightly caramelize using a blowtorch. Place a custard toward the front of each of eight dessert plates. Place a fritter next to each custard. Carefully lean a frozen terrine slice against each fritter. Pipe the sabayon and caramel sauces onto the plates. Decorate the plates with a milk chocolate garnish, chocolate tuile, and sugar garnish.

Caramelized Banana and Milk Chocolate Custard with Banana-Praline Terrine and Banana Fritters **95**

Warm Prune and Pignoli Tartlet with Ricotta Zeppoles

PRUNE AND PIGNOLI TARTLETS

Prune Tartlet

3 cups / 709 ml pitted prunes

3 cups / 709 ml water

1 cup / 236 ml granulated sugar

8 Sucre Dough disks (page 253),
3 inches in diameter

1½ cups / 354 ml pignoli nuts

Almond Financiers Batter

1¾ cups / 413 ml confectioners' sugar

¼ cup / 59 ml all-purpose flour

½ cup / 118 ml natural almond flour

3 egg whites

¼ cup / 55 g salted butter

Place the prunes in a bowl. In a small saucepan, combine water and sugar and bring to a boil. Pour over the prunes, cover, and allow to sit overnight.

The next day, preheat oven to 325 degrees.

Drain the prunes and cut into small dice. Using eight 2½-inch tartlet pans, blind bake the disks until golden brown, 15 minutes. Let cool.

Half-fill the disks with the diced prunes.

In an electric mixer bowl, combine the confectioners' sugar, flour, almond flour, and egg whites. Whisk until smooth. In a small saucepan, brown the butter and add to the batter. Place the batter in a small piping bag. Refrigerate.

Carefully pipe the batter on top of the prunes, filling the shells. Sprinkle pignoli nuts on top of the batter. Bake at 325 degrees until golden brown, 25 to 30 minutes. Store at room temperature. Reheat for 5 minutes in a 300-degree oven before serving.

FROZEN VANILLA SOUFFLÉS

4 eggs, separated

¾ cup / 777 ml granulated sugar

½ vanilla bean, split in half and seeds scraped

2 cups / 473 ml heavy cream

In an electric mixer bowl, combine egg yolks, ¼ cup of the sugar, and the vanilla seeds, and whisk until pale and thick. In a separate mixing bowl, whisk the egg whites until firm peaks are formed. Add the remaining ½ cup granulated sugar and continue to whisk for 1 minute. Fold egg whites into egg yolk mixture. In another bowl, whip the cream until firm peaks are formed and add to the egg mixture. Refrigerate.

Spread the soufflé on a parchment-lined sheet tray until ½ inch in thickness. Freeze for at least 3 hours, or overnight. Cut into eight 2-inch disks. Keep frozen until ready to use.

SERVES 8

Don't fear the prune! The prune has a bad reputation in the United States. This is my attempt to better the image of this unappreciated fruit. The tartlets and the zeppoles need to be prepared the same day that you serve them. All the other components can be prepared a day in advance.

RICOTTA ZEPPOLES

1 egg white

1 cup / 236 ml ricotta cheese

½ cup / 118 ml semolina flour

¼ cup / 59 ml cake flour

½ cup / 118 ml granulated sugar

Pinch of salt

3 teaspoons/15 ml baking powder

½ vanilla bean, split in half and seeds scraped

Vegetable oil, for deep-frying

½ cup confectioner's sugar, for dusting

Combine all the ingredients, except oil and confectioners' sugar, in an electric mixer and mix until incorporated.

Heat oil to 325 degrees and deep-fry zeppoles in hot oil until golden brown, 5 minutes. Remove and dust with confectioners' sugar.

PRUNE SAUCE

1 cup / 236 ml pitted prunes

2 tablespoons / 29 ml granulated sugar

1 cup water

Place the prunes in a bowl. In a small saucepan, combine sugar and water and bring to a boil. Pour over the prunes, cover, and allow to sit overnight. The next day, drain the prunes. Place in a blender with half of the steeping liquid and puree. Refrigerate.

ASSEMBLY

Prune Sauce

2 cups Vanilla Sabayon Sauce (page 250)

Prune and Pignoli Tartlets

Frozen Vanilla Soufflés

Ricotta Zeppoles

Honey Tuiles (page 247)

Sugar Garnish (page 253)

In the center of each of eight dessert plates, place a small pool of prune sauce. Carefully pipe dots of sabayon sauce around the border of the prune sauce. Place a warm tartlet in the center of the sauce. Place a disk of soufflé on top of the tart. Place three fried zeppoles around the plate. Garnish the plates with honey tuiles and a sugar garnish.

Red Wine Poached Pear and Pistachio Financier

PISTACHIO FINANCIERS

1¾ cups / 413 ml confectioners' sugar

¼ cup / 59 ml all-purpose flour

½ cup / 118 ml pistachio flour

3 egg whites

¼ cup / 55 g salted butter

2 teaspoons / 10 ml pistachio oil (page 259)

8 Red Wine Poached Seckel Pears ∎

∎ Red Wine Poached Seckel Pears

16 seckel pears

6 cups / 1418 ml concentrated red wine, reduced from 12 cups (see tip)

3 cups / 709 ml granulated sugar

1 vanilla bean, split in half

Peel of ½ orange

Juice of 1 lemon

1 cinnamon stick

MASCARPONE-FILLED PEARS

1 cup / 236 ml mascarpone cheese

½ cup / 118 ml heavy cream

¼ cup / 59 ml granulated sugar

1 vanilla bean, split in half and seeds scraped

8 Red Wine Poached Seckel Pears

Preheat oven to 325 degrees. Butter eight 2½-inch tartlet pans.

In an electric mixer bowl, combine the sugar, flours, and egg whites, and whisk until smooth. Brown the butter and add to the batter. Add the pistachio oil.

Place mixture in a piping bag and carefully pipe batter into tartlet pans. Cut poached pears into thin slices. Garnish each tartlet with sliced pears and bake until light golden brown and firm to the touch, 20 to 30 minutes. Allow to cool for 20 minutes. Store at room temperature.

Peel and core pears. In a small saucepan, combine ingredients and bring to a simmer. Cook until the pears are tender, 20 minutes. Remove pan from heat and place in an ice bath to cool. Refrigerate the pears in the poaching liquid.

In an electric mixer bowl, combine the mascarpone cheese, cream, sugar, and vanilla seeds, and whisk until firm. Place mixture in pastry bag and carefully pipe mixture into empty cores of the seckel pears. Set aside. Refrigerate.

SERVES 8

Warm, buttery-rich financiers are easy to make. When accompanied by the intense flavor of red wine poached pears and the smoothness of pistachio mascarpone, they make for a great combination of textures and temperatures. All components can be prepared one to two days ahead, but bake the financiers the same day you serve them.

CHEF'S NOTE

For the red wine poached seckel pears, use a full-bodied red wine, such as a Cabernet or Barolo of good quality, in a mid-price range. Don't waste your best wine, but then again don't try to make something good out of something that started off bad.

FROZEN PISTACHIO MOUSSE

1 cup / 236 ml mascarpone cheese

½ cup / 118 ml milk

½ cup / 118 ml pistachio paste

3 egg whites

1 cup / 236 ml granulated sugar

2 cups / 473 ml heavy cream

1 cup / 236 ml pistachio flour

Combine mascarpone cheese, milk, and pistachio paste in a bowl and whisk until smooth. In an electric mixer, whisk the egg whites until firm peaks are formed. Add the sugar and continue to whisk for 1 minute. Fold egg mixture into the mascarpone-pistachio base. Whip cream and also fold into the base. Place mixture in a pastry bag and carefully pipe into eight metal tubes 1 inch in diameter and 3 inches in length (see page 256). Freeze. Once the mousse is frozen, unmold and roll cylinders in the pistachio flour. Keep frozen.

RED WINE PEAR SORBET

6 Bartlett pears, ripe or overripe

1 cup / 236 ml granulated sugar

2 cups / 473 ml concentrated red wine, reduced from 4 cups

1 tablespoon / 15 ml lemon juice

1 vanilla bean, split in half

Peel, core, and quarter the pears. Combine the remaining ingredients in a saucepan and bring to a boil. Add pears, reduce heat, and simmer until pears are tender, 30 minutes. Place saucepan in an ice bath to cool, then puree the pears until smooth and pass through a fine sieve. Process in an ice cream machine according to the manufacturer's instructions. Keep frozen.

RED WINE SYRUP

4 cups / 946 ml red wine

1 tablespoon / 15 ml granulated sugar

2½ vanilla beans, split in half and seeds scraped

Combine ingredients in a small saucepan. Place over high heat and boil until there is only ½ cup liquid remaining. Set aside.

ASSEMBLY

Frozen Pistachio Mousse

Red Wine Pear Sorbet

Pistachio Financiers

Sucre Dough (page 253), four 3-inch round disks cut evenly in half

Mascarpone-Filled Pears

2 cups Pear Sabayon Sauce (page 250)

Red Wine Syrup

Honey Tuiles (page 247)

Sugar Garnish (page 253)

Place a frozen mousse slightly off center of each of eight dessert dishes. Place a scoop of sorbet on the opposite side of each plate. Place a financier on top of a sucre disk. Rest the disk on top of the frozen mousse and sorbet. Place a stuffed pear in front of the financier. Pipe sabayon sauce and red wine syrup on each plate. Garnish with honey tuiles and a sugar garnish.

Caramelized Banana Tart with Star Anise and Banana Fritters

ALMOND COOKIES

14 tablespoons / 200 g unsalted butter

1¾ cups / 413 ml granulated sugar

3½ cups / 827 ml finely ground almonds

1 cup / 236 ml all-purpose flour

¾ cup / 177 ml water

¼ cup / 59 ml almond flour

1 egg white

Preheat oven to 325 degrees.

Combine butter, sugar, and ground almonds in an electric mixer bowl. Cream until smooth. Stop the machine and add remaining ingredients, mixing until incorporated. Using a 4-inch round stencil (page 252), spread batter on a nonstick silicone baking sheet. Bake until golden brown, 20 minutes. Allow to cool, than store in airtight container.

FROZEN STAR ANISE SOUFFLÉ

2½ cups / 590 ml granulated sugar

1 cup / 236 ml water

½ cup / 118 ml corn syrup

¼ pound / 112 g star anise

4 eggs, separated

2 cups / 473 ml heavy cream

In a small saucepan, combine 2 cups of the sugar, the water, the corn syrup, and star anise and bring to a boil. Remove from heat and allow to steep for 2 to 3 hours. Once liquid has cooled, strain through a fine sieve.

In an electric mixer bowl, combine egg yolks and ¼ cup of the star anise syrup and whisk until pale and fluffy, 5 to 6 minutes. In a separate mixing bowl, whisk egg whites until firm peaks are formed. Add the remaining ½ cup sugar and continue to whisk for 1 minute, then fold whites into yolk mixture. Whip the cream and fold into egg mixture. Spread the mixture on a parchment-lined sheet tray until ½ inch in thickness. Freeze. Once frozen, cut into 3-inch disks. Keep frozen.

SERVES 8

Combining the flavors of banana and star anise was easy. There is something about the scent of the two that links them together. Stacking the components on this dish forces you to combine the flavors, textures, and temperatures when you eat it. All components except for the fritters can be prepared one to two days in advance.

BANANA FRITTERS

Vegetable oil, for deep-frying

2½ cups / 591 ml all-purpose flour

1 cup / 236 ml granulated sugar

2 tablespoons / 29 ml baking powder

2 cups / 473 ml cold water

16 bananas, peeled and cut into 2½-inch lengths

2 cups / 473 ml Panko bread crumbs (available in Japanese groceries)

Confectioners' sugar, for dusting

Heat the oil to 350 degrees.

Combine flour, sugar, and baking powder in a mixing bowl. Whisk in the cold water until smooth. Dip bananas into the fritter batter, coating lightly. Roll in the bread crumbs. Deep-fry until golden brown, about 5 minutes. Remove from oil. Drain on paper and trim the ends of the fritters. Dust lightly with confectioners' sugar.

BANANA CHIPS

1 banana, peeled and pureed until smooth

1 teaspoon / 5 ml granulated sugar

Preheat oven to 200 degrees.

On a nonstick silicone sheet tray, spread the puree, using a stencil (page 252). Sprinkle with sugar. Bake approximately 30 minutes, until light golden brown. While chips are still warm, carefully bend each over a large can to create a slightly curved chip. Store in air-tight container.

ASSEMBLY

8 bananas, peeled and sliced

Almond Cookies

1 cup Brûlée Sugar (page 244)

Frozen Star Anise Soufflé

2 cups Banana Caramel Sauce (page 246)

2 cups Star Anise Sabayon Sauce (page 250)

Banana Fritters

Spun Sugar (page 253)

Banana Chips

Thinly slice each banana and place in a fan pattern around an almond cookie to create the banana tarts. Sprinkle lightly with brûlée sugar and glaze with a blowtorch. Place a frozen soufflé on top of a second almond cookie. Place the banana tart on top of the soufflé, creating a sandwich. Place a small pool of banana caramel sauce in the center of each of eight dessert plates. Pipe star anise sabayon around the border. Place two banana fritters in the center of the sauce. Carefully place the soufflé assembly on top of the fritters. Garnish with the spun sugar and a banana chip.

Chilled Ginger and Pomegranate Parfait Served in a Shell

GINGER AND POMEGRANATE PARFAIT

8 medium pomegranates

Pomegranate Sorbet

1 cup / 236 ml granulated sugar

½ cup / 118 ml water

3 cups / 709 ml fresh pomegranate juice

Ginger Soufflé

2 eggs, separated

3 tablespoons / 44 ml Ginger Syrup ▪

¼ cup / 59 ml granulated sugar

1 cup / 236 ml heavy cream

▪ **Ginger Syrup**

1 cup / 236 ml granulated sugar

½ cup / 118 ml water

Juice of ½ lemon

½ cup / 118 ml corn syrup

½ cup / 118 ml fresh ginger, chopped

Cut the tops off of pomegranates, creating a lid. Hollow out the pomegranates and reserve the seeds for juice. Place the shells in the freezer until frozen.

In a saucepan, combine sugar and water for sorbet and bring to a boil. Remove from heat and allow to cool. Add pomegranate juice and process in an ice cream machine according to the manufacturer's instructions. Place in a pastry bag.

In an electric mixer bowl, combine egg yolks and ginger syrup. Mix until pale and fluffy. In a separate mixer bowl, whisk egg whites until firm peaks are formed. Add the sugar and continue to whisk for 1 minute. Fold whites into egg yolks. Whip the cream and fold into the egg mixture. Place the mixture in a pastry bag.

Remove pomegranate shells from the freezer and place a 1½-inch ring mold in the center of each shell. Line the ring with either plastic or parchment paper. Fill with alternating layers of sorbet and soufflé. Smooth the top. Place the shells back in the freezer and keep frozen until ready to serve.

Combine sugar, water, and lemon juice in a small saucepan and bring to a boil. Add corn syrup and ginger and bring to a second boil. Remove from the heat and allow to cool. Strain the ginger and set syrup aside.

SERVES 8

The sweet scent and flavor of ginger help counterbalance the often tannic bite of the pomegranate. Served in the shell, this makes a great party dessert, as it is prepared almost entirely in advance.

ASSEMBLY

Ginger and Pomegranate Parfait

Fresh pomegranate juice

Pomegranate seeds

Sugar Garnish (page 253)

Place a frozen parfait in the center of each of eight dessert plates. Pull off the metal rings and carefully remove the paper or plastic. Pour a very small amount of pomegranate juice around the soufflés inside shells. Place a few pomegranate seeds on top. Garnish with a sugar garnish that looks similar to a cage or netting (place the garnish on top in place of a lid).

Pan-Fried Apples with Nutmeg Ice Cream and Kumquat Compote

PAN-FRIED APPLES

8 Granny Smith apples

2 cups / 473 ml Brûlée Sugar (page 244)

2½ cups / 591 ml all-purpose flour

1 cup / 236 ml granulated sugar

2 tablespoons / 29 ml baking powder

2 cups / 473 ml cold water

2 cups / 473 ml Panko bread crumbs (available in Japanese groceries)

2 cups / 473 ml clarified butter

Confectioners' sugar, for dusting

Preheat oven to 275 degrees.

Peel apples and cut in half directly down center. Scoop out seeds using a Parisian scoop. Coat each apple half in brûlée sugar and place on a parchment-lined sheet tray. Bake 20 minutes, then remove from oven and allow to cool slightly.

Dredge apples once again in brûlée sugar. Place back in oven and continue to bake until the apples are tender and light golden in color, about 20 minutes. Remove from oven and allow apples to cool.

In a mixing bowl, combine flour, sugar, and baking powder. Whisk in cold water until the mixture is smooth. Once the apples are cool, dip them in the fritter batter, coating them lightly. Dredge in bread crumbs.

Preheat a sauté pan with clarified butter. Sauté the breaded apples until they are golden brown on each side, about 4 minutes on each side. Remove apples from pan and dust lightly with confectioners' sugar.

NUTMEG ICE CREAM

4 cups / 946 ml heavy cream

2 cups / 473 ml milk

1½ cups / 354 ml granulated sugar

½ nutmeg, grated

12 egg yolks

In a heavy saucepan, combine cream, milk, 1 cup of the sugar, and the nutmeg. Place over medium heat. In a separate bowl, combine egg yolks and remaining ½ cup sugar. Bring nutmeg cream to a boil, then quickly whisk the cream into the yolks and sugar. Strain through a fine-meshed sieve or chinois into a clean container. Place in an ice bath to cool.

Place cream in an ice cream machine and process according to the manufacturer's instructions. While the ice cream is still soft, place in a piping bag. Pipe the ice cream into eight ice cream bar molds that are ½ inch thick by 2 inches wide. Place in the freezer and allow to freeze solid. Unmold and keep in freezer until ready to use.

SERVES 8

Pan-frying gives a crisp buttery coating to soft roasted apples. Nutmeg is definitely my favorite spice of this season. When used in an ice cream, it is the perfect counter to the fragrant kumquats. All the components can be prepared a day in advance. Even the apples for the pan-fried apples can be roasted a day ahead, refrigerated, and then breaded and pan-fried when needed.

KUMQUAT COMPOTE

½ cup / 118 ml honey

2 cups / 473 ml sliced kumquats, in eighths, with seeds removed

½ cup / 118 ml diced apples

1 cup / 236 ml golden raisins

¼ cup / 59 ml Sauternes wine

Place honey in a saucepan and cook over medium heat until lightly caramelized. Add the kumquats, apples, and raisins and stir until hot. Add the Sauternes and cook over low heat until mixture becomes thick. Remove from heat and allow to cool. Refrigerate to store overnight.

ASSEMBLY

2 cups Vanilla Sabayon Sauce (page 250)

Pan-Fried Apples

Kumquat Compote

Nutmeg Ice Cream

Fresh apple, cut into fine julienne pieces

1 cup Spice Syrup (page 251)

Honey Tuiles (page 247)

Sugar Garnish (page 253)

In the center of each oval dessert plate, place a small pool of the sabayon sauce. Place two of the pan-fried apples, leaning against each other, on top of the sauce. To the left of the apples, place a small pile of the compote. To the right of the apples, place the mold of nutmeg ice cream standing straight up. Place a small amount of apple julienne on top of the pan-fried apples. Decorate the plates with the spice syrup, honey tuiles, and sugar garnish.

Frozen Torte of Pfeffernuss Spice and Honey with Port Cherries

SERVES 8

This torte has a chewy, creamy texture. Combined with the fragrant honey and spices, it is a powerhouse of flavors. It takes a strong sauce, such as the port with dried cherries, to accent this dish. All components should be made a day or two in advance for best results.

PFEFFERNUSS TORTE

Pfferernuss Meringue Disks

1 cup / 236 ml granulated sugar

1 cup / 236 ml sliced, blanched almonds

½ cup / 118 ml confectioners' sugar

¼ teaspoon / 1 ml black pepper

½ tablespoon / 7.5 ml ground cardamom

½ teaspoon / 2 ml ground anise seed

½ tablespoon / 7.5 ml ground cinnamon

¼ teaspoon / 1 ml ground cloves

¼ teaspoon / 1 ml ground nutmeg

Grated zest of 1 orange

1 tablespoon / 15 ml grated lemon zest

5 egg whites

FROZEN HONEY MOUSSE

4 eggs separated

¼ cup / 59 ml honey

¼ cup / 59 ml granulated sugar

2 cups / 473 ml heavy cream

Preheat oven to 250 degrees.

Create a stencil (page 252) that is 3 inches round to be used for the disk.

In a food processor, combine ½ cup of the granulated sugar, the almonds, confectioners' sugar, and all the spices and grated zests. Puree until smooth. In an electric mixer, whisk the egg whites until soft peaks are formed. Add the remaining ½ cup of sugar and continue to whisk until firm peaks are formed. Whisk for an additional minute, then fold in the dry ingredients. On a parchment-lined sheet tray, using the stencil you have created, spread the meringue. Bake until crisp and light golden brown in color, 30 minutes. Allow to cool. Store in airtight container.

In an electric mixer bowl, combine yolks and honey for mousse and whisk until pale and thick. In a separate mixer bowl, whisk whites until soft peaks are formed. Add sugar and continue to whisk until firm peaks are formed. Fold whites into yolk mixture. In another bowl, whip cream until firm peaks are formed and add to egg mixture. Place in a piping bag.

Place eight ring molds 3 inches in diameter and 1 inch tall on a flat sheet tray. Place a meringue disk on the bottom of each mold. Carefully pipe, on top of the disk, the mousse until it is ¼ inch thick. Cover with another meringue disk. Alternate the layers until you have four layers of meringue and three layers of mousse. Place in freezer. Once tortes are frozen, carefully use a 1-inch round cutter to cut a slightly off-center hole in each torte. (Dip cutter in hot water first to make cutting easier.) Keep frozen.

PORT CHERRIES

3 cups / 709 ml concentrated Ruby Port wine, reduced from 4 cups

1 cup / 236 ml granulated sugar

2 cups / 473 ml whole dried cherries

In a small saucepan, combine the port and sugar and bring to a boil. Pour mixture over the dried cherries, cover, and allow to cool at room temperature. Refrigerate to store overnight.

ASSEMBLY

Port Cherries

Pfeffernuss Torte

Honey Tuiles (page 247)

Sugar Garnish (page 253)

2 cups Vanilla Sabayon Sauce (page 250)

In the center of each dessert plate, place a small pool of cherries and sauce. Unmold a torte and place upright on its edge in the center of the sauce. Carefully place a honey tuile through the hole in the torte. Garnish the plate with a sugar garnish and some sabayon sauce.

Date Strudel Cake with Vanilla Soufflé

SERVES 8

Layering cakes and tortes is a wonderful way of combining flavors. I often thought that some of them might taste good served warm or hot. Unfortunately, heating most cakes or tortes tends to dry them out. I came up with the idea of wrapping a layered cake or torte in strudel dough. This, I felt, would retain the moisture and give it a flaky exterior. All the components can be made in advance, but the strudel cakes should be refrigerated for only an hour or two before baking.

DATE STRUDEL CAKE

Frangipane Cake Layers

1 cup / 236 ml almond paste

1¾ cup plus 2 tablespoons / 200 g unsalted butter

1 cup / 236 ml granulated sugar

4 eggs

½ cup / 118 ml cake flour

Date Puree with Almonds

1 pound / 455 g pitted dates

1 cup / 236 ml toasted and finely chopped almonds

6 sheets strudel dough

1 cup / 236 ml clarified butter

Preheat oven to 325 degrees.

In an electric mixer bowl, cream the almond paste, butter, and sugar until pale and fluffy. Add the eggs and flour and mix until ingredients are blended. Place mixture in a parchment-lined, 8-inch round cake pan. Bake until golden brown and firm to the touch, 30 minutes. Allow to cool, then refrigerate overnight.

Place the dates in a medium saucepan and cover with cold water. Bring to a quick boil and drain immediately. Pass the dates through a food mill while still warm. Add the almonds to the date puree, and allow to cool. Place in a pastry bag.

Cut cake into quarter-inch slices using a round metal cutter 2½ inches in diameter to create 24 2½-inch disks.

Carefully spread a sheet of strudel dough on a flat surface and brush lightly with clarified butter. Place a second sheet of strudel dough on top and again brush with butter. Place a third sheet of strudel dough and butter. Cut 9-inch disks of strudel dough from the sheets. You should get four disks per sheet. Repeat with remaining three sheets of dough.

Place eight metal ring molds, which are 3 inches in diameter and 1½ inches in height, on a sheet tray. Carefully line the rings with the strudel disks. Place a disk of the frangipane cake inside each ring mold on top of the strudel dough. Pipe a ¼-inch-thick layer of date puree on top of each cake. Alternate the cake and date layers until you have three layers of cake and two layers of puree. Carefully fold the strudel dough on top of the cake. Each cake should now be encased within the strudel dough, creating a shape that is 1½ inches in height and 3 inches round. Leave in the metal ring molds and place a piece of parchment paper on top. Lay another sheet tray on top for weight.

Preheat oven to 350 degrees. Bake until golden brown, 20 minutes.

ALMOND COOKIES

1¾ cups / 413 ml granulated sugar

3½ cups / 827 ml sliced, blanched almonds

14 tablespoons / 200 g unsalted butter

1 cup / 236 ml all-purpose flour

¼ cup / 59 ml almond flour

1 egg white

¾ cup / 177 ml water

Preheat oven to 300 degrees.

In a food processor, combine sugar and almonds. Puree until smooth. Put into an electric mixer bowl and cream butter until smooth. Add flours, egg white, and water and mix until incorporated. Using a stencil (page 252) to create 2-inch round cookies, spread batter onto a silicone sheet tray. Bake until light golden brown in color, 20 minutes. Allow to cool; then store in airtight container.

FROZEN VANILLA SOUFFLÉ

2 eggs separated

6 tablespoons / 89 ml granulated sugar

¼ vanilla bean, split in half and seeds scraped

1 cup / 236 ml heavy cream

In an electric mixer bowl, combine egg yolks, 2 tablespoons sugar, and the vanilla seeds. Whisk until pale and thick. Using a separate mixer bowl, whip egg whites until firm peaks are formed. Add the remaining ¼ cup sugar and continue to whip for 1 minute. Fold whites into yolk mixture. Whip the cream until firm peaks are formed, then fold into egg mixture. Pipe the mixture into eight dome-shaped molds 2 inches in diameter. Place on 2-inch round metal rings, and freeze.

ASSEMBLY

2 cups Vanilla Sabayon Sauce (page 250)

1 cup Clear Caramel Sauce (page 246)

Date Strudel Cake

Frozen Vanilla Soufflé

Almond Cookies

Sugar Garnish (page 253)

On each round dessert plate, pipe a small pool of sabayon sauce in the center. Pipe a thin line of caramel sauce around the sabayon. Carefully slice each strudel cake in half. Turn slices around and place in the center of each plate on the sabayon—the inside of the cake should be facing outward. Carefully unmold the frozen soufflés on top of the almond cookies. Place on top of the strudel cakes. Decorate with a sugar garnish.

Pineapple Tartlet

YIELDS 12 TARTLETS

Slow-cooking the pineapple with vanilla and cinnamon gives it an almost spiced heat. It needs the soothing counter that the crème fraîche provides. The tartlets can be assembled and refrigerated for two to four hours without the kataifi strips. Just place them on top when you are ready to serve.

2 cups / 473 ml diced pineapple

½ cup / 118 ml granulated sugar

½ vanilla bean, split in half

2 cinnamon sticks

12 Sucre Dough disks (page 253), 2 inches in diameter

¼ cup / 59 ml crème fraîche, whipped

15 to 20 strands kataifi dough, toasted

In a small saucepan, combine the pineapple, sugar, vanilla bean, and cinnamon sticks. Simmer until the pineapple is tender, 10 minutes. Remove the vanilla bean and cinnamon sticks and puree the pineapple in a food processor until smooth. Place the puree back in the pan and reduce until thickened, about 5 minutes.

Preheat oven to 300 degrees.

Place the disks of sucre dough in small tartlet pans and bake 20 minutes. Allow to cool.

Carefully pipe the pineapple puree into the tartlet shells. Using a demitasse spoon, carefully place small quenelles of the crème fraîche on top of the pineapple. Place a few strands of the toasted kataifi dough on top of the crème fraîche and serve.

Prune and Pistachio Financiers

YIELDS 24 FINANCIERS

The natural sweetness of the prune is a great addition to an already wonderful, nutty cake. These can be baked two to four hours ahead.

1¾ cups / 413 ml confectioners' sugar

¼ cup / 59 ml all-purpose flour

½ cup / 118 ml pistachio flour

3 egg whites

¼ cup / 55 g salted butter

6 pitted prunes, cut into quarters

1 cup / 236 ml ground pistachios

Preheat oven to 325 degrees.

In an electric mixer bowl, combine the sugar, flours, and egg whites, whisking until smooth. In a small saucepan, brown the butter and add to the mixture. Place in a piping bag.

Lightly butter 24 petit four tartlet pans. Pipe the batter into each pan until it is half filled. Place one piece of prune into the center of each. Sprinkle the surface of each tartlet with the ground pistachios. Bake until light golden brown in color, 15 to 20 minutes. Cool briefly, then serve.

Speculaas Spiced Cookies with Praline Filling

1 cup plus 2 tablespoons/285 g unsalted butter

1½ cups / 354 ml granulated sugar

1 egg

3¾ cups / 886 ml cake flour

4 teaspoons / 20 ml baking powder

Pinch of salt

1 tablespoon / 15 ml ground cinnamon

¼ teaspoon / 1 ml ground nutmeg

¼ teaspoon / 1 ml ground cloves

½ teaspoon / 2 ml ground ginger

¼ teaspoon / 1 ml ground cardamom

2 tablespoons / 29 ml water

3 egg whites, lightly beaten

1 cup / 236 ml Brûlée Sugar (page 244)

70 g cocoa butter

4½ ounces / 130 g milk chocolate

8 ounces / 225 g praline paste

In an electric mixer bowl, cream butter and sugar until smooth. Add egg, flour, baking powder, salt, cinnamon, nutmeg, cloves, ginger, cardamom, and water. Mix until well blended. Allow to rest for 1 hour.

Preheat oven to 300 degrees.

Roll dough into a sheet ⅛ inch thick. Carefully brush dough with beaten egg white and sprinkle with brûlée sugar. Cut into 1-inch rounds or squares. Bake until light golden brown, 20 minutes. Allow to cool.

In a double boiler combine cocoa butter and milk chocolate. Melt over hot water. Whisk in the praline paste until smooth and thick.

Reverse cookies so that the sugar side is facing down. Pipe the praline mixture into the center of each cookie. Place another cookie on top, creating a sandwich. Allow to cool before serving. Any unused dough can be frozen for later use.

YIELDS 25 COOKIES

A traditional Christmas cookie from Holland, with the added touch of praline. Store in a cool place for up to two days.

LEFT TO RIGHT: *Banana Fritters with Jicama Salad, Chocolate Praline Pops, Kumquats Filled with Chilled Vanilla Mascarpone, and Almond Fruit Cake*

Banana Fritters with Jicama Salad

Juice of 3 limes

1¼ cups / 295 ml water

¼ cup / 59 ml granulated sugar

4 mint leaves, minced

1 cup / 236 ml julienned jicama

2 to 3 ripe bananas

1¼ cups / 295 ml all-purpose flour

1 tablespoon / 15 ml baking powder

1 cup / 236 ml Panko bread crumbs (available in Japanese groceries)

Vegetable oil, for deep-frying

½ cup /118 ml confectioners' sugar

To make the jicama salad, combine the lime juice, sugar, ¼ cup water, and mint and pour over the jicama. Allow to sit for at least 1 hour.

Heat the oil to 350 degrees.

To make the fritters, cut the bananas into 1-inch lengths. In a small bowl, combine the flour, baking powder, and 1 cup water, whisking until smooth. Dip each banana into the batter, coating lightly. Coat with the bread crumbs. Deep-fry the bananas for 5 minutes. Remove from the fryer, drain, and dust lightly with confectioners' sugar. Place a small pile of the jicama salad directly on top of the banana fritter and serve.

YIELDS 12 FRITTERS

Bananas always taste great with a touch of lime. The jicama salad here provides that acidic accent plus a great crunchy texture. The salad should be prepared one to two hours prior to serving. Deep-fry the bananas when ready to serve.

Chocolate Praline Pops

½ cup / 118 ml chopped white chocolate, tempered (page 245)

2 cups / 473 ml extra-bitter chocolate, tempered (page 245)

½ cup / 118 ml heavy cream

4 tablespoons /58 ml praline paste

1½ cups / 354 ml extra-bitter chocolate, finely chopped

½ cup / 118 ml dry chocolate cake crumbs (page 33)

24 Chocolate Tuiles (page 247)

Use 1-inch round or square chocolate molds. Place the white chocolate in a piping bag and pipe an abstract pattern into the chocolate molds. Allow to set. Pour the tempered extra-bitter chocolate into the molds. Drain the molds and tap out excess chocolate. Allow to set, then trim the tops and edges smooth.

In a small saucepan, combine the cream and praline paste. Bring to a boil and pour over the chopped chocolate. Whisk until smooth. Once this ganache mixture has cooled, pipe it into the chocolate molds, filling molds to the top. Sprinkle with cake crumbs. Place a lollipop stick in the center of each mold. Refrigerate until set. Remove from the molds and garnish each stick with a chocolate tuile.

YIELDS 24 POPS

A basic molded chocolate that, when placed on a stick, has a nice look and is also fun to eat. Refrigerate to store, but allow to sit at room temperature for 30 minutes before serving.

Kumquats Filled with Chilled Vanilla Mascarpone *(photograph on page 116)*

YIELDS 12 SERVINGS

These are petit fours with classic popsicle flavors that have been refined. Make them in advance and store them in the freezer.

12 kumquats

4 cups plus 3 tablespoons / 990 ml granulated sugar

2 cups / 473 ml water

Juice of 1 lemon

½ cup / 118 ml mascarpone cheese

¼ cup / 59 ml heavy cream

½ vanilla bean, split in half and seeds scraped

Carefully cut the tops off the kumquats, creating an opening in each. Scoop out the insides with a small Parisian scoop until hollow. Place the hollowed-out kumquats in a small bowl.

In a small saucepan, combine 4 cups of the sugar, the water, and lemon juice and bring to a boil. Pour over the kumquats. Cover immediately and allow to cool, at least 3 hours. Remove the hollowed-out kumquats and drain on a towel until semi-dry. Place the shells in a pan and place in the freezer to chill.

In an electric mixer, bowl, combine the mascarpone cheese, cream, remaining 3 tablespoons sugar, and vanilla seeds. Whip until stiff and place in a piping bag. Carefully pipe mixture into the hollowed-out kumquat shells. Poke a toothpick through the cream and into the kumquat so that it is standing straight up. Store in freezer until ready to serve.

Almond Fruit Cake *(photograph on page 116)*

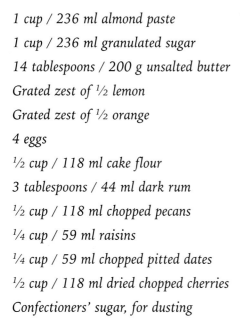

1 cup / 236 ml almond paste

1 cup / 236 ml granulated sugar

14 tablespoons / 200 g unsalted butter

Grated zest of ½ lemon

Grated zest of ½ orange

4 eggs

½ cup / 118 ml cake flour

3 tablespoons / 44 ml dark rum

½ cup / 118 ml chopped pecans

¼ cup / 59 ml raisins

¼ cup / 59 ml chopped pitted dates

½ cup / 118 ml dried chopped cherries

Confectioners' sugar, for dusting

Preheat oven to 300 degrees.

In an electric mixer bowl, cream the almond paste, sugar, butter, and grated zests until pale and fluffy. Add the eggs and flour and mix until smooth. Add the rum, nuts, and fruit, mixing until well blended. Spread the batter on a parchment-lined sheet tray until ½ inch thick. Bake until golden brown, 20 to 30 minutes. Allow to cool. Cut into shapes and dust with confectioners' sugar.

YIELDS 12 SERVINGS

Not old and dry, but moist and fresh, this is hardly a traditional fruit cake. It can be baked in advance and stored in the refrigerator.

Just when everyone has had enough of winter and the long stretch of nothing new in the markets, along comes spring to begin the year's cycle once again. For me growing up, the most important aspect of spring was that school was coming to an end. But once I started cooking, I noticed a whole new world. Produce comes to life at this time of year, and I start to look forward to certain fruits and herbs. If you are lucky enough to have a local farmer's market, you can get the first crack at fresh produce. To see and smell large bins and stacks of fresh fruits and herbs is inspirational—the sight attacks your senses and starts your creative juices flowing. The varieties and quality cannot be beat because often the produce is organic, picked at the peak of ripeness. The downside is that the produce and herbs come and go very fast. Local produce can have unpredictable seasons, which makes it difficult to rely on. While working at large restaurants, I have always treated local fruit as a bonus when I can get it. Realistically, I must rely on commercial purveyors. ■ **Spring also means that great** fresh herbs are starting to grow. Though I try to use herbs year-round, in the warmer weather they add a fresh, almost floral fragrance to my desserts. I started using herbs early in my pastry career, but I was really inspired after a meal at Mondrian restaurant in New York City. Tom Collicchio used a wide variety of herbs in his desserts. The natural fragrance and sweetness of the herbs complemented the fruits and chocolate so well. Since then, herbs have always been included in my creative process for desserts. Some chefs may consider herbs a fad, but they have become a standard ingredient in my pastry work. ■

The tart characteristics of spring fruits give these desserts a lighter and more acidic quality than ones on my winter menu. In spring and summer, guests like to be refreshed with dessert, so many of the dishes include fresh fruit. When writing this book, I had to draw a line between spring and summer fruits in an attempt to categorize them. The truth is, many fruits share the two seasons. Weather and your geographical region more accurately determine the seasons for fruit. ■ **I have always handled fruit** the same way a chef would handle vegetables. A chef will use vegetables as a garnish, an accompaniment, or a main component of a dish, adding texture, taste, substance, and presentation to the plate. Skills such as making a thin slice or perfect dice and such attention to detail not only make the presentations beautiful but also can determine how the food is eaten, how it combines with other components, and the texture and the feel of the food. I like seeing fresh or cooked fruit on a dessert because it shows the fruit in its natural state. No matter how wild the finished dessert may look, I like to have a link to the fruit's original form. ■ **In spring as well as** the other seasons, I have tried to showcase the most popular fruits and show you a few approaches to each. No matter what you make for dessert, the key to the best flavor is to start with the best fruit available.

Glazed Ricotta Cheese Tart with Fresh Cherries

RICOTTA CHEESE TART

Spiced Crust

10 tablespoons / 140 g unsalted butter

¾ cup / 177 ml granulated sugar

1 egg white

1½ cups / 354 ml cake flour

2 teaspoons / 10 ml baking powder

Pinch of salt

½ tablespoon / 7.5 ml ground cinnamon

⅛ teaspoon / .62 ml ground nutmeg

⅛ teaspoon / .62 ml ground cloves

¼ teaspoon / 1 ml ground ginger

⅛ teaspoon / .62 ml ground cardamom

1 tablespoon / 15 ml water

Ricotta Cheese Base

1½ cups / 354 ml cream cheese

¾ cup / 177 ml ricotta cheese

½ cup / 118 ml granulated sugar

½ vanilla bean, split in half and seeds scraped

2 whole eggs

1 egg white

¾ cup / 170 g heavy cream

In a mixing bowl, combine and cream the butter and sugar. Add the remaining ingredients for crust and mix until well incorporated. Place the dough on a sheet tray and refrigerate until chilled, approximately 3 hours. Once dough is chilled, roll the crust out until it is ⅛ inch thick. Cut into eight 3½-inch disks.

In an electric mixer bowl, combine cream cheese, ricotta cheese, sugar, and vanilla seeds; cream until smooth. Add the whole eggs, egg whites, and cream. Mix until smooth and pass through a fine sieve.

Preheat oven to 300 degrees.

Place the spiced dough disks on a sheet pan. Gently indent a 3-inch ring into each disk, making sure not to cut through the disks. Bake the disks with the rings until lightly golden brown, 20 minutes. Remove the disks from the oven and allow to cool slightly.

Lower the oven to 225 degrees.

Fill the rings until they are three-fourths full with the ricotta cheese base. Return the disks to the oven and bake until the cheese is set, 30 minutes. Remove from the oven and allow to cool.

Carefully trim around the edge of the metal rings and remove the rings from the cheese. Set aside. Keep in a cool place until served.

SERVES 8

I always prefer raw cherries over cooked. I like their texture, tartness, and freshness. The fresh cherries, along with the soft cheese tart and flaky strudel dough, enhance the light feel of this dessert. The sauce and strudel rings can be prepared a day in advance, but the cheese tart should be baked the same day you serve it.

STRUDEL RINGS

3 sheets strudel dough

½ cup / 118 ml clarified butter

Preheat oven to 350 degrees.

Carefully spread a sheet of strudel dough on a flat surface. Brush the sheet with butter and place another sheet of strudel dough on top. Brush once again with butter and place the third sheet on top. Cut into long, 1-inch-wide strips. Roll the strips onto metal rings that are 3 inches in diameter and 1 inch wide and refrigerate. Bake until golden brown, 15 minutes. Allow to cool and slide the dough circles off of the metal rings. Set aside. Store in an airtight container.

CHERRY SAUCE

4 cups / 946 ml cherries, pitted

1 cup / 236 ml water

Juice of ½ lemon

1 cup / 236 ml granulated sugar

Combine the ingredients in a saucepan and bring to a boil. Simmer for 4 to 5 minutes, then remove from heat and puree until fine. Pass through a fine sieve. Refrigerate.

ASSEMBLY

1 cup Brûlée Sugar (page 244)

Ricotta Cheese Tart

Strudel Rings

Honey Tuiles (page 247)

Fresh cherries

Cherry Sauce

1 cup Vanilla Sabayon Sauce (page 250)

Sugar Garnish (page 253)

Sprinkle the brûlée sugar on top of the cheese tarts and lightly glaze with a blowtorch. Place a tart in the center of each of eight dessert bowls and place a strudel ring around it. Carefully lift one end of each cheese tart in order to place a tuile end underneath it. This will allow the tuile to stand straight up. Place the fresh cherries around the cheese tarts. Add the cherry sauce and sabayon sauce. Finish the plates with a sugar garnish.

Cherry and Spice Custard with Warm Financier

CHERRY AND SPICE CUSTARD

Cherry Puree

3 cups / 709 ml Bing cherries, pitted

Juice of ½ lemon

1 cup / 236 ml granulated sugar

Spiced Custard

2 cups / 473 ml milk

1 cup / 236 ml heavy cream

1 cup / 236 ml crème fraîche

½ cup / 118 ml granulated sugar

1 cinnamon stick

Pinch of grated nutmeg

½ vanilla bean, split in half

½ cardamom pod

9 egg yolks

Place puree ingredients in a small saucepan and simmer until the cherries are soft, 5 minutes. Puree until smooth and pass through a fine sieve. Allow to cool, then spread puree evenly on the bottom of eight 4-inch shallow dishes or bowls until ¼ inch thick. Place bowls in freezer until the puree is frozen, at least 2 hours.

In a small saucepan, combine milk, cream, crème fraîche, sugar, and spices. Place over medium heat and simmer for 3 to 5 minutes. Remove from heat and allow to steep for 20 minutes.

Whisk in egg yolks and pass mixture through a fine sieve. Cool the liquid in an ice bath.

Preheat oven to 250 degrees.

Remove the bowls of cherry puree from the freezer and fill till three-quarters full with the custard. Create a water bath and bake until the custard is set, 40 minutes. Remove from oven and allow to cool. Place the bowls in the refrigerator.

CHERRY SAUCE

2 cups / 473 ml cherries, pitted

½ cup / 118 ml water

Juice of ½ lemon

½ cup / 118 ml granulated sugar

Combine ingredients in a saucepan. Simmer for 4 to 5 minutes, then puree until smooth. Pass through a fine sieve. Refrigerate.

WARM FINANCIER

1¾ cups / 413 ml confectioners' sugar

¼ cup / 59 ml all-purpose flour

½ cup / 118 ml natural almond flour

3 egg whites

¼ cup / 55 g salted butter

Preheat oven to 325 degrees.

In an electric mixer bowl, combine the sugar, flours, and egg whites. Whisk until smooth. In a small saucepan, brown the butter and add to the mixture. Place the batter in a piping bag. Butter eight small savarin molds, then pipe batter into the molds until three-quarters full. Bake until firm and golden brown, 25 minutes.

To reheat, place in 325-degree oven for 3 minutes.

SERVES 8

With the bilevel custard, you are almost certain to combine the smooth spice custard and rich cherry puree in every spoonful. It is accompanied by a warm financier and a creamy vanilla soufflé to round out the dish. All components can be made one to two days in advance. The batter for the financiers can be made ahead, but bake them just before serving.

FROZEN VANILLA SOUFFLÉ

4 eggs, separated

³⁄₄ cup / 177 ml granulated sugar

½ vanilla bean, seeds scraped

2 cups / 473 ml heavy cream

In an electric mixer bowl, combine egg yolks, ¼ cup of the sugar, and the vanilla seeds. Whisk until pale and thick. In a separate mixing bowl, whisk egg whites until firm peaks are formed. Add the remaining ½ cup sugar and continue to whisk for 1 minute. Fold the whites into the egg yolk mixture. In another bowl, whip the cream until firm peaks are formed, then add to the egg mixture.

Spread the mixture on a parchment-lined sheet tray until ½ inch in thickness. Freeze until firm, then cut into eight 2-inch disks.

MERINGUE CRISPS

½ cup / 118 ml granulated sugar

½ cup / 118 ml sliced, blanched almonds

½ cup / 118 ml confectioners' sugar

2 egg whites

Preheat oven to 250 degrees.

Create a round stencil (page 252) 2½ inches in diameter. In a food processor, combine ¼ cup of granulated sugar, the almonds, and confectioners' sugar. Puree until smooth. In an electric mixer bowl, whisk egg whites until soft peaks are formed. Add the remaining ¼ cup sugar and continue to whisk until firm peaks are formed. Whisk for an additional minute and remove from the machine. Fold in the dry ingredients.

On a parchment-lined sheet tray, using the stencil you have created, spread the meringue batter into the stencil, making disks. Bake until light golden brown, 20–30 minutes. Remove from oven and allow to cool.

ASSEMBLY

1 cup Brûlée Sugar (page 244)

Spiced Custard

Honey Tuiles (page 247)

Fresh cherries

Financiers

Frozen Vanilla Soufflé

Meringue Crisps

Cherry Sauce

2 cups Vanilla Sabayon Sauce (page 250)

Sugar Garnish (page 253)

Lightly sprinkle the brûlée sugar on top of each custard and glaze with a blowtorch. Place a honey tuile on top of each custard and place on one side of each of eight oval plates. On the opposite side of the oval plates, place a small bed of fresh cherries. Reheat and place a financier on top of the fresh cherries. Place a disk of vanilla soufflé on top of each meringue crisp. Place these on top of the financiers. Pipe cherry sauce and sabayon sauce around the fresh cherries. Decorate with a sugar garnish.

Spring Cherry and Vanilla Cocktail with Warm Cherry Cobbler

FROZEN VANILLA SOUFFLÉS

4 eggs, separated

³/₄ cup / 177 ml granulated sugar

½ vanilla bean, split in half and seeds scraped

2 cups / 473 ml heavy cream

Place eight martini glasses in the freezer and allow to freeze. In an electric mixer bowl, combine the egg yolks, ¼ cup of the sugar, and vanilla seeds. Whisk until pale and thick. In a separate bowl, using an electric mixer, whisk egg whites until firm peaks are formed. Add the remaining ½ cup sugar and continue to whisk for 1 minute. Fold the whites into the yolk mixture. In a third bowl, whip the cream until firm peaks are formed and add to the egg mixture.

Place the mixture in a piping bag. Carefully pipe the soufflé into the bottom of the martini glasses, approximately one-third of the way. Place the glasses into the freezer and freeze 2 to 3 hours.

CHERRY SAUCE

4 cups / 946 ml cherries, pitted

1 cup / 236 ml water

Juice of ½ lemon

1 cup / 236 ml granulated sugar

Combine the ingredients in a saucepan and bring to a simmer. Cook 4 to 5 minutes, then puree until smooth. Pass through a fine sieve and cool in an ice bath. Refrigerate until needed.

MARINATED JICAMA

1 medium jicama

1 cup / 236 ml white verjus

½ cup / 118 ml granulated sugar

Juice of ½ lemon

1 cup / 236 ml water

Clean and peel the jicama and cut into julienne strips. In a small bowl, combine the verjus, sugar, lemon juice, and water. Whisk well and pour over the jicama. Marinate 2 to 3 hours.

SERVES 8

Two opposite views of cherries on one plate: the light, ice-cold refreshing cocktail and the warm, homey cherry cobbler. Sometimes it is difficult to decide which way to go on a dessert, so I did a little of both. The cocktail, jicama, and cobbler need to be prepared the same day you serve them. The other components can be prepared ahead.

CHERRY COBBLER

2 cups / 473 ml cherries, pitted

1 cup / 236 ml all-purpose flour

1 cup / 236 ml semolina flour

1 cup / 236 ml granulated sugar

1 tablespoon / 15 ml baking powder

4 egg whites

1 cup / 236 ml milk

½ teaspoon / 2 ml salt

¼ cup / 59 ml finely chopped dried cherries

½ cup / 115 g unsalted butter, melted

Preheat oven to 325 degrees.

Using eight 4-inch bowls or dishes, place a scattered layer of fresh cherries on the bottom of each bowl. In an electric mixer bowl, combine the flours, sugar, baking powder, egg whites, milk, salt, and dried cherries. Mix until smooth, then stir in the melted butter. Pour batter over cherries in the bowls and bake until golden brown and firm, 25 minutes.

MERINGUE CRISPS

½ cup / 118 ml granulated sugar

½ cup / 118 ml sliced, blanched almonds

¼ cup / 59 ml confectioners' sugar

2 egg whites

Preheat oven to 250 degrees. Create a round stencil (page 252) 2 inches in diameter.

In a food processor, combine ¼ cup of the granulated sugar, the almonds, and confectioners' sugar. Puree until smooth. In an electric mixer bowl, whisk the egg whites until soft peaks are formed. Add the remaining ¼ cup of sugar, and continue to whisk until firm peaks are formed. Whisk for an additional minute and remove from the machine. Fold the dry ingredients into the egg mixture.

On a parchment-lined sheet tray, spread the mixture over the stencil you have made, creating disks. Bake until light golden brown, 20–25 minutes. Remove from the oven and allow to cool.

ASSEMBLY

Frozen Vanilla Soufflés

Meringue Disks

Marinated Jicama

Cherry Sauce

Cherry Cobbler

Strudel Crisps (page 252)

Sugar Garnish (page 253)

Honey Tuiles (page 247)

Remove the martini glasses from the freezer and place a meringue disk over each soufflé. Place a small mound of marinated jicama on top of each meringue disk. Pour cherry sauce around the jicama. Place the martini glasses off to one side on eight round plates. Place the warm cherry cobblers next to them. Garnish each plate with a strudel crisp, sugar garnish, and honey tuile.

Rhubarb with Crisp Rice Pudding

CRISP RICE PUDDING

Pudding

1 cup / 236 ml short-grain rice

4 cups / 946 ml milk

1 vanilla bean, split in half

1 cinnamon stick

1½ cups / 354 ml granulated sugar

4 egg yolks

Vanilla Crepes

¾ cup / 177 ml all-purpose flour

2 egg yolks

2 whole eggs

1 cup / 236 ml milk

¼ cup / 55 g unsalted butter

½ vanilla bean, split in half

8 Vietnamese spring roll wrappers

1 egg, lightly beaten

Vegetable oil, for deep-frying

Confectioners' sugar, for dusting

Place the rice in a small saucepan and cover with cold water. Bring to a quick boil and drain off the water. Run the rice under cold water for 1 to 2 minutes to rinse off excess starch. Shake the rice dry and place into a new saucepan. Add milk, vanilla bean, cinnamon stick, and 1 cup of the sugar. Stir to incorporate and place over medium heat. Reduce heat and simmer until rice is tender, about 25 minutes. Remove from the heat.

In a medium mixing bowl, combine the remaining ½ cup sugar and the egg yolks and whisk until smooth. Temper the hot rice pudding into the eggs and sugar, mixing well. Place everything back in the saucepan and cook over medium heat, stirring constantly, until thick, about 3 minutes. Remove and pour into a clean pan, cover with plastic wrap, and refrigerate immediately. Allow to cool before use. Set 2 cups pudding aside for recipe.

Place flour in a medium mixing bowl. In a separate mixing bowl, combine yolks, whole eggs, and milk. Slowly whisk the wet ingredients into flour until smooth. Combine the butter and vanilla bean in a saucepan. Melt and whisk together, then add the melted butter to the crepe batter. Using an 8-inch nonstick sauté pan, make the crepes (page 247). You will need eight for this recipe.

Place the eight crepes on a flat surface and spoon onto each 4 tablespoons of rice pudding. Fold the edges over, creating puck-shaped crepes. Spread out the spring roll wrappers. Place the crepes in the middle of each wrapper. Brush the edges of each wrapper with beaten egg. Fold the edges over into a square package. Allow to rest in the refrigerator for 1 hour.

Heat oil to 350 degrees. Deep-fry the puddings until golden brown and crisp, 5 minutes. Remove from the fryer and lightly powder with confectioners' sugar.

SERVES 8

Rice pudding tastes great when matched with rhubarb. Whether to serve it hot or cold was the big question. I decided to provide both, with an additional crunch of the spring roll wrapper on the warm rice pudding. Everything in this recipe can be prepared in advance, except for the crepes and the assembly of the crisp rice pudding.

CHEF'S NOTE

Vietnamese spring roll wrappers (for the crisp rice pudding) can be found in the frozen section of Asian markets. They have a very thin, crisp skin when fried.

RHUBARB COMPOTE

2 cups / 473 ml diced rhubarb

½ cup / 236 ml granulated sugar

Juice of 1 lemon

Combine ingredients in a small saucepan and cook over medium heat until thick, 15 minutes. Pour into a bowl and allow to cool. Refrigerate.

RHUBARB AND VANILLA PARFAITS

2 stalks rhubarb, peeled

¾ cup plus 2 tablespoons / 177 ml granulated sugar

2 eggs, separated

¼ vanilla bean, split in half and seeds scraped

1 cup / 236 ml heavy cream

2 cups / 473 ml Rhubarb Sorbet ▪

Preheat oven to 200 degrees.

Cut the rhubarb stalks into 2-inch lengths, then carefully slice lengthwise into thin strips. Sprinkle ½ cup of the sugar onto a silicone sheet tray and place the rhubarb on top. Sprinkle again with sugar and bake for 10 minutes. Remove from oven and allow to cool.

Line eight 3-inch metal tart pans with disks of parchment paper. Carefully place rhubarb strips around the inside edge of each tartlet pan. Place the tartlet pans in the freezer and allow to freeze.

In an electric mixer bowl, combine the egg yolks, 2 tablespoons of the sugar, and the vanilla seeds, whisking until pale and thick. Using a separate mixing bowl, whip the egg whites until firm peaks are formed. Add the remaining ¼ cup sugar and continue to whisk for 1 minute. Fold the whites into the yolk mixture. Whip the cream until firm peaks are formed and fold into the egg mixture.

Pipe the mixture into the tartlet pans, filling halfway. Place in the freezer and once again allow to freeze.

Remove tartlet pans from the freezer and fill with rhubarb sorbet. Smooth the tops and place back in the freezer until ready to use.

▪ Rhubarb Sorbet

4 cups / 946 ml diced rhubarb

2 cups / 473 ml granulated sugar

1½ cups / 354 ml water

Juice of 1 lemon

Place ingredients in a saucepan and bring to a quick boil. Cook until the rhubarb is soft, 6–8 minutes. Puree until smooth, then pass through a fine chinois. Freeze in an ice cream machine according to the manufacturer's instructions. Keep frozen.

RHUBARB SAUCE

2 cups / 473 ml sliced rhubarb, with peels
in ¼-inch slices

1 cup / 236 ml granulated sugar

½ cup / 118 ml water

Juice of 1 lemon

Combine the ingredients in a saucepan and bring to a simmer. Simmer until the rhubarb starts to break up, 5 minutes. Using a whisk, stir the rhubarb until completely broken up. Remove from heat and allow to cool. Pass the sauce through a large-holed china cap strainer. Keep the sauce cool until ready to use.

LINZER BISCUITS

1 cup / 236 ml granulated sugar

1½ cups / 354 ml blanched hazelnuts, skinned

¾ cup / 340 g unsalted butter

2 eggs

2½ cups / 590 ml cake flour

1 tablespoon / 15 ml ground cinnamon

2 teaspoons / 10 ml baking powder

Preheat oven to 300 degrees.

In a food processor, combine the sugar and nuts and puree until smooth. Transfer to an electric mixer bowl and add the butter. Cream the butter, sugar, and nuts until smooth. Add the eggs, flour, cinnamon, and baking powder. Roll out the dough until ⅛ inch thick. Cut into eight 3-inch squares. Bake until light golden brown, 20 minutes.

ASSEMBLY

Rhubarb Sauce

1 cup Vanilla Sabayon Sauce (page 250)

Crisp Rice Pudding

Rhubarb and Vanilla Parfaits

Linzer Biscuits

Rhubarb Compote

Honey Tuiles (page 247)

Sugar Garnish (page 253)

In the centers of eight round dessert plates, place a small pool of rhubarb sauce. Pipe lines of the sabayon sauce, then place the deep-fried puddings on top of the sauce. Unmold the rhubarb and vanilla parfaits and place one on each linzer biscuit. Place a honey tuile in the center of the parfait. Fill the bottom half of the tuile with rhubarb compote. Fill the remaining half of the tuile with rice pudding. Place the entire assembly on top of the crisp rice pudding. Decorate the plates with another honey tuile and sugar garnish.

Chilled Rhubarb and Banana Charlotte with Banana Fritters

RHUBARB AND BANANA CHARLOTTES

Rhubarb Strips

2 stalks rhubarb

½ cup / 118 ml granulated sugar

Banana Mousse

4 eggs, separated

¾ cup / 77 ml granulated sugar

½ cup / 118 ml pureed banana

2 cups / 473 ml heavy cream

Preheat oven to 200 degrees.

Cut the rhubarb stalks into 2½-inch lengths. Carefully slice the lengths to create long, thin slices that are ⅛ inch thick. Lightly sprinkle a silicone baking sheet with the sugar. Place the rhubarb slices on the sugar and carefully sprinkle more sugar on top of the rhubarb. Bake for 10 minutes, then remove and allow to cool.

Using metal rings that are 1½ inches in diameter and 2½ inches in length, carefully line the inner edges of the rings with the sliced rhubarb. The rhubarb should be placed completely around the inside edge of the molds. Once the rings are lined with rhubarb, place the rings in the freezer to freeze.

In an electric mixer bowl, combine the egg yolks and ¼ cup of the sugar, mixing until pale and thick. Remove from the machine and fold in the banana puree. In a separate mixing bowl, whisk the egg whites until firm peaks are formed. Add the remaining ½ cup sugar and continue to whisk for 1 minute. Remove from the machine and fold the whites into the yolk-banana mixture. Whip the cream and fold into the egg mixture.

Place the mousse in a pastry bag and fill the frozen rhubarb shells. Place the charlottes back in the freezer and allow to freeze.

SERVES 8

The sweet creaminess of bananas and tartness of rhubarb have been a favorite combination of mine for years. I have tried presenting it in several different ways, but find that this version is the best. All the components can be prepared one to two days in advance, with the exception of the banana fritters and the rhubarb-apple salad.

BANANA SORBET

3 cups / 709 ml chopped bananas

2 cups / 473 ml granulated sugar

4 cups / 946 ml water

Juice of 1 lemon

Combine the ingredients in a saucepan and bring to a simmer. Remove from the heat and puree until smooth. Pass the mixture through a fine sieve. Process in an ice cream machine according to the manufacturer's instructions. Keep frozen.

RHUBARB-APPLE SALAD

Juice of 3 limes

1/2 cup / 118 ml water

1/4 cup / 59 ml granulated sugar

1/2 banana, peeled and diced

1 stalk rhubarb, peeled

1/2 Granny Smith apple, peeled

Combine the lime juice, water, sugar, and banana. Allow to sit for 20 minutes, then strain the juice into a new container. Cut the rhubarb into 1½-inch lengths and julienne fine; add to the liquid. Cut the apple into 1½-inch lengths and julienne fine also; add to the liquid. Let mixture rest for 4 to 5 minutes, softening the fruit slightly, then toss lightly in the liquid. Allow the fruit salad to macerate for 30 minutes before use.

RHUBARB AND BANANA SAUCE

2 cups / 437 ml diced rhubarb, not peeled

1 cup / 236 ml granulated sugar

1 cup / 236 ml water

1 banana, peeled and diced

Combine the ingredients in a saucepan and bring to a simmer, then cool until the rhubarb is soft, 5 minutes. Remove from heat and puree. Pass through a fine sieve and place in an ice bath to cool. Refrigerate.

BANANA FRITTERS

1¼ cups / 295 ml all-purpose flour

1/2 cup / 118 ml granulated sugar

1 tablespoon / 15ml baking powder

1 cup / 236 ml cold water

4 bananas, peeled and cut into 1-inch lengths

1 cup / 236 ml Panko bread crumbs (available in Japanese groceries)

Vegetable oil, for deep-frying

Confectioners' sugar, for dusting

Heat the oil to 350 degrees.

Combine flour, sugar, and baking powder in a mixing bowl. Whisk in cold water until smooth. Place bananas in the fritter batter, coating lightly. Roll in the bread crumbs. Deep-fry until golden brown, 5 minutes. Dust lightly with confectioners' sugar.

SPICED MERINGUES

1 cup / 236 ml sliced, blanched almonds

1 cup / 236 ml granulated sugar

¼ teaspoon / 1 ml ground cinnamon

⅛ teaspoon / .62 ml ground cardamom

Pinch of ground nutmeg

½ cup / 118 ml confectioners' sugar

5 egg whites

Preheat oven to 225 degrees. Generously butter mini muffin pans for a total of 16 muffins.

Combine the almonds, ½ cup of the sugar, the spices, and the confectioners' sugar in a food processor and puree until fine. Whisk the egg whites until soft peaks are formed. Add the remaining ½ cup of sugar and continue to whisk until stiff peaks are formed. Fold the dry ingredients into the egg whites.

Pipe the mixture into muffin pans. Bake for 5 minutes, remove from the oven, and gently press meringues to flatten slightly. Place back in the oven and bake until dry and light golden brown, approximately 1 hour. Allow to cool and store in an airtight container.

ASSEMBLY

Rhubarb and Banana Sauce

Rhubarb and Banana Charlottes

Banana Sorbet

Spiced Meringues

Rhubarb-Apple Salad

1 cup Vanilla Sabayon Sauce (page 250)

Banana Fritters

Honey Tuiles (page 247)

Sugar Garnish (page 253)

Pour a small pool of rhubarb sauce into the center of each of eight dessert plates. Unmold the charlottes and place one slightly off center on each plate. Place a scoop of sorbet between two spiced meringues, creating a sandwich. Place a small mound of the rhubarb-apple salad on top of the sandwich, which is lying down. Place the salad-sandwich ensemble next to the charlotte. Put a small dot of sabayon sauce on the rhubarb sauce and place two banana fritters on top of the sabayon on each plate. Decorate the dishes with honey tuiles and a sugar garnish.

Warm Ricotta and Lemon Thyme Soufflé with Strawberry-Rhubarb Compote

RICOTTA AND LEMON THYME SOUFFLÉ

1 cup / 236 ml granulated sugar

4 egg yolks

1¾ cups / 413 ml ricotta cheese

¼ cup / 59 ml all-purpose flour

1 tablespoon / 15 ml fresh lemon thyme leaves, coarsely chopped

Pinch of salt

8 egg whites

Preheat oven to 350 degrees. Butter and sugar eight 4-inch ramekins. Chill the ramekins.

Combine ½ cup of the sugar and egg yolks, whisking by hand until pale and thick. Add the ricotta cheese, flour, thyme, and salt. Mix until well blended. In an electric mixer bowl, whisk egg whites at medium speed until foamy. Add the remaining ½ cup of sugar and continue to whisk until soft peaks are formed. Carefully fold the egg whites into the cheese mixture.

Fill the ramekins with the soufflé mix and bake until soufflés have risen and are light golden brown, 10 minutes.

STRAWBERRY-RHUBARB COMPOTE

1 cup / 236 ml diced rhubarb, not peeled

2 cups / 472 ml quartered strawberries

¼ cup / 59 ml lemon juice

½ cup / 118 ml granulated sugar

1 tablespoon / 15 ml unsalted butter

1 cup / 236 ml diced, peeled rhubarb

In a small saucepan, combine the unpeeled rhubarb, 1 cup of the strawberries, the lemon juice, and sugar. Bring to a simmer and cook until soft, 8 minutes. Puree until smooth, then add butter. Pass through a fine sieve and transfer to a new saucepan. Add the peeled rhubarb and remaining 1 cup strawberries. Bring to a low simmer and cook until the rhubarb is tender, 4 minutes. Be careful not to boil, as this will cause the rhubarb to break up. Keep warm.

ASSEMBLY

Ricotta and Lemon Thyme Soufflé

Confectioners' sugar, for dusting

Strawberry-Rhubarb Compote

Divide the strawberry-rhubarb compote among eight small ramekins. Dust soufflés lightly with confectioners' sugar and serve immediately with the warm compotes.

SERVES 8

The cheese in the soufflé retains the moisture well, and the fresh fragrance of the lemon thyme is wonderful. The sweet and acidic blend of strawberry and rhubarb makes the perfect complement. This dessert requires last-minute preparation, but you can prepare the compote first and keep it warm.

Classic Crème Brûlée with Warm Berries

SERVES 8

Crème brûlée is a dessert that will always appear on my menu. One reason is its familiarity. It is a safe alternative for someone who is not feeling adventurous enough to try a dish such as Roasted Pineapple Tart with Basil Ice Cream (page 167). Another reason is that it is a good standard test for a pastry chef. It sounds simple but there are a lot of bad brûlées out there. All the elements of this recipe can be prepared a day in advance. Just glaze the brûlée and warm the sauce when needed.

CRÈME BRÛLÉE

2 cups / 473 ml milk
2 cups / 473 ml heavy cream
½ cup / 118 ml granulated sugar
1 vanilla bean, split in half
Pinch of ground nutmeg
1 cinnamon stick
9 egg yolks

In a saucepan, combine milk, cream, sugar, vanilla, nutmeg, and cinnamon stick. Bring to a quick boil, remove from heat, and allow to steep for 20 minutes. Cool in an ice bath.

Preheat oven to 300 degrees.

Whisk in the yolks, then pass the mixture through a fine sieve. Pour the mixture into eight shallow bowls, or ramekins, 4 inches in diameter. Bake in water bath until set, 40 minutes. Allow to cool, then store in the refrigerator.

BERRY SAUCE

2 cups / 473 ml chopped fresh strawberries
2 cups / 473 ml fresh raspberries
1½ cups / 354 ml granulated sugar
2 cups / 473 ml water
Juice of 1 lemon

Combine ingredients in a saucepan and bring to a quick boil, then simmer for 10 minutes. Remove from heat and pass through a fine sieve. Refrigerate.

LINZER BISCUITS

1 cup / 236 ml granulated sugar
1½ cups / 354 ml hazelnuts, toasted
1½ cups / 340 g unsalted butter
2 whole eggs
2½ cups / 590 ml cake flour
1 tablespoon / 15 ml ground cinnamon
2 teaspoons / 10 ml baking powder
2 egg whites
½ cup / 118 ml Brûlée Sugar (page 244)

Preheat oven to 300 degrees.

In a food processor, combine sugar and hazelnuts; puree until smooth. Transfer to an electric mixer bowl and add the butter. Cream until smooth, then add whole eggs, cake flour, cinnamon, and baking powder and blend well.

Roll out dough until ⅛ inch in thickness. Cut into sixteen 2-inch disks, and brush each disk with egg white. Sprinkle on the brûlée sugar. Bake until light golden brown, 20–30 minutes. Allow to cool, and store in an airtight container.

ASSEMBLY

Crème Brûlées

2 cups Brûlée Sugar (page 244)

Berry Sauce

Fresh strawberries, raspberries, and blackberries

1 cup Vanilla Sabayon Sauce (page 250)

Linzer Biscuits

Sprinkle the brûlée sugar on top of the crème brûlées and glaze with a blowtorch. Leave crème brûlées in ramekins and place on eight dessert plates. In a saucepan, warm the berry sauce. Place the diced berries in eight separate small bowls. Pour the warm berry sauce over the fresh berries, then pipe a small amount of sabayon sauce on top of the berries. Garnish each plate with two linzer biscuits.

Raspberry Tart with Crème Fraîche and Lemon Thyme

RASPBERRY SORBET

4 cups / 946 ml fresh raspberries

1½ cups / 354 ml water

1½ cups / 354 ml granulated sugar

Combine ingredients in a blender and puree until smooth. Pass through a fine sieve, then freeze the mixture in an ice cream machine according to the manufacturer's instructions. Keep frozen.

RASPBERRY TARTS

8 disks Sucre Dough (page 253), 3½ inches in diameter

¼ cup / 59 ml crème fraîche, whipped

3 cups / 709 ml fresh raspberries

¼ cup / 59 ml honey

Preheat oven to 300 degrees.

Place the disks on a parchment-lined sheet tray and bake until light golden brown, 20 minutes. Set aside to cool.

Carefully pipe thin lines of crème fraîche around the top of each disk. Line the raspberries around the tarts in a circular pattern. Quickly drizzle the honey on top of the raspberries by placing a fork in the honey and allowing the honey to flow off the fork in a fine stream.

FROZEN CRÈME FRAÎCHE SOUFFLÉS

4 eggs, separated

¾ cup / 177 ml granulated sugar

½ cup / 118 ml heavy cream

1½ cups / 354 ml crème fraîche

In an electric mixer bowl, combine egg yolks and ¼ cup of the sugar and whisk until pale and thick. In a separate mixing bowl, whisk egg whites until firm peaks are formed. Add the remaining ½ cup sugar and continue to whisk for one minute. Fold the whites into the yolk mixture. In a third bowl, whip cream and crème fraîche together until firm peaks are formed. Add to the egg mixture.

Pipe mixture into eight 3-inch metal rings until ½ inch thick. Place rings in freezer.

SERVES 8

Honey is the best way to sweeten raspberries: it tames the acidity without oversweetening the dessert. Honey also has the same aromatic quality that I find in lemon thyme. Here, the honey and herbal qualities create a light and fresh dessert. The raspberry tarts must be assembled just before being served, but all the other components can be prepared ahead of time.

CHEF'S NOTE

Drizzling the honey to create small beads on the raspberry tarts is a technique that can also be used on large berry or fruit tarts instead of the traditional apricot glaze.

LEMON THYME MERINGUE CRISPS

½ cup / 118 ml granulated sugar

½ cup / 118 ml sliced, blanched almonds

1 tablespoon / 15 ml fresh lemon thyme leaves

¼ cup / 59 ml confectioners' sugar

2 egg whites

Preheat oven to 250 degrees.

Create a stencil (page 252) 1-inch by ¾-inch rectangle.

In a food processor, combine ¼ cup of the granulated sugar, the almonds, lemon thyme, and confectioners' sugar. Puree until smooth. In an electric mixer bowl, whisk egg whites until soft peaks are formed. Add the remaining ¼ cup sugar and continue to whisk until firm peaks are formed. Whisk for an additional minute, then fold in the dry ingredients.

On a parchment-lined sheet tray, using the stencil that you have created, spread the meringue in small rectangular shapes. Bake until light golden brown, 30 minutes. Remove from the oven and allow to cool.

HONEYED RASPBERRIES

3 cups / 709 ml fresh raspberries

¼ cup / 59 ml honey

Combine the raspberries and honey, carefully folding with a spoon. You want to coat the raspberries lightly with the honey. Refrigerate.

ASSEMBLY

Honeyed Raspberries

2 cups Lemon-Thyme Sabayon Sauce (page 250)

Honey

Fresh raspberries

Lemon thyme leaves

Frozen Crème Fraîche Soufflés

2 cups Meringue Crumbs (page 248)

Raspberry Sorbet

Raspberry Tarts

Lemon Thyme Meringue Crisps

Sugar Garnish (page 253)

On each of eight round plates, place a small mound of the honeyed raspberries in the center. Pipe the sabayon sauce and honey around the raspberries in a circular pattern. Garnish the sauces with fresh raspberries and lemon thyme leaves. Place soufflés in the meringue crumbs and coat lightly. Place the soufflés on top of the honeyed raspberries in the center of each plate. Place a small scoop of raspberry sorbet on top of each raspberry tart. Lean the meringue crisps against the sorbet. Place the assembled raspberry tarts on top of the soufflés. Decorate the plates with a sugar garnish.

Strawberry Tart with Vanilla Shortcake and Warm Strawberry Sauce

VANILLA SHORTCAKE BISCUITS

2 cups / 473 ml all-purpose flour

1 vanilla bean, split in half and seeds scraped

1¼ tablespoons / 18.75 ml baking powder

5 tablespoons / 75 ml granulated sugar

½ teaspoon / 2 ml salt

½ cup / 115 g cold unsalted butter, in small pieces

¾ cup / 170 g heavy cream

In an electric mixer bowl, combine flour, vanilla seeds, baking powder, sugar, salt, and butter. Mix at a medium speed with a paddle attachment until mixture resembles meal. Add cream all at once and mix until incorporated. Knead dough slightly, then refrigerate for 1 to 2 hours.

Preheat oven to 300 degrees.

Roll the dough out on a flat surface until ½ inch thick. Using eight 3-inch metal rings, cut out disks. Place rings with dough on a sheet pan and bake until light golden brown and firm to the touch, 20 minutes. Remove from oven and allow to cool. When cool, trim tops off the biscuits. Store in an airtight container.

STRAWBERRY TARTS

Strudel Layer

6 sheets strudel dough

¾ cup / 177 ml clarified butter

½ cup / 118 ml granulated sugar

12 to 16 fresh strawberries

1 cup / 236 ml Vanilla Mascarpone Filling ▪

Carefully place a sheet of strudel dough on a flat surface and lightly brush with clarified butter. Place another sheet of strudel dough on top. Repeat until all six sheet are used. Using a round cutter 3¼ inches in diameter, cut out disks.

Preheat oven to 350 degrees.

On a parchment-lined sheet tray, place the strudel dough disks, cover with another sheet of parchment paper, and place another sheet tray on top—the disks should be sandwiched between parchment paper and sheet trays. Bake until golden brown, 15 minutes. Remove and allow to cool. Set aside. Store in airtight container.

Line eight 3-inch metal tart pans with parchment paper. Sprinkle the pans lightly with sugar. Carefully slice the strawberries and place in a fan pattern on top of the sugar in the tart pans. Sprinkle again lightly with sugar. Pipe a thin line of mascarpone filling on top of the berries. Place a strudel disk on top of the mascarpone and press gently. Flip the tarts over and remove the metal pan and paper, revealing the fanned strawberries on top.

The American classic strawberry shortcake reconstructed. Whipped mascarpone replaces the whipped cream, and some crunchy textures are added. This dessert needs to be prepared the same day it is served.

Vanilla Mascarpone Filling

2 cups / 472 ml mascarpone cheese

1 cup / 236 ml heavy cream

½ cup / 118 ml granulated sugar

1 vanilla bean split in half and seeds scraped

Combine ingredients in an electric mixer bowl and whisk until stiff. Place in a piping bag ready to use. Refrigerate.

WARM STRAWBERRY-VANILLA SAUCE

3 cups / 709 ml diced fresh strawberries

1 vanilla bean

1 cup / 236 ml granulated sugar

½ cup / 118 ml water

Juice of ½ lemon

Place the strawberries in a small saucepan. Chop the vanilla bean and add to the strawberries. Add the sugar, water, and lemon juice. Place over low heat and bring to a simmer. Cook until the strawberries are soft, 8 minutes. Keep warm, or simmer to reheat before serving.

ASSEMBLY

Warm Strawberry-Vanilla Sauce

Vanilla Shortcake

Vanilla Mascarpone Filling

Snap Cookies (page 251)

Strawberry Tarts

Kataifi dough strands, toasted

Sugar Garnish (page 253)

Carefully spoon some of the warm sauce onto the centers of eight round dessert plates. Place a shortcake on top in the center of each. For each serving, pipe the mascarpone cream onto two snap cookies and place on top of the shortcake. Carefully set a strawberry tart on top of the snap cookies on each plate. Sprinkle the toasted kataifi strands on top of the strawberry tarts. Decorate plates with the sugar garnish.

Fresh Blackberries with Lemon Verbena Panna Cotta

LEMON VERBENA PANNA COTTA

2 cups / 473 ml milk

2 cups / 473 ml heavy cream

1 cup / 236 ml granulated sugar

Zest of 1 lemon

8 to 12 lemon verbena leaves, chopped

4 teaspoons powdered gelatin bloomed in
4 tablespoons water, or 4 sheets gelatin

In a saucepan, combine all ingredients except the gelatin. Bring to a quick boil. Remove from the heat and allow to steep for 20 to 30 minutes. Soften or bloom the gelatin in cold water and add to the pan. Pass the mixture through a chinois into a metal container. Place the container in the refrigerator and allow to cool.

BLACKBERRIES WITH SOFT LEMON VERBENA JELLY

2 cups / 473 ml Sauternes

½ cup / 118 ml granulated sugar

6 to 8 fresh lemon verbena leaves, chopped

Juice of 1 lemon

2 teaspoons powdered gelatin bloomed in
4 tablespoons water, or 2 sheets gelatin

16 to 24 fresh blackberries

In a small saucepan, combine the Sauternes, sugar, lemon verbena, and lemon juice, warming gently over low heat. Remove from the heat and allow to steep for 20 to 30 minutes.

Soak the gelatin in cold water and add to the pan. Pass through a fine chinois and reserve.

Place two to three blackberries at the bottom of eight martini glasses, depending on the size. Gently pour the strained herb mixture over the berries just enough to cover them, about 1 inch in depth. Place in the refrigerator and allow to set.

MERINGUE DISKS

1 cup / 236 ml sliced, blanched almonds

1 cup / 236 ml granulated sugar

½ cup / 118 ml confectioners' sugar

5 egg whites

Preheat oven to 250 degrees.

Combine the almonds, ½ cup of the sugar, and the confectioners' sugar in a food processor and grind until smooth. In an electric mixer bowl, whisk the egg whites until firm peaks are formed. Add the remaining ½ cup of sugar and continue to whisk for 1 minute. Then fold the dry ingredients into the egg whites.

On a parchment-lined sheet tray, using a small round stencil (page 252) 2½ inches in diameter, spread the meringue—eight disks are needed. Bake until light golden brown in color, 20 to 30 minutes. Remove from the oven and allow to cool. Store in airtight container.

SERVES 8

I still remember my first encounter with lemon verbena: I stuck my face into a two-pound bag of it and inhaled deeply. What an incredible smell! I am still amazed by this herb. I usually infuse its flavor into custards, ice creams, or sauces and match it with berries, apricots, or peaches. The blackberry and lemon verbena jelly can be set early in the day, but the rest should be finished about an hour before being served.

ASSEMBLY

Blackberries with Soft Lemon Verbena Jelly

Meringue Disks

2 cups Lemon Curd (page 248)

Fresh blackberries

Granulated sugar

Lemon Verbena Panna Cotta

Honey Tuiles (page 247)

Sugar Garnish (page 253)

Remove the martini glasses from the refrigerator and gently place a meringue disk on top of the jelly in each. Carefully pipe the lemon curd around the edge of the meringue disks. Also pipe some lemon curd into the center of each meringue disk just enough to cover the disk. Gently cut some fresh blackberries in half and toss with some sugar. Place a small mound of the blackberries on top of the lemon curd in each glass. Place the panna cotta in a warm water bath long enough to soften, then into an ice bath. Puree with a hand blender, moving the blender around to create air pockets and bubbles as mixture cools. Once it is foamy and cool, gently skim off the foam and spoon panna cotta into the martini glasses over the black-berries and lemon curd. Return the glasses to the refrigerator and allow to set, approximately 20 minutes. Decorate the plates with honey tuiles and a sugar garnish.

Angel Food Cake with Fresh Strawberries and Fried Berries

STRAWBERRY-CRÈME FRAÎCHE PARFAIT

Strawberry Sorbet

3 cups / 709 ml diced fresh strawberries

2 cups / 473 ml granulated sugar

1 cup / 236 ml water

Juice of ½ lemon

Crème Fraîche Soufflé

2 eggs, separated

6 tablespoons / 79 ml granulated sugar

¾ cup / 177 ml crème fraîche

¼ cup / 59 ml heavy cream

8 slices Angel Food Cake ▪

Combine ingredients for sorbet and puree until smooth. Pass through a fine sieve, then freeze in an ice cream machine according to the manufacturer's instructions. Keep frozen.

In an electric mixer bowl, combine egg yolks and 2 tablespoons of the sugar. Whisk until pale and thick. In a separate mixing bowl, whip egg whites until firm peaks are formed. Add the remaining ¼ cup sugar and continue to whip for 1 minute. Fold the whites into the yolk mixture. Whip the crème fraîche and cream together until firm peaks are formed. Fold into the egg mixture. Place the mixture in a piping bag.

Using eight metal tubes 1½ inches in diameter and 2 inches in height, place a slice of angel food cake on the bottom of each tube. Place the tubes, with the cake inside, in the freezer to chill, about 30 minutes.

Remove tubes from freezer and pipe the soufflé into the tubes, filling halfway. Return tubes to freezer and freeze until soufflé is firm, about 30 minutes. Fill remainder of the tubes with sorbet. Smooth the tops and keep in the freezer until ready to serve.

SERVES 8

The moist, springy quality of fresh angel food cake always seems so light. The best match for it, naturally, is juicy fruit. In this case, some fresh strawberries are simply sliced, while a few are batter-fried for their crisp shells with warm and juicy interiors. The parfait, strudel rings, and garnishes can be prepared a day ahead, but the angel food cake and fried strawberries should be prepared when needed.

Angel Food Cake

5 / 170g egg whites, at room temperature

Pinch of salt

½ teaspoon / 2 ml cream of tartar

½ vanilla bean, split in half and seeds scraped

½ cup / 118 ml superfine sugar

½ cup / 118 ml sifted cake flour

2 tablespoons / 29 ml superfine sugar, sifted

Preheat oven to 350 degrees.

In an electric mixer bowl, combine egg whites, salt, cream of tartar, and vanilla seeds. Whisk at medium speed until soft peaks begin to form. Add the ½ cup superfine sugar and increase the speed slightly, whisking egg whites until shiny soft peaks are formed. Do not overwhip, allowing the egg whites to go to firm peaks. Combine the flour and 2 tablespoons sifted sugar. Gently fold into the egg whites.

Pour batter into a 4-inch by 9-inch ungreased loaf pan and bake until light golden brown and springy to the touch, 30 minutes. Remove from oven and turn pan upside down. Lean the pan against something so that the cake cools upside down. Once cake has cooled, unmold with a paring knife. Store in airtight container. Cut into 1-inch-thick slices. You will need 8 slices.

STRUDEL RINGS

3 sheets strudel dough

½ cup / 118 ml clarified butter

Preheat oven to 350 degrees.

Carefully spread a sheet of strudel dough on a flat surface. Brush lightly with the clarified butter. Place another sheet of strudel dough on top. Continue until all three sheets of strudel dough have been used. Cut into 1½-inch-wide strips. Roll the strudel dough strips onto pipes measuring 2 inches by 1½ inches in diameter. Bake until golden brown, 15 minutes. Allow to cool. Slide the rings off the pipes. Store in an airtight container.

FRIED STRAWBERRIES

Vegetable oil, for deep-frying

24 medium strawberries, hulled

2½ cups / 591 ml all-purpose flour

1 cup / 236 ml granulated sugar

2 tablespoons / 29 ml baking powder

2 cups / 473 ml cold water

Confectioners' sugar for dusting

Heat the oil to 350 degrees.

Hull the strawberries and dry well. Combine flour, sugar, and baking powder in a mixing bowl. Slowly add the water until the batter becomes smooth. Dip the strawberries into the batter. Deep-fry until golden brown, 5 minutes. Drain and dust with confectioners' sugar.

STRAWBERRY SAUCE

2 cups / 473 ml chopped fresh strawberries

1 cup / 236 ml granulated sugar

½ vanilla bean, split in half and seeds scraped

3 tablespoons / 44 ml water

Combine ingredients in a small saucepan and bring to a simmer. Puree and pass through a fine sieve. Set aside to cool. Store in refrigerator.

ASSEMBLY

Slices of Angel Food Cake

Fried Strawberries

Strudel Rings

Fresh strawberries, hulled and sliced

Strawberry-Crème Fraîche Parfait

Strawberry Sauce

2 cups Vanilla Sabayon Sauce (page 250)

Honey Tuiles (page 247)

Sugar Garnish (page 253)

Using eight oval plates, place a slice of the cake in the center of each plate. Put fried berries on the cake. To the left, place a strudel ring and fill with fresh strawberries. Place a few fresh berries among the fried strawberries. Unmold the parfaits and place to the right of the cake slice. Pipe the strawberry sauce and sabayon sauce on the plates. Decorate with the honey tuiles and sugar garnish.

Frozen Raspberry Roulade with Fresh Berries

FROZEN RASPBERRY ROULADE

Lemon Genoise

½ cup / 118 ml granulated sugar

5 eggs

Grated zest of 1 lemon

½ cup / 118 ml sifted cake flour

4 tablespoons / 60 ml sifted cornstarch

Filling

2¾ cups / 650 ml granulated sugar

1 cup / 236 ml water

1 cup / 236 ml fresh raspberries

4 eggs, separated

1½ cups / 354 ml crème fraîche

½ cup / 118 ml heavy cream

Preheat oven to 300 degrees.

Place sugar, eggs, and zest for the genoise in an electric mixer bowl. Place over hot water and whisk by hand until warm. Transfer to mixer and whisk at high speed for 8 to 10 minutes. Carefully fold in flour and cornstarch. Spread the batter onto a parchment-lined sheet pan until ¼ inch thick. Bake until lightly golden brown and firm, 15 minutes. Allow the cake to cool, then cut into 2 rectangles 10 inches by 12 inches.

Place 2 cups of the sugar and the water for the filling in a saucepan and bring to a boil. Pour over the raspberries and allow to sit and cool. Drain completely.

In an electric mixer bowl, combine the 4 yolks and ¼ cup sugar, whisking until pale and thick. In a separate bowl, whisk whites until firm peaks are formed. Add the remaining ½ cup sugar and continue to whisk for 1 minute. Fold into the yolk mixture. In a third bowl, whisk the crème fraîche and cream until firm peaks are formed; fold into the egg mixture.

Carefully fold the drained raspberries into the mixture. Spread onto the cooled genoise rectangles until ¼ inch in thickness. Carefully roll the genoise into a roll 4 inches in diameter. The roll will be 10 inches long when finished. Trim edges and wrap in plastic wrap, then place in the freezer. Once the rolls are frozen, cut them into ½-inch slices. Keep frozen.

RASPBERRY SORBET

4 cups / 946 ml fresh raspberries

1½ cups / 354 ml water

1½ cups / 354 ml granulated sugar

Combine ingredients and puree until smooth. Pass through a fine sieve, then process in an ice cream machine according to the manufacturer's instructions. Keep frozen.

SERVES 8

Here's nothing but fresh berries and cream, with the added soft texture of lemon genoise. A cool, light, and fragrant finish to a big meal. All the components should be prepared one day in advance for best results.

ASSEMBLY

Fresh raspberries in a bowl, sprinkled lightly with sugar

Frozen Raspberry Roulade

Snap Cookies (page 251)

Snap Cookie Cones (page 251)

Raspberry Sorbet

Sugar Garnish (page 253)

Honey Tuiles (page 247)

2 cups Lemon Verbena Sabayon Sauce (page 250)

Place the raspberries in the centers of eight dessert plates. Cut a ½-inch hole in the centers of eight roulade slices. For each serving, place a roulade slice on top of a snap cookie, then place the roulade and cookie on top of the raspberries. Place a snap cookie cone in the hole in each roulade slice. Scoop some raspberry sorbet onto the cones. Decorate the plates with a sugar garnish, honey tuiles, and sabayon sauce.

Warm Blackberries with Goat Cheese Cream and Toasted Brioche

SERVES 8

The mild touch of the goat cheese blends well with the blackberries. The toasted brioche and warm blackberries start to melt the frozen crème fraîche soufflé, giving this dessert an even smoother texture. The brioche and the frozen soufflé should be prepared one to two days in advance.

GOAT CHEESE CREAM

½ cup / 118 ml mascarpone cheese

½ cup / 118 ml fresh goat cheese

¾ cup / 177 ml heavy cream

½ cup / 118 ml granulated sugar

1 tablespoon / 30 ml grated orange rind

Combine ingredients in an electric mixer bowl and whisk until stiff. Place in a pastry bag for use later.

BRIOCHE SLICES

¼ cup / 59 ml milk

2 tablespoons fresh yeast or 1 tablespoon dry yeast

2¼ cups / 511 ml all-purpose flour

4 eggs

2 tablespoons / 30 ml granulated sugar

1 teaspoon / 5 ml salt

1 cup / 225 g unsalted butter, at room temperature

In a small mixer bowl, gently warm the milk, then add the yeast and ¼ cup of the flour. Whisk until smooth and cover with plastic wrap. Allow to rise in a warm place until double in size, 10–15 minutes.

Transfer dough to a large mixing bowl. Add the eggs, remaining 2 cups flour, sugar, and salt. Using a dough hook attachment, mix the ingredients until smooth and elastic, approximately 10 minutes. On medium speed, slowly add the butter a little at a time, allowing it to incorporate each time. Continue to mix for 1 to 2 minutes, then cover dough with a damp towel and allow to rise until doubled, about 10 minutes. Punch dough down and refrigerate for 4 to 6 hours.

The brioche is baked in a loaf pan 4 inches in height and 9 inches in length. Roll dough into a long log and place log in pan. Cover and allow to rise once again in a warm place, about 30 minutes.

Preheat oven to 350 degrees.

Bake brioche until golden brown, 30 minutes. Cool the brioche, then cut into ½-inch-thick slices. Trim slices with an oval cutter into oval shapes that are approximately 3 inches in length. Set aside. Refrigerate until needed.

FROZEN CRÈME FRAÎCHE SOUFFLÉ

2 eggs, separated

6 tablespoons / 79 ml granulated sugar

¼ cup / 59 ml heavy cream

¾ cup / 177 ml crème fraîche

In an electric mixer bowl, combine egg yolks with 2 tablespoons of the sugar and whisk until pale and thick. In a separate mixer bowl, whisk egg whites until firm peaks are formed. Add the remaining 4 tablespoons sugar and continue to whisk for 1 minute. Fold whites into yolk mixture. Whip cream and crème fraîche together until firm peaks are formed; add to the egg mixture.

Pipe the mixture into eight 2½-inch metal rings to a ½-inch depth. Place rings in the freezer.

BLACKBERRY SAUCE

4 cups / 946 ml fresh blackberries

1 cup / 236 ml granulated sugar

Combine ingredients in a blender and puree until smooth. Pass the mixture through a chinois. Refrigerate.

SKEWERED BLACKBERRIES

24 fresh blackberries

½ cup / 118 ml Vanilla Sabayon Sauce (page 250)

1 cup / 236 ml Meringue Crumbs (page 248)

Using eight small 3-inch skewers, place three blackberries onto each skewer in a row. Drizzle a small amount of sauce onto the blackberries, then roll skewers in the meringue crumbs. Refrigerate.

ASSEMBLY

Frozen Crème Fraîche Soufflé

Brioche Slices

16 tube-shaped Snap Cookies (page 251)

Goat Cheese Cream

Skewered Blackberries

Fresh blackberries

Blackberry Sauce

2 cups Vanilla Sabayon Sauce (page 250)

Sugar Garnish (page 253)

½ cup Candied Orange Rinds, julienned (page 244)

Place the soufflés in the center of each of eight dessert bowls. Toast the brioche slices and place one on top of each soufflé. Fill snap cookie tubes with the goat cheese cream. Lay 2 tubes side by side on top of the brioche slices. Lay the skewered blackberries in top of the tubes. Combine the fresh blackberries and the blackberry sauce in a small saucepan. Gently warm and pour around the structure in the bowls. Decorate the bowls with the sabayon sauce, sugar garnish, and candied orange rinds.

Chocolate Cake Round with Chocolate Tea Ice Cream

CHOCOLATE CAKE ROUNDS

Chocolate Mousse

1½ cups / 354 ml bittersweet chocolate, finely chopped

½ cup / 118 ml milk

½ cup / 118 ml unsalted butter

2 egg yolks

½ tablespoon / 7.5 ml granulated sugar

2 cups / 473 ml heavy cream

Chocolate Cake

1 cup / 236 ml unsalted butter

2¼ cups / 528 ml granulated sugar

1 cup / 236 ml black cocoa powder (see page 258)

2 teaspoons / 10 ml baking powder

2¾ cups / 645 ml all-purpose flour

½ tablespoon / 7 ml baking soda

15 g salt

3 eggs

2 cups / 473 ml warm water

1½ cups / 354 ml bittersweet chocolate, melted

Combine the chocolate, milk, and butter in a double boiler and place over hot water to melt. In a mixer bowl, whisk the yolks and sugar until pale ribbons form. Fold into the chocolate. Whip cream until firm peaks are formed and carefully fold into chocolate. Place the mousse in a clean bowl and refrigerate until firm, 1 to 2 hours.

Preheat oven to 325 degrees. Butter two 8-inch round cake pans.

Cream the butter, sugar, and cocoa for the cake. Add flour, baking powder, baking soda, and salt and mix until smooth. Add eggs, then slowly add water. Pour batter into cake pans and bake until firm and springy to the touch, 30 to 40 minutes. Allow the cake to cool, then refrigerate for 2 to 3 hours.

Carefully cut each cake into three ¼-inch-thick layers. Using a 3-inch round cutter, cut 3 disks out of each layer. You should have 18 disks, although need only 16 for this recipe. Set aside.

Place the mousse in a piping bag. Using eight 3-inch metal rings, place a disk of cake in the bottom of each ring. Carefully pipe a ½-inch layer of mousse on top of each cake. Place another layer of cake on top of the mousse and press down on cake until flat. Put rings in refrigerator and allow to set. Using a ½-inch round cutter, cut a hole in each cake that is slightly off center. Place cakes back in refrigerator.

Spread the melted chocolate onto the back of a warm sheet tray. Refrigerate the chocolate until solid, then remove from refrigerator and allow to sit out until chocolate is pliable. Using a paring knife, cut 1-inch strips into the chocolate. Peel the strips off the pan with the paring knife. Remove the cakes from the rings and wrap chocolate strips around each one. Place immediately back in the refrigerator.

SERVES 8

Earl Grey tea has a fragrance and a slight bitterness that I find similar to chocolate. It is a perfect match as long as the balance of flavors is correct. Too much tea can be bitter and may overwhelm the chocolate. The chocolate mousse can be assembled with the cake a day in advance, but don't wrap with the chocolate till the day you serve it. All the other components can also be made a day in advance.

CHEF'S NOTE

For the chocolate mousse, before you fold in the whipped cream, make sure that the chocolate egg base is slightly warm but not hot. This will prevent the chocolate from seizing up when it meets the cream.

CHOCOLATE TEA ICE CREAM

4 cups / 946 ml heavy cream

2 cups / 473 ml milk

1½ cups / 354 ml granulated sugar

8 bags Earl Grey tea

12 egg yolks

1½ cups / 354 ml extra-bitter chocolate, finely chopped

In a saucepan, combine cream, milk, 1 cup of the sugar, and the tea bags. Warm over medium heat, then remove from heat and allow to steep for 20 minutes.

Place egg yolks and remaining ½ cup sugar in a mixing bowl, stirring to combine. Strain tea bags from the cream mixture and bring the cream to a full boil. Quickly whisk the cream into the yolk mixture. Add chocolate and stir until smooth. Strain through a fine sieve. Cool mixture in an ice bath. Once it has cooled, process in an ice cream machine according to the manufacturer's instructions. Keep frozen.

EARL GREY TEA SYRUP

3 cups / 709 ml water

4 bags Earl Grey tea

1 cup / 236 ml granulated sugar

½ cup / 118 ml corn syrup

In a small saucepan, combine water and tea bags and bring to a simmer. Turn off heat and allow tea to steep for 10 minutes. Strain out the tea bags and add sugar. Bring to a full boil, add corn syrup, and continue to cook until 230 degrees is reached on a candy thermometer. Cool in an ice bath, then place syrup in a squeeze bottle for later use.

ASSEMBLY

2 cups Chocolate Sauce (page 246)

Earl Grey Tea Syrup

Chocolate Cake Rounds

Chocolate Tea Ice Cream

Chocolate Tuiles (page 247)

Chocolate Garnish (page 245)

Using eight round dessert plates, pipe lines of chocolate sauce and dots of tea syrup onto the plates. Stand the chocolate cake rounds upright and slightly off center on the plates. Place an oval scoop of ice cream next to each. Decorate the plates with the chocolate tuiles and chocolate garnish.

Frozen Banana Timbale with Jicama, Lime, and Mint

FROZEN BANANA TIMBALES

5 ripe bananas

3 cups Banana Sorbet ▪

Trim both ends of each banana and cut into 2-inch lengths. Carefully thinly slice each banana lengthwise, then arrange the bananas on the inside of eight 2½-inch ring molds, creating a circle. Place the rings in the freezer and freeze until firm. Remove from freezer and carefully pipe on the sorbet. Place back in the freezer until ready to use.

▪ **Banana Sorbet**

3 cups / 709 ml chopped ripe bananas

2 cups / 473 ml granulated sugar

4 cups / 946 ml water

Juice of 1 lemon

Combine ingredients in a saucepan and bring to a quick boil. Remove from heat and allow to sit for 5 to 10 minutes. Puree mixture until smooth and pass through a fine sieve. Freeze in an ice cream machine according to the manufacturer's instructions. Keep frozen.

JICAMA SALAD

2 medium jicamas

1 cup / 236 ml lime juice

½ cup / 118 ml granulated sugar

1 to 1½ cups / 354 ml water

6 mint leaves, finely chopped

Peel and trim the jicamas. Cut into julienne pieces 1 inch in length. In a bowl, combine the lime juice, sugar, water, and mint. Adjust the water according to the acidity of the limes; the mixture should have a light limeade flavor. Pour mixture over the jicamas and allow to sit for 2 to 3 hours.

BANANA CHIPS

1 banana, peeled and pureed

1 teaspoon / 5 ml granulated sugar

Preheat oven to 200 degrees.

Create a small, rectangular stencil (page 252). On a nonstick silicone sheet tray, spread the puree using the stencil. Sprinkle with the sugar. Bake until dry and light golden brown, approximately 30 minutes.

SERVES 8

This dish was inspired by the many meals that I have had at Vietnamese restaurants. I love the fresh, lively flavors. The crunchy sprouts and noodles with fresh lime, mint, and peanuts challenged me to create a dessert with some of these components. I came up with this combination of sweet bananas, crunchy jicama, fresh lime juice, fresh mint, and a touch of roasted peanut. It's extremely refreshing, with no dairy products and, except for a few peanuts, no fat. The sorbet and frozen banana timbales can be prepared a day in advance, but the rest should be prepared on the day the dish is served.

ASSEMBLY

Ripe bananas

4 cups Meringue Crumbs (page 248)

Frozen Banana Timbales

Jicama Salad, drained and marinade reserved

Orange sections

Chopped roasted peanuts

Banana Sorbet

Banana Chips

Sugar Garnish (page 253)

Cut a banana into 2 pieces for each serving. Coat the sections in meringue crumbs and place in the centers of eight large dessert bowls. Unmold and place the timbales on top of the bananas. Arrange a small mound of jicama salad on top of each timbale, reserving the lime marinade; also place some salad around the base of each bowl. Add the orange sections, peanuts, and some banana slices to the jicama around the bowl. Carefully pour the reserved lime marinade into the bowls. Place a scoop of sorbet on top of each timbale. Stick two banana chips into each sorbet scoop and decorate servings with a sugar garnish.

Roasted Pineapple Tart with Basil Ice Cream

ROASTED PINEAPPLE RINGS

1 large pineapple

2 vanilla beans, split in half

4 cinnamon sticks

½ cup / 118 ml granulated sugar

Preheat oven to 275 degrees.

Peel and core the pineapple, then cut into eight ½-inch-thick rings. Trim each ring, making it hexagonal in shape and 3 inches in diameter. Place the pineapple rings in a small roasting pan with the vanilla and cinnamon. Sprinkle sugar on top of the pineapple rings. Bake in the roasting pan until tender, 20 minutes. Store pineapple rings in liquid until ready to use. Refrigerate.

PINEAPPLE CURD

½ cup / 118 ml Roasted Pineapple Puree ▪

½ cup / 118 ml granulated sugar

3 whole eggs

2 egg yolks

1 cup / 225 ml unsalted butter, at room temperature

▪ **Roasted Pineapple Puree**

1 large, golden pineapple

2 vanilla beans, split in half

4 cinnamon sticks

½ cup / 118 ml granulated sugar

Combine puree, sugar, whole eggs, and egg yolks and mix until smooth. Place in double boiler over hot water and whisk mixture until pale and thick, 5 to 8 minutes. Remove from heat and whisk in butter. Pour mixture into a clean bowl and refrigerate for 2 to 3 hours.

Preheat oven to 275 degrees.

Clean and core the pineapple. Dice in 1-inch pieces. Place pineapple in a small roasting pan, then add the vanilla beans, cinnamon, and sugar. Bake until tender, 20 minutes. Remove from oven and drain off liquid. Discard vanilla beans and cinnamon sticks, and puree pineapple in a food processor. Place puree in a saucepan and, over low heat, cook until reduced and thickened and dry. Remove from heat and transfer to a bowl to cool. Refrigerate.

SERVES 8

Pineapple and basil are two very fragrant ingredients, with a sweet floral quality. The fragrant flavors of vanilla and cinnamon in the roasted pineapple here are the links in joining the pineapple and basil ice cream. All the components can be prepared a day in advance.

CHEF'S NOTE

Once you have used all the pineapple rings, save the cooking liquid to pour over the next batch.

KATAIFI DISKS

¼ package kataifi dough

¼ cup / 59 ml clarified butter

1 tablespoon / 15 ml confectioners' sugar

Preheat oven to 350 degrees.

Carefully separate the strands of dough. Toss dough with clarified butter and sugar to coat lightly. Fill eight 4-inch metal tartlet pans with enough dough to cover bottoms. Place another tartlet pan on top of the dough to sandwich it. Bake until golden brown, 15 minutes. Let cool and set aside. Store in an airtight container.

STRUDEL TART SHELLS

3 sheets strudel dough

¼ cup / 59 ml clarified butter

Preheat oven to 350 degrees.

Carefully spread a sheet of dough on a flat surface and brush with clarified butter. Place a second sheet on top; brush again with the butter. Place the third sheet on top and once again brush with butter. Using a 5-inch round cutter, cut the strudel dough into disks. Press the disks into 3-inch metal tartlet pans, creating tart shells. Use the scrap dough to fill in shells by folding and bunching together. Fold excess dough into the center.

Place tart shells on a sheet pan and cover with a sheet of parchment. Place a second sheet tray on top of the paper and bake until golden brown, 20 minutes. Let cool, then set aside. Store in an airtight container

BASIL ICE CREAM

4 cups / 946 ml heavy cream

2 cups / 473 ml milk

1½ cups / 354 ml granulated sugar

12 egg yolks

4 cups / 946 ml fresh basil

½ cup / 118 ml corn syrup

Place the cream, milk, and 1 cup of the sugar in a heavy saucepan. In a medium bowl, combine egg yolks and remaining ½ cup sugar. Place cream over medium heat and bring to a full boil, then quickly whisk into the yolks and sugar. Stir until smooth. Pass through a fine sieve. Place in a clean mixing bowl and into an ice bath to cool.

Place about 6 cups of water in a saucepan and bring to a full boil. Add the basil and cook for 30 seconds. Drain the basil and shock in ice water. Squeeze dry and place in a blender with the corn syrup. Puree smooth, then add puree to the ice cream mixture.

Pass the ice cream mixture one more time through a fine sieve, then process in an ice cream machine according to the manufacturer's instructions. Keep frozen.

BASIL SYRUP

4 cups / 946 ml fresh basil

¾ cup / 177 ml corn syrup

Place about 6 cups of water in a saucepan and bring to a full boil. Add the basil and cook for 30 seconds. Remove the basil and shock in ice water. Squeeze excess water out of basil, then place in a blender with the corn syrup. Puree until smooth; adjust with a little cold water if necessary. Pass through a fine sieve and pour into a squeeze bottle. Refrigerate.

ASSEMBLY

Roasted Pineapple Rings

Basil Ice Cream

4 cups Meringue Crumbs (page 248)

Strudel Tart Shells

Roasted Pineapple Puree

Kataifi Disks

Pineapple Curd

Sugar Garnish (page 253)

Basil Syrup

2 cups Pineapple Sabayon Sauce (page 250)

Drain the pineapple rings and place in the centers of eight large round dessert plates. Scoop eight large balls of the ice cream and bread them in the meringue crumbs. Place on top of the pineapple rings. Place the tart shell directly on top of the ice cream. Spread a thin layer—¼ inch thick—of the pineapple puree on the shell. Place a kataifi disk on top of the puree, then pipe a small dot of pineapple curd in the center of each disk. Decorate plates with a sugar garnish. Pipe the basil syrup and sabayon sauce around the pineapple rings.

Frozen Banana Terrine with Banana Fritters

FROZEN BANANA TERRINE

Caramel Genoise Layer

3/4 cup / 177 ml granulated sugar

5 eggs

1/2 cup / 118 ml sifted cake flour

4 tablespoons / 60 ml cornstarch

Banana Mousse Filling

4 eggs, separated

3/4 cup / 177 ml granulated sugar

1 cup / 236 ml pureed ripe banana

1 cup / 236 ml mascarpone cheese

2 cups / 473 ml heavy cream

2 cups / 473 ml Sesame Nougat ▪

In a small saucepan, combine 1/4 cup of the sugar and just enough water to dissolve it. Place over medium heat and bring to a boil, then boil until caramelized, 5–8 minutes.

While the sugar is cooking, place eggs and remaining 1/2 cup sugar in an electric mixer bowl. Place over hot water and whisk by hand until mixture is warm. Once warm, whisk with mixer at high speed for 5 to 8 minutes. Add caramelized sugar to egg mixture, then stop machine. Fold in cake flour and cornstarch.

Preheat oven to 300 degrees.

Spread batter onto a parchment-lined sheet pan until 1/4 inch thick. Bake until lightly golden brown and firm, 15 minutes. Let cool slightly.

Line a U-shaped metal or plastic terrine, 3 inches by 17 inches, with parchment paper. Cut genoise into long strips and line terrine with them. Place terrine in the freezer.

In an electric mixer bowl, combine yolks and 1/4 cup of the sugar. Whisk until pale and fluffy. Stir the banana puree and mascarpone cheese together until smooth. Fold yolk mixture into banana mixture. Whisk egg whites until firm peaks are formed. Add the remaining 1/2 cup sugar and continue to whisk for 1 minute. Fold the whites into the banana mixture. Whip the cream and fold into the banana mixture. Add the nougat and fold until all ingredients are well incorporated.

Spoon the mousse into the genoise-lined terrine and freeze overnight. The next day, using a hot knife, carefully slice terrine into 1-inch-thick slices. Keep frozen. Freeze leftover terrine for future use.

SERVES 8

Caramel and bananas are great! Caramel, bananas, and crunchy sesame nougat are even better. The frozen terrine and sorbet can be prepared one to two days in advance, but the fritters should wait till the last moment.

Sesame Nougat

3/4 cup / 177 ml granulated sugar

6 tablespoons / 85 g unsalted butter

1 cup / 236 ml sesame seeds, toasted

Pinch of salt

Place sugar in a saucepan and cook over medium heat until it begins to melt. Stir and continue to cook the sugar until deep amber. Add butter and stir. Add sesame seeds and salt. Pour mixture onto an oiled sheet pan and allow to cool. Crush and chop with a fine knife. Set aside. Store in an airtight container.

BANANA FRITTERS

Vegetable oil, for deep-frying

3 ripe bananas

2½ cups / 591 ml all-purpose flour

1 cup / 236 ml granulated sugar

2 tablespoons / 29 ml baking powder

2 cups / 473 ml cold water

2 cups / 473 ml Panko bread crumbs (available in Japanese groceries)

Confectioners' sugar, for dusting

Heat the oil to 350 degrees.

Peel the bananas and cut into 1-inch lengths. Combine flour, sugar, and baking powder in a bowl. Whisk in the cold water until smooth. Dip the bananas into the fritter batter, coating lightly, then into the bread crumbs. Deep-fry bananas until golden brown, 3 minutes. Remove and dust with confectioners' sugar.

BANANA SORBET

3 cups / 709 ml chopped ripe bananas

2 cups / 473 ml granulated sugar

4 cups / 946 ml water

Juice of 1 lemon

Combine ingredients in a saucepan and bring to a simmer. Remove from heat and puree until smooth. Pass through a fine sieve, then cool in an ice bath. Process in an ice cream machine according to the manufacturer's instructions. Keep frozen.

BANANA CHIPS

1 ripe banana, pureed

1 teaspoon / 5 ml granulated sugar

Preheat oven to 200 degrees.

On a nonstick silicone sheet tray, spread the banana puree with a stencil (page 252). Sprinkle with the sugar and bake until light golden brown, approximately 30 minutes. Bend the chips into shapes while they are still warm.

ASSEMBLY

2 cups Banana Sesame Caramel Sauce (page 246)

2 cups Star Anise Sabayon Sauce (page 250)

Frozen Banana Terrine

Banana Fritters

Banana Sorbet

Honey Tuiles (page 247)

Banana Chips

Sugar Garnish (page 253)

In the centers of eight round dessert plates, pipe a spiral of caramel sauce. Pipe a spiral of sabayon on top of that. Place a slice of terrine in the center of each plate. Put one banana fritter next to the terrine and one under one end of the terrine. Place one small scoop of sorbet next to the terrine and one small scoop on top of the terrine. Decorate the plates with honey tuiles, banana chips, and sugar garnish.

Lemon Mango Tartlets *(photograph on page 174)*

12 2-inch disks of Sucre Dough *(page 253)*

½ cup / 118 ml lemon juice

½ cup / 118 ml granulated sugar

3 whole eggs

3 egg yolks

Grated zest of ½ lemon

1 cup / 225 g unsalted butter

1 mango, peeled and diced brunoise *(finely)*

2 to 3 mint leaves, very finely minced

Preheat oven to 300 degrees.

Place pastry disks in metal tartlet pans and blind bake 20 minutes. Let cool.

In a bowl, combine lemon juice, sugar, eggs, and egg yolks, mixing until smooth. Pass through a chinois into a double boiler. Add the lemon zest, place over hot water, and cook, whisking, until pale and thick, 8 to 10 minutes. Remove from heat and whisk in butter. Pour into a clean bowl and refrigerate for at least 2 hours.

Place lemon curd in a piping bag and pipe a small amount into each tartlet shell. Mix the mango and mint, then place a small amount of the mixture on top of the lemon curd in the tartlet shells.

YIELDS 12 TARTLETS

The tangy lemon curd is just the right accompaniment for the sweet mango. The mint adds a touch of freshness. The curd and the tart shells can be prepared a day in advance, but don't assemble the tart until one to two hours before it is served.

Coconut Basil Macaroons *(photograph on page 174)*

5½ cups / 1300 ml unsweetened coconut, finely chopped

¾ cup / 177 ml corn syrup

½ cup / 118 ml granulated sugar

9 egg whites (about 1½ cups)

½ cup / 118 ml all-purpose flour

8 to 12 basil leaves, finely chopped

In a mixing bowl, combine 3½ cups of the coconut, the corn syrup, sugar, 3 egg whites, and flour, mixing until well blended. Add the basil and mix just enough to incorporate. Form into 1-inch balls and place in freezer to harden.

Preheat oven to 300 degrees.

Coat balls lightly with remaining 6 egg whites and dredge in remaining 2 cups coconut, and place on parchment-lined baking sheet. Bake macaroons until very light golden brown, 20 minutes.

YIELDS 30 COOKIES

The combination of coconut and basil is common in spicy Thai food. I was curious to see if it would work in pastry. These macaroons, a longtime favorite of mine, are the result. The macaroons may surprise diners at first, but they always get great reviews. These can be prepared ahead. Store in the freezer.

CLOCKWISE FROM TOP LEFT: *Ricotta Brûlée with Honeyed Raspberries, Lemon Mango Tartlets, Coconut Basil Macaroons, and Espresso Chocolates*

Espresso Chocolates

2 tablespoons / 29 ml white chocolate,
tempered (page 245)

1 cup / 236 ml bittersweet chocolate,
tempered (page 245)

½ cup / 118 ml heavy cream

2 tablespoons plus 1 teaspoon / 34 ml espresso

8 ounces / 225 g extra-bitter chocolate,
finely chopped

1 tablespoon / 15 ml coffee-flavored liqueur

¼ cup / 59 ml crème fraîche

½ teaspoon / 2 ml granulated sugar

1 cup bittersweet chocolate shavings

Using 12 1-inch round chocolate molds, pipe the white chocolate into them and allow to set. Carefully brush a thin layer of the tempered bittersweet chocolate over the piped white chocolate.

In a small saucepan, bring the cream and 2 tablespoons espresso to a boil and pour over the chopped chocolate. Whisk until smooth and add the liqueur. Place the mixture in a piping bag and pipe into the chocolate molds. Smooth the tops. Place in the refrigerator to set.

Unmold the chocolates onto a clean sheet tray. In an electric mixer, combine the crème fraîche, remaining 1 teaspoon espresso, and sugar, whisking until stiff peaks are formed. Using a small demitasse spoon, place a quenelle of the mixture on top of the chocolate. Decorate and garnish with chocolate shavings. Refrigerate.

YIELDS 12

The whipped espresso crème fraîche adds a needed touch of creaminess to the rich espresso filling. Prepare the chocolates one to two days in advance and top with the crème fraîche and shavings before serving.

Ricotta Brûlée with Honeyed Raspberries

2 cups / 473 ml fresh raspberries

3 tablespoons / 44 ml honey

¾ cup / 177 ml cream cheese

¼ cup plus 2 tablespoons / 89 ml ricotta cheese

¼ cup / 59 ml granulated sugar

¼ vanilla bean, split in half

1 whole egg

1 egg white

¾ cup / 85 g heavy cream

½ cup / 118 ml Brûlée Sugar (page 244)

Place the raspberries in a small bowl and drizzle with the honey. Gently fold to lightly coat the raspberries.

Place a small number of raspberries (three or four) at the bottom of 12 small ceramic or glass cups approximately 1 inch in diameter. Fill only halfway with the raspberries. Place the cups in the freezer until raspberries are frozen solid.

Preheat oven to 300 degrees.

In an electric mixer bowl, cream the cream cheese, ricotta cheese, sugar, and vanilla bean until smooth. Add the whole egg, egg white, and cream and mix until smooth. Pass through a sieve. Pour the cheese mixture over the frozen raspberries just enough to fill the dishes. Bake in a water bath until set and cheese is firm to the touch, 20–30 minutes. Allow to cool, then refrigerate. When ready to serve, sprinkle the tops with brûlée sugar and glaze lightly using a blowtorch.

YIELDS 12

A small taste of a dessert that also works well in larger form. The crunchy layer of caramelized sugar slightly warms the ricotta cheese that tops the honey-sweetened raspberries. Bake earlier in the day and glaze when served.

Fresh Strawberries with Sour Cream Ice Cream and Strawberry Chip

YIELDS 12 SERVINGS

The key here is to obtain great berries. It's flavorful berries with some sour cream ice cream and a potent little strawberry chip, all in one bite. The chips can be prepared ahead, along with the ice cream. Cut and set the berries as you serve them.

Strawberry Chips

3 fresh strawberries

¼ cup / 59 ml granulated sugar

Sour Cream Ice Cream

4 cups / 946 ml heavy cream

1½ cups / 354 ml granulated sugar

12 egg yolks

2 cups / 473 ml sour cream

12 large strawberries

Preheat oven to 200 degrees.

Carefully cut the strawberries into thin slices. Sprinkle sugar onto a silicone baking sheet and place the sliced strawberries on top of the sugar. Sprinkle another layer of sugar on top of the strawberries. Bake until dry and crisp, 30 to 40 minutes. Set aside. Store in an airtight container.

Combine cream and 1 cup of the sugar in a saucepan and bring to a boil. Place egg yolks and remaining ½ cup sugar in a large bowl. In one motion, pour and whisk hot cream into yolks. Stir in sour cream. Pass the mixture through a fine sieve, then chill briefly. Process in an ice cream machine according to the manufacturer's instructions. Keep frozen.

Trim tops and bottoms of 12 fresh strawberries. Scoop out a small amount of each strawberry using a Parisian scoop. This should create a hole in the top of each strawberry. Using a Parisian scoop, put some ice cream into the holes. Place a strawberry chip on top of the ice cream and serve.

Strawberry and Rhubarb Tartlets

YIELDS 12

The whipped crème fraîche provides a needed creaminess that mellows the intense strawberry and rhubarb filling. These tarts can be assembled and refrigerated one to two hours in advance.

1 cup / 236 ml peeled and diced rhubarb

½ cup / 118 ml diced strawberries

¼ cup / 59 ml granulated sugar

Juice of ½ lemon

12 disks of Sucre Dough (page 253), 2 inches in diameter

¼ cup / 59 ml crème fraîche, whipped

15 to 20 strands kataifi dough, toasted

Combine the rhubarb, strawberries, sugar, and lemon juice in a small saucepan. Cook over low heat, simmering until soft and thick, 5–8 minutes. Pour into a clean bowl and allow to cool.

Preheat oven to 300 degrees.

Press the pastry disks into 12 metal tartlet pans and bake until golden brown, 20 minutes. Let cool.

Carefully spoon the filling into the shells. Using a small demitasse spoon, place a quenelle of crème fraîche on top of the filling, then garnish with toasted dough strands.

Blackberry and Lemon Semolina Cakes

½ cup / 118 ml semolina flour

½ cup / 118 ml all-purpose flour

½ cup / 118 ml granulated sugar

½ tablespoon / 7.5 ml baking powder

¼ teaspoon / 1 ml salt

2 egg whites

½ cup / 118 ml milk

Grated zest of 1 lemon

¼ cup / 55 g unsalted butter, melted

12 fresh blackberries

Confectioners' sugar, for dusting

Preheat oven to 325 degrees. Generously butter 12 metal tartlet pans.

In an electric mixer bowl, combine all ingredients except the melted butter and blackberries, and mix until smooth. Add the melted butter. Pipe the batter into tartlet pans, filling only halfway. Place a blackberry in the center of each tartlet. Bake until lightly golden brown and firm to the touch, 20 minutes. Let cool briefly, then lightly dust tartlets with confectioners' sugar.

YIELDS 12 CAKES

These petit fours are best when served warm. The soft semolina cake with the juicy blackberry is just simple and great tasting. Prepare the batter a day in advance, but bake just before serving.

Strudel Cup with Vanilla Mascarpone and Fresh Cherries

2 sheets strudel dough

¼ cup / 59 ml clarified butter

½ cup / 118 ml mascarpone cheese

¼ cup / 59 ml heavy cream

3 tablespoons / 44 ml granulated sugar

½ vanilla bean, split in half and seeds scraped

1 cup / 236 ml fresh cherries, pitted and quartered

Preheat oven to 325 degrees.

Carefully place a sheet of strudel dough on a flat surface and brush lightly with clarified butter. Place the other sheet of strudel on top and brush again with the butter. Fold the dough in half, and cut into 3-inch disks using a metal cutter. Place in mini muffin pan and bake until golden brown, 15 minutes. Let cool.

In an electric mixer bowl, combine mascarpone cheese, cream, sugar, and vanilla seeds, whisking until stiff peaks are formed. Place in a piping bag and pipe into the shells. Arrange the quartered cherries on top.

YIELDS 12

A crisp strudel shell filled with smooth vanilla mascarpone and a touch of tart cherries. The strudel cups can be prepared ahead, but don't assemble with cream and cherries until needed.

Summer is one huge battle against heat and humidity. Nothing benefits from these conditions. My tuiles become soggy, the sugar garnishes are sticky, sauces ferment sooner, and anything frozen melts quickly. The weather is a constant challenge that has to be met by using creative production techniques. ■ **When I work with chocolate** and sugar, the high temperatures of the kitchen force me to alter my production schedule and location. The ideal space for working with chocolate and sugar in winter may become the worst place in summer. I usually schedule chocolate and sugar production earlier in the day and sometimes use an empty, cool dining room. Proper storage containers

SUMMER

and location of storage are critical in the summer heat. Sugar work, tuiles, and chocolate must be in containers that are absolutely airtight—the slightest exposure to heat and humidity can cause chocolate to melt and sugar garnishes and tuiles to become soft and sticky. Also, hot room temperatures can encourage fermentation and spoilage of fresh fruit and dairy sauces—sauces must be stored on ice or in the refrigerator. Handling frozen items, such as ice cream, sorbet, and frozen mousses, is probably the biggest challenge. Temperature of the plates also plays a major role in presenting desserts. Hot plates don't work for obvious reasons, but some people may be surprised to learn that cold plates are no good either—they build condensation immediately in contact with a hot kitchen. In the heat, some freezers perform better than others. I tend to shift frozen components for my desserts from one freezer to the next to maintain proper temperature. Over time, you learn how to troubleshoot disaster and juggle multiple problems in order to make your desserts work. ■ **If you are cooking at** home, it's a different world. Turn on the air-conditioning, relax, organize well first, and take your time. Summer heat is not so bad when you are looking at it through your window in your 70-degree kitchen. ■ **Although it seems as if** making desserts in the summer is a major hassle, the results are worth it. This time of year has the best fruit to work with. There are great peaches, plums, melons, apricots, and berries, each with so many varieties that it provides an endless supply of possibilities. As in spring, I tend to keep summer desserts refreshing, with a light feel. Some have simple chocolate and sugar garnishes and a streamlined design.

Frozen Peach Coupe with Hyssop and Citrus-Poached Peaches

FROZEN PEACH COUPE

Peach Sorbet

4 cups / 946 ml diced peaches,
(overripe peaches are best)

2 cups / 473 ml granulated sugar

1 cup / 236 ml water

Juice of 1 lemon

Frozen Crème Fraîche Soufflé

4 eggs, separated

¾ cup / 177 ml granulated sugar

2 cups / 473 ml crème fraîche, whipped

Combine the sorbet ingredients in a saucepan and bring to a simmer. Cook until the peaches are tender, 15 minutes, then remove from the heat. Puree until smooth and pass through a fine chinois. Cool the mixture in an ice bath. Freeze in an ice cream machine according to the manufacturer's instructions. Keep frozen.

Combine the egg yolks and ¼ cup of the sugar for soufflé in an electric mixer bowl and whisk until pale and fluffy. In a separate mixer bowl, whisk the egg whites until firm peaks are formed. Add the remaining ½ cup sugar and continue to whisk for 1 minute. Fold into egg yolks. Fold in whipped crème fraîche until incorporated.

Using eight metal ring molds 2½ inches in diameter, pipe the mixture into the bottom half of each mold. Place in freezer to set.

Remove rings from freezer and pipe on a layer of peach sorbet. The molds should now be full. Smooth the tops. Place molds back in freezer to set. Keep molds in the freezer until ready to serve.

PEACH GRANITÉ

1 cup / 236 ml lemon juice

1 cup / 236 ml water

¾ cup / 177 ml granulated sugar

1 bag orange pekoe tea

2 to 3 mint leaves

1 large peach, diced

Zest and juice of ½ orange

Combine ingredients in a saucepan and bring to a quick simmer. Remove from the heat and allow to steep 20 minutes. Strain the mixture through a chinois and then strain through a cloth. Pour the liquid into a low, shallow pan and place in the freezer. Every 10 to 15 minutes, stir the pan, mixing in the ice crystals. Repeat until small ice crystals are distributed throughout.

SERVES 8

Poaching the peaches in citrus gives them a sharp accent. The meringue crumbs provide a crunchy coating, and the soft peaches are enhanced by the touch of anise-scented hyssop. The frozen coupe and the granité should be prepared one day in advance. The other components may be prepared one to two days ahead.

CHEF'S NOTE

When you're stirring the peach granité, use a stiff whisk to scrape up the ice crystals. Any small lumps can be crushed with a fork.

CITRUS-POACHED PEACHES

1 cup / 236 ml lemon juice

1 cup / 236 ml orange juice

1 cup / 236 ml water

2 cups / 473 ml granulated sugar

2 to 3 hyssop leaves

4 large peaches

Combine all ingredients, except peaches, in a saucepan. Split the peaches in half and discard pits. Place the peach halves in the liquid. Bring to a quick simmer, reduce the heat, and simmer until peaches are tender, 10 minutes. Remove from the heat and allow the peaches to cool.

Remove peach halves and pull off skins. Place peach halves in a new pan or bowl and strain the poaching liquid over them.

ASSEMBLY

Citrus-Poached Peaches

Frozen Peach Coupe

2 cups Meringue Crumbs (page 248)

Peach Granité

Honey Tuiles (page 247)

Sugar Garnish (page 253)

Cut peach halves into ¼-inch slices and place in the bottoms of eight dessert bowls. Remove molds from coupes and gently coat with meringue crumbs. Place a scoop of peach granité on top of each coupe. Place the coupes on top of the sliced peaches in the bowls. Pour the peach poaching liquid around the bowls. Decorate the bowls with honey tuiles and sugar garnish.

Roasted Apricots with Lychee Sauce, Ginger Ice Cream, and Jicama Chips

ROASTED APRICOTS

16 fresh apricots

1 cup / 236 ml granulated sugar

Preheat oven to 250 degrees.

Cut the apricots in half and remove the pits. On a stainless steel sheet pan, sprinkle the sugar evenly over the surface. Place the apricots, cut side down, on the sugar. Roast for 10 minutes, then flip apricots over onto skin side and roast until tender, 15 to 20 minutes. Allow to cool. Wrap with plastic wrap and store at room temperature.

LYCHEE SAUCE

3 cups / 709 ml peeled and pitted lychees

1½ cups / 354 ml granulated sugar

Juice of 1 lemon

Combine the ingredients in a small saucepan and simmer until lychees are soft, 5 minutes. Puree until smooth and pass through a fine chinois. Cool in an ice bath. Refrigerate.

JICAMA CHIPS

2 jicamas

½ cup / 118 ml granulated sugar

Preheat oven to 200 degrees.

Use an electric meat slicer to cut jicamas into wide, thin, flat sheets. With a 3-inch metal cutter, cut out 24 disks. Sprinkle the sugar on a nonstick silicone sheet tray and lay the disks on top of the sugar. Sprinkle more sugar on top, then bake until dry and crisp, 30 minutes. Set aside. Store in an airtight container.

GINGER ICE CREAM

4 cups / 946 ml heavy cream

2 cups / 473 ml milk

1½ cups / 354 ml granulated sugar

1½ cups / 354 ml chopped fresh ginger

12 egg yolks

Place the cream, milk, 1 cup of the sugar, and the ginger in a saucepan over medium heat. Bring to a simmer, then remove from heat and allow to steep for 20 to 30 minutes.

Place the egg yolks and remaining ½ cup sugar in a medium bowl and stir to combine. Put the ginger mixture back on the heat and bring to a full boil. Quickly whisk the boiling mixture into the yolks and sugar. Strain the mixture through a fine chinois and place into an ice bath to cool.

SERVES 8

Lychees are one of my favorite fruits. They have a very short season, but when they are available, you can find them in Chinatowns, either piled high on a shelf or hanging on branches. They have a unique perfumelike flavor and a texture that most people dislike. I find that the best solution is to make a simple puree and serve lychees with some sharp-flavored apricots, creamy ginger ice cream, and nutty jicama chips. All these components can be prepared one to two days in advance and assembled when being served.

CHEF'S NOTE

Cook the lychees for the lychee sauce just until tender. Overcooking the lychees can cause them to turn brown.

Transfer the mixture to an ice cream machine and process according to the manufacturer's instructions. Put in freezer to harden.

Scoop and press ice cream into eight 2-ounce triangular molds. Keep molds in freezer until ready to use.

ASSEMBLY

Roasted Apricots

Ginger Ice Cream

Meringue Crumbs (page 248)

Lychee Sauce

Jicama Chips

Sugar Garnish (page 253)

In the bottoms of eight dessert bowls, place four apricot halves. Unmold the ice cream triangles and coat the bottom in meringue crumbs. Place ice cream on top of apricots. Pour the lychee sauce around the apricots. Place the jicama chips in the ice cream and decorate bowls with a sugar garnish.

Warm Peach Strudel with Sweet Corn Panna Cotta

SERVES 8

Some ideas happen when you least expect them. I was eating a bowl of Corn Pops and fresh peaches with my sons one morning and I started to think about the two flavors together. This dish is the end result. The frozen timbale and sorbet can be prepared two days in advance, but the panna cotta and other components should be prepared one day ahead.

CHEF'S NOTE

For the roasted peach halves, always use ripe peaches for the best results. An underripe peach will not only have less flavor, it will not release its skin when roasted.

CREPE-WRAPPED PEACH STRUDELS

¾ cup / 177 ml all-purpose flour

2 egg yolks

2 whole eggs

1 cup / 236 ml milk

¼ cup / 55 g unsalted butter, melted

½ vanilla bean, split in half

12 Roasted Peach Halves ■

6 sheets strudel dough

1 cup / 236 ml clarified butter

■ **Roasted Peach Halves**

7 ripe peaches

1 cup / 236 ml granulated sugar

Place the flour in a medium mixer bowl. In a separate small bowl, whisk together the yolks, whole eggs, and milk. Slowly whisk the wet ingredients into the flour until smooth.

Combine the butter and vanilla bean, then add the vanilla butter to the batter. Use an 8-inch nonstick sauté pan to make the crepes (page 247).

Cut peach halves in half and place three of the quarters in the center of each crepe. Fold the sides of the crepe over to wrap the peaches.

Carefully place a sheet of dough on a flat surface. Brush with clarified butter and place another sheet of strudel dough on top. Brush with butter. Cut the sheets of dough into three equal pieces. Place a crepe-wrapped peach in the center of each piece, then fold over the sides and fold from front to back. This should completely wrap the crepe bundle with the strudel dough. Brush the tops with clarified butter and place on a parchment-lined sheet tray. Repeat the process with the four remaining strudel sheets.

Preheat oven to 350 degrees, then bake until golden brown, 20 minutes. Let cool. (You should end up with an extra piece of strudel dough, which you can use if one of the others tears.)

Preheat oven to 250 degrees.

Halve the peaches and remove the pits. Spread the sugar on top of a parchment-lined sheet tray. Place the peaches flesh side down on top of the sugar. Bake for 10 minutes, remove from oven, and turn the peaches over so that the skin side is down. Place back in the oven and roast until the peaches are tender, 20 to 30 minutes more. Let the peaches cool, then

Cut the roasted peach halves.

Place the peaches in the center of the crepes.

Fold over the two sides of the crepe.

Fold ends of the crepe over and form into a rectangular package.

Spread and cut the strudel dough and place the peach-filled crepes at the end nearest you.

Fold over the first side of the strudel dough.

Fold over the second and align the dough.

Fold over the peach-filled crepe once.

Butter the strudel dough slightly if needed and continue to fold.

Once the strudels are folded, place them on a parchment-lined pan and butter the tops.

peel the skins off. Keep twelve halves for the strudel and reserve the other two for the peach sauce. Refrigerate it stored overnight.

SWEET CORN PANNA COTTA

2 cups / 473 ml heavy cream

3 cups / 709 ml milk

1 cup / 236 ml granulated sugar

¹/₂ ear fresh corn

1 cup / 236 ml dehydrated corn

1 vanilla bean, split in half

4 teaspoons powdered gelatin, bloomed in 4 tablespoons water, or 4 sheets gelatin

Combine all of the ingredients, except gelatin, in a saucepan and bring to a quick boil. Remove from the heat and allow to steep for 20 to 30 minutes. Soften or bloom the gelatin in cold water, then add to the pan. Pass the mixture through a chinois and pour the panna cotta into eight 3-ounce metal cups. Chill until set. Refrigerate.

FROZEN PEACHES AND CREAM TIMBALE

3 ripe peaches

³/₄ cup plus 2 tablespoons / 207 ml granulated sugar

2 eggs, separated

³/₄ cup / 177 ml crème fraîche

¹/₄ cup / 59 ml heavy cream

Preheat oven to 200 degrees.

Halve the peaches and remove the pits. Cut the halves into ¹/₈-inch-thick slices. Sprinkle ¹/₂ cup of the sugar onto a silicone baking sheet and arrange the peach slices on top of the sugar. Bake for 8 to 12 minutes or until peach slices are tender. Remove and allow to cool.

Arrange peach slices in a fan pattern inside eight 2-ounce plastic or metal timbale molds. Place in freezer and freeze until hard, approximately 30 minutes.

In an electric mixer bowl, combine egg yolks and 2 tablespoons of sugar. Whisk until mixture is pale and thick. In a separate mixing bowl, whisk egg whites until firm peaks are formed. Add the remaining ¹/₄ cup sugar and continue to whisk for 1 minute. Fold whites into yolk mixture. Whisk the crème fraîche and cream together until firm peaks are formed. Fold into the egg mixture.

Place the mousse in a piping bag. Remove the timbale molds from the freezer and pipe the mousse into the molds, filling them completely. Carefully bend the peach slices over the top of the mousse. Place molds back in freezer and freeze 2 to 3 hours.

PEACH SORBET

2 cups / 473 ml diced ripe peaches

1 cup / 236 ml granulated sugar

¹/₂ cup / 118 ml water

Juice of ¹/₂ lemon

Combine ingredients in a saucepan and simmer until peaches are tender, 15 minutes. Puree until smooth, then pass through a chinois and place in an ice bath to cool. Transfer to an ice cream machine and process according to the manufacturer's instructions. Keep frozen.

MERINGUE DISKS

1 cup / 236 ml sliced, blanched almonds

1 cup / 236 ml granulated sugar

¹/₂ cup / 118 ml confectioners' sugar

5 egg whites

Preheat oven to 250 degrees.

Combine the almonds, ¹/₂ cup of the granulated sugar, and the confectioners' sugar in a food processor until smooth. In an electric mixer bowl, whisk the egg whites until soft peaks are formed. Add the remaining ¹/₂ cup sugar and continue to whisk until firm peaks are formed. Whisk for an additional minute, then remove from the machine. Fold the dry ingredients into the egg whites.

On a parchment-lined sheet tray, using a small round stencil (page 252) which is $1^1/_2$ inches in diameter that you have created, spread the meringue over the stencil. Bake until light golden brown in color, 20 to 30 minutes. Allow to cool, then set aside. Store in an airtight container.

PEACH SAUCE

2 halves roasted peaches (page 186)

$^1/_2$ cup / 118 ml water

$^1/_2$ cup / 118 ml granulated sugar

Place the ingredients in a blender and puree until smooth. Pass through a chinois, then refrigerate for later use.

CORN SAUCE

2 cups / 473 ml half-and-half

$^1/_2$ cup / 118 ml granulated sugar

$^1/_2$ cup / 118 ml fresh corn kernels

$^1/_2$ cup / 118 ml dried corn

1 tablespoon / 15 ml instant polenta

Combine all of the ingredients except the polenta in a saucepan and bring to a simmer. Remove from the heat and allow to steep for 10 to 20 minutes. Puree until smooth. Add the polenta and place back over medium heat. Bring the mixture to a simmer, then cook, stirring, until mixture is slightly thickened. Remove from heat and place in an ice bath to cool. Refrigerate.

ASSEMBLY

Corn Sauce

Crepe-Wrapped Peach Strudels

Sweet Corn Panna Cotta

Frozen Peaches and Cream Timbales

Meringue Disks

Peach Sorbet

Peach Sauce

Honey Tuiles (page 247)

Sugar Garnish (page 253)

Place a small pool of corn sauce slightly off center on each of eight dessert plates. Place a peach strudel on top of the corn sauce. Unmold the corn panna cottas and place behind the strudels to the left sides. Unmold the timbales and place behind the strudels on the right sides. Place a meringue disk on top of each frozen timbale. Place a scoop of peach sorbet on top of the meringue disk. Pipe some peach sauce around the timbales and panna cottas. Decorate the plates with honey tuiles and sugar garnish.

Iced Plum and Nectarine Soups with Orange Mousse

PLUM SOUP

2 cups / 473 ml diced red plums

1 cup / 236 ml granulated sugar

1 cup / 236 ml water

Juice of ½ lemon

Combine the ingredients in a saucepan and bring to a simmer. Cook until plums are soft, 10 minutes. Puree until smooth and pass through a chinois. Place in an ice bath to cool. Refrigerate.

NECTARINE SOUP

2 cups / 473 ml diced nectarines

1 cup / 236 ml granulated sugar

1 cup / 236 ml water

Juice of ½ lemon

Combine ingredients in a saucepan and bring to a simmer. Cook until the nectarines are soft, 10 minutes. Remove from heat and puree until smooth. Pass through a chinois. Place in an ice bath to cool. Refrigerate.

MARINATED PLUMS AND JICAMA

1 cup / 236 ml white verjus

½ cup / 118 ml granulated sugar

Juice of ½ lemon

½ cup / 118 ml water

1 jicama, julienned

1 plum, very thinly sliced, with peel

In a bowl, combine verjus, sugar, lemon juice, and water. Whisk until sugar is dissolved, then add jicama and plum slices and marinate for 2 to 3 hours. Refrigerate.

FROZEN ORANGE MOUSSES

4 eggs, separated

Grated zest of 1 orange

¾ cup / 177 ml granulated sugar

2 cups / 473 ml heavy cream

In an electric mixer bowl, combine egg yolks, zest, and ¼ cup of the sugar. Whisk until pale and fluffy. In a separate mixing bowl, whisk egg whites until firm peaks are formed. Add the remaining ½ cup of sugar and continue to whisk for 1 minute. Add the whites to the yolk mixture. Whip the cream and fold into egg mixture.

Place in a piping bag. Put eight metal or plastic rings, 2 inches in diameter, into the bottom of eight glass bowls. Pipe the mousse into the rings until 1 inch deep. Place in freezer for 3 to 5 hours.

Cut around the interiors of the rings to remove the rings. Put mousses (in the bowls) back in freezer.

SERVES 8

Here are two smooth purees served ice cold, both with intense flavor. The nectarine is smooth and sweet; the plum is tangy and refreshing. The jicama adds crunchy texture, as the frozen mousse adds creamy balance. All components can be prepared one to two days in advance, with the exception of the sliced plums and jicama.

CHEF'S NOTE

For the marinated plums and jicama, you can substitute muscato wine or plum wine for the white verjus.

MERINGUE DISKS

1 cup / 236 ml sliced, blanched almonds

1 cup / 236 ml granulated sugar

½ cup / 118 ml confectioners' sugar

5 egg whites

Preheat oven to 250 degrees.

In a food processor, combine the almonds, ½ cup of the granulated sugar, and the confectioners' sugar. Puree until smooth. In an electric mixer, whisk egg whites until soft peaks are formed. Add the remaining ½ cup sugar and continue to whisk until firm peaks are formed. Whisk for an additional minute, then add dry ingredients to the egg whites.

On a parchment-lined sheet tray, using a stencil (page 252) that you have created, make eight 3-inch disks. Bake until light golden brown in color, 20 to 30 minutes. Let disks cool completely, then set aside. Store in airtight container.

ASSEMBLY

Crushed ice

Frozen Orange Mousses

Meringue Disks

Marinated Plums and Jicama

Nectarine Soup

Plum Soup

Sugar Garnish (page 253)

Fill each of eight glass dessert bowls a third of the way with crushed ice. Place the bowls of mousse on top of the crushed ice. Place a meringue disk on top of each mousse. Put a small amount of the marinated plums and jicama on top of each meringue disk. Carefully pour in the plum and nectarine soups simultaneously so that you have equal amounts of each in each bowl. Decorate with the sugar garnish.

Peach Trio

PEACH TART

Almond Financier

1¾ cups / 413 ml confectioners' sugar

¼ cup / 59 ml all-purpose flour

1 cup / 118 ml natural almond flour

3 egg whites

¼ cup / 55g salted butter

8 disks Sucre Dough, 3 inches in diameter (page 253)

8 halves roasted peaches (page 186)

In an electric mixer bowl, combine the confectioners' sugar, flours, and egg whites. Whisk until smooth. In a small saucepan, brown the butter and add to the batter. Place the batter in a small piping bag. Set aside.

Preheat the oven to 300 degrees.

Using eight 2½-inch metal tartlet pans, blind bake the sucre disks until golden brown, 20 minutes. Let cool. Keep oven at 300 degrees.

Place a peach half, flesh side down, into each tartlet shell. Pipe a small amount of batter around the border of each peach—this should fill the gap between the peach and the pastry shell. Bake until batter is golden brown, 15 minutes. Allow to cool. Set aside.

PEACH DACQUOISE

Meringue Sheets

1 cup / 236 ml granulated sugar

1 cup / 236 ml sliced, blanched almonds

½ cup / 118 ml confectioners' sugar

5 egg whites

Preheat the oven to 250 degrees.

Create a stencil (page 252) that will be the width and length of the terrine or loaf pan you will be using to mold the dacquoise. In a food processor, combine ½ cup of the sugar, the almonds, and confectioners' sugar, and puree until smooth. In an electric mixer bowl, whisk egg whites until soft peaks are formed. Add the remaining ½ cup sugar and continue to whisk until firm peaks are formed. Whisk for an additional minute and then remove from the machine. Fold in the dry ingredients.

In a parchment-lined sheet tray, using the stencil you have created, spread the meringue to make five long rectangles. Bake until light golden brown, 20 to 30 minutes. Remove from the oven and allow to cool.

Peach Mousse

4 eggs, separated

¾ cup / 177 ml granulated sugar

½ cup / 118 ml Peach Sauce ▪

2 cups / 473 ml heavy cream

In an electric mixer bowl, combine the yolks and ¼ cup of the sugar, whisking until pale and thick. Fold in peach sauce. In a separate mixing bowl, whisk egg whites until firm peaks are formed. Add the remaining ½ cup sugar and continue to whisk for 1 minute. Fold whites into peach mixture. In another mixing

SERVES 8

I set out to combine the elements of warm and cold fresh peaches. The fresh peaches ended up being a nice complement to the warm peach tart. The chilled dacquoise adds a refreshing note. The peach dacquoise needs to be prepared one day in advance. The tart and fresh peaches should be prepared the day you need them.

bowl, whip the cream until firm peaks are formed and fold into the peach mixture. Place into a piping bag.

Place a sheet of meringue on the bottom of a 4-inch by 10-inch terrine or loaf pan. Spread an even layer of mousse on top of the meringue. Alternate layers of meringue and mousse until you have five layers of meringue and four layers of mousse. Place in the freezer and allow to freeze overnight. Once frozen, slice into 1-inch-thick slices.

■ **Peach Sauce**

2 halves roasted peaches (page 186)

$\frac{1}{2}$ cup / 118 ml water

$\frac{1}{2}$ cup / 118 ml granulated sugar

Place ingredients in a blender and puree until smooth. Pass through a chinois. Refrigerate for use later.

FRESH PEACHES WITH CRÈME FRAÎCHE

3 ripe unpeeled peaches, diced

6 tablespoons / 79 ml granulated sugar

Juice of $\frac{1}{2}$ lemon

4 to 6 mint leaves, minced

1 cup / 236 ml crème fraîche

In a bowl, combine the peaches, 4 tablespoons of the sugar, the lemon juice, and mint and toss together gently. Allow to sit for 15 to 20 minutes.

Using eight metal or plastic rings $1\frac{1}{2}$ inches in diameter and 2 inches tall, fill the rings almost completely with the diced peaches. Leave a $\frac{1}{4}$-inch space at the top of each mold. In a bowl, combine the crème fraîche and remaining 2 tablespoons sugar and whisk until stiff. Fill the molds with the crème fraîche and smooth the tops. Refrigerate.

ASSEMBLY

Peach Tart

Fresh Peaches with Crème Fraîche

Peach Dacquoise

Peach Sauce

2 cups Vanilla Sabayon Sauce (page 250)

Honey Tuiles (page 247)

Sugar Garnish (page 253)

Place a peach tart in the centers of eight oval dessert plates. To one side of the peach tart, unmold the peaches and crème fraîche. On the other side of the peach tart, place a slice of dacquoise, standing on end. Pipe the peach sauce and sabayon sauce around the plates. Decorate with the honey tuiles and sugar garnish.

Warm Plum Cake with Jasmine Ice Cream

PLUM CAKE

1 cup / 236 ml semolina flour

1 cup / 236 ml all-purpose flour

1 cup / 236 ml granulated sugar

1 tablespoon / 15 ml baking powder

$^1\!/_2$ teaspoon / 2 ml salt

$^1\!/_8$ teaspoon / .62 ml ground cinnamon

$^1\!/_8$ teaspoon / .62 ml ground ginger

4 egg whites

1 cup / 236 ml milk

Grated zest of 1 orange

$^1\!/_2$ cup / 115 g unsalted butter, melted

2 red plums, pitted and thinly sliced

Preheat oven to 325 degrees. Butter a 9-inch by 3-inch loaf pan.

In an electric mixer bowl, combine all the ingredients except the melted butter and plums. Mix until smooth. Add the butter and plums, and pour the batter into the loaf pan. Fill the loaf pan three-quarters full. Bake until light golden brown and firm to the touch, 30–40 minutes. Remove from oven and unmold cake. Allow to cool. Once it has cooled, cut into $^1\!/_2$-inch-thick slices. When ready to serve, heat cake slices in 325-degree oven for 2 minutes.

SERVES 8

The fragrant jasmine ice cream works well with the warm plum cake and the tart roasted plums. The sesame and ginger are Asian accents that fit right in. All components can be prepared one to two days in advance, but the plum cake should be baked the day you serve it for best results.

JASMINE ICE CREAM MOLDS

Baked Plum Slices

5 red plums

$^1\!/_2$ cup / 118 ml granulated sugar

Preheat oven to 225 degrees.

Halve the plums and remove the pits. Cut into thin slices $^1\!/_8$ inch thick. Spread an even layer of sugar on a parchment-lined sheet tray. Arrange plum slices on top of the sugar and sprinkle lightly with sugar. Bake until tender, 10 to 15 minutes. Remove from the oven and allow the slices to cool.

Line the interior of eight 3-ounce metal dome molds with the plum slices. Place the molds in the freezer.

Ice Cream

4 cups / 946 ml heavy cream

2 cups / 473 ml milk

$1^1\!/_2$ cups / 354 ml granulated sugar

$^1\!/_2$ cup / 118 ml jasmine tea

Zest of 1 orange

12 egg yolks

Combine the cream, milk, sugar, tea, and orange zest in a saucepan and bring to a simmer. Remove from heat and allow to steep for 20 minutes. Place back on the stove and bring to a boil. Place the egg yolks in a large bowl. In one motion, pour and whisk the cream mixture into the egg yolks. Pass through a fine sieve. Chill, then process in an ice cream machine according to the manufacturer's instructions.

While the ice cream is still soft, pipe it into the plum-lined molds in the freezer. Allow to set solid in the freezer overnight.

ROASTED PLUMS AND PLUM PUREE

12 ripe plums

1¹/₂ cups / 354 ml granulated sugar

Preheat oven to 250 degrees.

Halve the plums and remove the pits. Evenly spread the sugar on a parchment-lined sheet tray. Arrange the plums flesh side down on the sugar. Roast for 10 minutes, then remove tray from oven and turn the plums over so that the skin sides are facing down. Return to oven and roast for an additional 10 to 15 minutes or until the plums are tender. Allow the plums to cool slightly, then peel the skins off 16 plum halves. Reserve these skinless plums for finishing the dessert. Place remaining plums in a food processor and puree until smooth. Put puree in a pastry bag. Refrigerate.

PLUM AND ORANGE SAUCE

5 plums, pitted and cut into eighths

¹/₂ cup / 118 ml water

1 cup / 236 ml orange juice

1¹/₂ cups / 354 ml granulated sugar

Zest of ¹/₂ orange

Combine ingredients in a saucepan and bring to a simmer. Continue to simmer for 15 minutes. Remove from heat and strain through a large-holed sieve. Pass the liquid through a fine chinois and chill in an ice bath. Keep the sauce refrigerated until ready to use.

ASSEMBLY

Plum and Orange Sauce

Roasted Plums and Plum Puree

Plum Cake

Jasmine Ice Cream Molds

Sesame Snap Cookie (page 251)

Honey Tuiles (page 247)

2 cups Ginger Sabayon Sauce (page 250)

Sugar Garnish (page 253)

Pour a pool of the plum and orange sauce onto each of eight dessert plates. Place a couple of roasted plum halves toward the front of each plate. Heat a slice of the plum cake and gently place on top of the plum halves. Unmold the ice cream molds and place, plum side down, on the plates behind the plum cakes. Place a sesame snap cookie on top of each ice cream. Place a honey tuile in the snap cookie. Fill the honey tuiles with plum puree. Decorate the plates with the sabayon sauce and sugar garnish.

Poached White Peach with Vanilla Ice Cream and Glazed Crème Fraîche Custard

SERVES 8

Some peaches can be so amazing in size that it is a shame to cut them up. These white peaches were so huge that I decided simply to stuff them with ice cream and top them with a custard, leaving the whole peach intact. All these components can be prepared one to two days in advance.

POACHED WHITE PEACHES

8 large white peaches

8 cups / 1892 ml water

6 cups / 1419 ml granulated sugar

Juice of 2 lemons

2 cinnamon sticks

2 vanilla beans, split in half

Cut $^1/_2$ inch off the top of each peach, making a flat, level surface. Using a metal tube 1 inch in diameter, core the peaches from the flat top and remove the pits. Place the cored peaches in a large saucepan and add the remaining ingredients. Bring to a simmer and simmer until peaches are tender, 10 minutes. Remove from the heat and allow the peaches to cool in the liquid. Drain peaches, peel, and place in refrigerator. Discard the poaching liquid, or save to use again.

CRÈME FRAÎCHE CUSTARD

2 cups / 473 ml heavy cream

2 cups / 473 ml crème fraîche

$^1/_2$ cup / 118 ml granulated sugar

$^1/_2$ vanilla bean, split in half

1 cinnamon stick

9 egg yolks

1 whole egg

In a saucepan, combine the cream, crème fraîche, sugar, vanilla bean, and cinnamon stick. Bring to a simmer and remove from heat. Steep for 10 to 15 minutes, then cool the liquid in an ice bath. Whisk in the egg yolks and whole egg. Pass through a chinois and pour into a clean container.

Preheat oven to 300 degrees.

Using $2^1/_2$-inch metal tart pans, line the interior of each pan with plastic wrap—the wrap should fit tightly against the molds. Fill each pan with the custard. Bake in a water bath until the custard is set and firm, 20–30 minutes. Allow to cool, then place in refrigerator for at least 1 hour. Gently pull custards out of pans to unmold. Refrigerate.

WHITE PEACH SAUCE

2 large white peaches, pitted and cut into eighths

1 cup / 236 ml water

$^1/_2$ cup / 118 ml granulated sugar

1 vanilla bean, split in half and seeds scraped

Juice of $^1/_2$ lemon

Combine ingredients in a saucepan and bring to a simmer. Simmer for 5 minutes, then remove from heat and strain through a sieve. Pass the liquid through a fine chinois, then cool in an ice bath. Refrigerate until ready to use.

ASSEMBLY

White Peach Sauce

Honey Tuiles (page 247)

Poached White Peaches

Vanilla Ice Cream (page 254)

Almond Cookies (page 243)

Crème Fraîche Custard

1 cup Brûlée Sugar (page 244)

Fresh peaches, julienned

2 cups Vanilla Sabayon Sauce (page 250)

Sugar Garnish (page 253)

Pour a small pool of peach sauce in the center of each of eight round dessert plates. Place a small round honey tuile in the center of the peach sauce. Stand a poached peach, with the open end up, on the honey tuile. Place a small scoop of vanilla ice cream in the hollowed peach. Place an almond cookie on top of the peach, covering the vanilla ice cream. Place a custard on top of the almond cookie. Sprinkle the brûlée sugar on top of the custard and glaze with a blowtorch. Place a small mound of julienned peach on top of the custard. Put dots of sabayon sauce around each plate, then decorate with the honey tuile and sugar garnish.

Frozen Peach Parfait

FROZEN PEACH PARFAIT

Peach Sorbet

4 cups / 946 ml diced ripe peaches

2 cups / 473 ml granulated sugar

1 cup / 236 ml water

Juice of 1/2 lemon

YOGURT MOUSSE

4 eggs, separated

3/4 cup / 177 ml granulated sugar

1/2 cup / 118 ml heavy cream

1 1/2 cups / 354 ml plain yogurt

Combine ingredients for sorbet in a medium saucepan and bring to a simmer. Cook the peaches until tender, 15 minutes. Remove from the heat and puree until smooth. Pass through a chinois and cool in an ice bath. Process in an ice cream machine according to the manufacturer's instructions. Keep frozen.

In an electric mixer bowl, combine the yolks and 1/4 cup of the sugar, whisking until pale and thick. Using a separate mixing bowl, whisk egg whites until firm peaks are formed. Add the remaining 1/2 cup of sugar and continue to whisk for 1 minute. Fold the whites into the yolk mixture. Whip the heavy cream until firm peaks are formed. Fold into the egg mixture. Last, fold in the plain yogurt. Place the mixture in a piping bag.

Using eight metal tubes 1 1/2 inches in diameter and 3 inches tall, pipe a layer of the mousse, filling the tubes one-fourth of the way. Place in the freezer and allow to freeze until solid. Remove from the freezer and pipe the sorbet into the tubes until half filled. Return to the freezer and allow to freeze solid. Remove from the freezer and pipe another layer of the mousse until the tubes are three-fourths full. Return to the freezer again and freeze until solid. Remove from the freezer and pipe another layer of the sorbet, filling the tubes. The tubes should consist of alternating layers of mousse and sorbet—two layers of each. Return to the freezer and allow to freeze solid, 2 to 3 hours. Keep frozen in the tubes until ready to use. Reserve remaining sorbet for finishing the dessert.

SERVES 8

The yogurt adds a great tangy accent to the peaches while giving the dessert a light feel. The parfait is cool and refreshing, and the strudel crisps add a flaky crunch. All these components should be prepared one to two days in advance.

MINT SYRUP

20 large spearmint leaves

1 cup / 236 ml light corn syrup

1 teaspoon / 5 ml cold water

Bring a small saucepan of water to a full boil and blanch the mint leaves. Cook for 30 seconds, drain, and shock in ice water. Squeeze the leaves dry, trying to remove as much excess water as possible. Chop very fine with a sharp knife.

Place the chopped mint leaves, corn syrup, and water in a blender and puree until very smooth. Pass through a chinois and place in a squeeze bottle.

PEACH SAUCE

2 to 3 Roasted Peach Halves ■

1/2 cup / 118 ml water

1/2 cup / 118 ml granulated sugar

Place ingredients in a blender and puree until smooth. Pass through a chinois and place in a squeeze bottle. Refrigerate.

■ Roasted Peach Halves

1/2 cup / 118 ml granulated sugar

6 small ripe peaches, split in half and pitted

Preheat oven to 250 degrees.

Sprinkle an even layer of sugar on a parchment-lined sheet tray. Place the peaches flesh side down. Bake for 10 minutes, remove from the oven, and turn the peaches over so that the skin side is down. Return to the oven and bake for an additional 20 to 30 minutes or until the peaches are tender. Remove from the oven, allowing to cool slightly, and peel off the skins. Reserve eight peach halves for garnish and the rest for sauce. Cover the halves with plastic wrap and refrigerate.

CANDIED PEACHES

4 medium peaches

3 cups / 709 ml granulated sugar

2 cups / 473 ml water

Juice of 1/2 lemon

Cut the peaches in half and remove the pits. Cut the halves into quarters. In a saucepan, combine the peaches, sugar, water, and lemon juice. Bring to a boil and boil until the temperature reaches 230 degrees. Drain and cool. Cover and store at room temperature until ready to use.

ASSEMBLY

Frozen Peach Parfait

Strudel Crisps (page 252)

Roasted Peach Halves

Mint Syrup

Plain yogurt

Peach Sauce

Candied Peaches

Peach Sorbet

Fresh peaches

Sugar Garnish (page 253)

Using eight round plates, unmold the parfaits and place off center on the plates. Arrange and lean the strudel crisps against the parfaits. Place a roasted peach half on top of each parfait—that will help to hold down the strudel crisps. Place dots of mint syrup, yogurt, and peach sauce around the plate. Place pieces of the candied peaches around the plate. Carefully place a small scoop of sorbet on top of the horizontal strudel crisp. Arrange a few slices of fresh peaches in the center of the plates. Decorate with a sugar garnish.

Warm Plum Strudel with Ginger Ice Cream

PLUM STRUDELS

Vanilla Crepes

³/₄ cups / 177 ml all-purpose flour

2 egg yolks

2 whole eggs

1 cup / 236 ml milk

¹/₄ cup / 55 g unsalted butter, melted

¹/₂ vanilla bean, split in half

24 Roasted Plum Halves ▪

6 sheets strudel dough

³/₄ cup / 177 ml clarified butter, melted

Place the flour in a medium mixer bowl. In a separate small mixing bowl, combine and whisk the egg yolks, whole eggs, and milk. Add the wet ingredients to the flour and mix until smooth. Combine and whisk the melted butter and vanilla bean. Add the vanilla butter to the rest of the crepe batter. Strain the batter to remove vanilla bean. Use an 8-inch nonstick sauté pan to make the crepes (page 247).

Preheat oven to 350 degrees.

Lay out eight crepes and place three roasted plum halves in the center of each. Fold over each side of the crepe, creating a square packet. Carefully spread out a sheet of strudel dough and lightly brush with the clarified butter. Place another sheet of strudel dough on top. Continue until there are three sheets of strudel dough together. Cut the strudel dough into squares that are 7 by 7 inches. Place each crepe packet in the middle of the strudel dough square. Fold over two sides and then the other two sides, creating a square. Brush the top with clarified butter. Bake until golden brown, 20 minutes. Allow to cool on tray. Reheat in oven for 4 minutes when ready to serve.

▪ Roasted Plum Halves

12 plums

1¹/₂ cups / 354 ml granulated sugar

Preheat oven to 250 degrees.

Cut the plums in half and pit them. On a parchment-lined sheet tray, sprinkle the sugar evenly. Face the plums, flesh side down, on the sugar. Bake for 10 minutes, remove from the oven, and turn the plums over. The skin side should be on the sugar. Continue to bake until the plums are tender, 10 to 20 minutes. Remove from the oven. Transfer the plums to a perforated pan, allowing the excess liquid to drain. Allow to cool. Place once again on a parchment-lined sheet tray.

SERVES 8

Smooth ginger ice cream sits upon warm crepes and roasted plums that are wrapped in flaky strudel dough. The strudel sits on a small bed of fruit and an intense plum sauce. The crepe acts as a moisture barrier between the roasted plums and the flaky strudel dough, leaving the strudel crisp and not soggy. The ginger ice cream and linzer cookies can be prepared one to two days in advance, but the strudels should be assembled the same day that you serve them.

GINGER ICE CREAM

4 cups / 946 ml heavy cream

2 cups / 473 ml milk

1¹/₂ cups / 354 ml granulated sugar

1 cup / 236 ml finely chopped fresh ginger

12 egg yolks

Combine the cream, milk, sugar, and ginger in a saucepan and bring to a boil. Remove from the heat and allow to steep for 20 minutes. Place the egg yolks in a large bowl and bring the ginger milk mixture to a full boil. In one motion, pour and whisk the hot milk mixture into the yolks. Pass through a chinois. Chill in an ice bath. Process in an ice cream machine according to the manufacturer's instructions. Keep frozen.

LINZER BISCUITS

1 cup / 236 ml granulated sugar

1¹/₂ cups / 354 ml hazelnuts, toasted and skinned

1¹/₂ cups / 340 g unsalted butter

2 whole eggs

2¹/₂ cups / 590 ml cake flour

1 tablespoon / 15 ml ground cinnamon

2 teaspoons / 10 ml baking powder

Preheat oven to 300 degrees.

In a food processor, combine the sugar and hazelnuts, and puree until smooth. Transfer to an electric mixer bowl. Add the butter, and cream until smooth. Add the eggs, flour, cinnamon, and baking powder and blend well.

Roll out the dough until it is ¹/₈ inch thick. Cut into oval shapes 3 inches long. Bake until light golden brown in color, 15 minutes. Store in an airtight container.

BAKED PLUM SLICES

4 red plums

¹/₂ cup / 118 ml granulated sugar

Preheat oven to 225 degrees.

Halve the plums and remove the pits. Carefully slice the plums ¹/₈ inch thick. Spread the sugar evenly on a parchment-lined sheet tray. Arrange the plum slices on top of the sugar. Sprinkle more sugar on top of the plums. Bake until the plum slices are tender, 10 to 15 minutes.

PLUM SAUCE

3 cups / 709 ml diced red plums

1¹/₂ cups / 354 ml granulated sugar

1 cup / 236 ml water

Juice of ¹/₂ lemon

Combine all ingredients in a saucepan and bring to a simmer. Continue to cook until the plums are tender, about 8 minutes. Puree until smooth. Pass through a chinois. Place in an ice bath to cool. Keep the sauce refrigerated until ready to use.

ASSEMBLY

Plum Sauce

Peeled white grapes

Fresh apricots, sliced

Red plums, thinly sliced

Plum Strudels

Linzer Biscuits

Baked Plum Slices

Ginger Ice Cream

Sugar Garnish (page 253)

2 cups Vanilla Sabayon Sauce (page 250)

Pour a small pool of the plum sauce into the center of each of eight round plates. Arrange a small mound of white grapes and apricot and plum slices. Place the warm strudel on top of each mound. Place a linzer biscuit on top of the plum strudel. Arrange the baked plum slices in a fan pattern on top of the linzer biscuits. Place a scoop of ginger ice cream on top of the fanned plum slices. Decorate the plate with a sugar garnish and dots of the vanilla sabayon.

Frozen Cantaloupe Parfait with Lavender Meringue Disks

SERVES 8

Fresh melon is always cool and refreshing. I wanted to create a dessert that had the same feel. I like to match two fragrant components together, so I thought lavender would go well with the melon. The lavender meringue disks and the frozen parfait should be prepared one day in advance.

LAVENDER MERINGUE DISKS

1 cup / 236 ml sliced, blanched almonds

1 cup / 236 ml granulated sugar

Zest of $1/2$ orange

2 teaspoons / 10 ml dried lavender

$1/2$ cup / 118 ml confectioners' sugar

5 egg whites

Preheat oven to 250 degrees.

In a food processor, combine the almonds, $1/2$ cup of the sugar, the zest, lavender, and confectioners' sugar. Puree until smooth. In an electric mixer, whisk the egg whites until soft peaks are formed. Add the remaining $1/2$ cup sugar and continue to whisk until firm peaks are formed. Whisk for an additional minute and remove from the machine. Fold the dry ingredients into the egg mixture.

On a parchment-lined sheet tray, using a stencil (page 252) you have created ($3^1/2$ inches round), spread the meringue mixture. Bake until light golden brown, 20 to 30 minutes. Remove the disks while still hot. Using a $1/2$-inch metal cutter, cut a hole into the center of each disk. Store in an airtight container.

FROZEN CANTALOUPE PARFAITS

Cantaloupe Sorbet

4 cups / 946 ml diced cantaloupe

$1^1/2$ cups / 354 ml granulated sugar

Juice of $1/2$ lemon

Place sorbet ingredients in a blender and puree until smooth. Pass through a chinois. Process in an ice cream machine according to the manufacturer's instructions. Keep frozen.

FROZEN CANTALOUPE MOUSSE

4 eggs, separated

$3/4$ cup / 177 ml granulated sugar

$1/4$ of the grated zest of 1 orange

1 cup / 236 ml concentrated cantaloupe puree (reduced from 2 cups puree)

2 cups / 473 ml heavy cream

Meringue Crumbs (page 248)

In an electric mixer bowl, combine the egg yolks, $1/4$ cup of the sugar, and the grated zest. Whisk until pale and fluffy, 5 to 6 minutes. Fold in the cantaloupe puree. In a separate mixer bowl, whisk the egg whites until firm peaks are formed. Add the remaining $1/2$ cup sugar and continue to whisk for 1 minute. Whisk for an additional minute. Fold into the egg yolk and cantaloupe mixture. Whisk the heavy cream until firm peaks are formed and fold into the cantaloupe mixture.

Using eight metal oval ring molds 1 inch deep, pipe

the mousse mixture into the bottom of the molds, filling halfway. Place in the freezer to freeze solid.

Once the cantaloupe mousse molds are frozen solid, sprinkle a thin layer of meringue crumbs on top of each mousse. Fill the remainder of the molds with the sorbet and smooth the top. Return to the freezer until ready to use. Reserve rest of sorbet for assembling the dessert.

CANTALOUPE SAUCE

1 cup / 236 ml cantaloupe puree

$^1/_4$ cup / 59 ml granulated sugar

$^1/_8$ teaspoon / .62 ml grated orange rind

$^1/_2$ cup / 118 ml crème fraîche

In a blender, combine the cantaloupe puree, sugar, and grated rind. Puree until smooth. Add the crème fraîche and continue to puree until frothy. Refrigerate.

ASSEMBLY

Cantaloupe balls made with melon baller

Frozen Cantaloupe Parfait

Candied Orange Rind (page 244)

Cantaloupe Sorbet

Lavender Meringue Disks

Honey Tuiles (page 247)

Sugar Garnish (page 253)

Cantaloupe Sauce

In the centers of eight dessert plates, place a small mound of cantaloupe balls. Unmold and place the parfaits on top. Place a few strands of candied orange rinds on top of the parfaits. Add a small scoop of the cantaloupe sorbet on top of the rinds. Rest a meringue disk on top of each cantaloupe sorbet. Decorate with a honey tuile and sugar garnish. Carefully pour the cantaloupe sauce around the border of the plate.

Summer Melon Sorbet Cocktail

FROZEN ORANGE MOUSSE

4 eggs, separated

³/₄ cup / 177 ml granulated sugar

1 teaspoon / 5 ml grated orange rind

2 cups / 473 ml heavy cream

In an electric mixer bowl, combine the egg yolks, ¹/₄ cup of the sugar, and the grated rind. Whisk until pale and fluffy, 5 to 6 minutes. In a separate mixing bowl, whisk the egg whites until firm peaks are formed. Add the remaining ¹/₂ cup sugar and continue to whisk for 1 minute. Remove the whites from the machine and fold into the yolks. Whip cream until firm peaks are formed and fold into the egg mixture.

Place the mousse in a piping bag. Pipe a ¹/₂-inch layer into the bottom of eight martini or similar shaped glasses. Place the glasses in the freezer and freeze until solid, 2 to 3 hours. Keep frozen until served.

CANTALOUPE SORBET

4 cups / 946 ml diced cantaloupe

1¹/₂ cups / 354 ml granulated sugar

Juice of ¹/₂ lemon

Combine ingredients in a blender and puree until smooth. Pass through a fine chinois. Process in an ice cream machine according to the manufacturer's instructions. Keep frozen.

WATERMELON SORBET

4 cups / 946 ml seeded and diced watermelon

1¹/₂ cups / 354 ml granulated sugar

Combine the watermelon and sugar in a blender and puree until smooth. Pass through a chinois. Process in an ice cream machine according to the manufacturer's instructions. Keep frozen.

LEMONGRASS SAUCE

2 cups / 473 ml milk

1 cup / 236 ml granulated sugar

2¹/₂ stalks lemongrass

³/₄ cup / 85 g lemon juice

In a saucepan, combine the milk, ¹/₂ cup of the sugar, and 2 stalks of lemon grass, finely chopped. Place over medium heat and bring to a quick simmer. Remove from the heat and allow to steep for 20 minutes. Place in an ice bath to cool. In a small saucepan, combine the lemon juice, remaining ¹/₂ cup sugar, and remaining half stalk of chopped lemongrass. Bring to a quick simmer. Remove from the heat and steep for 15 to 20 minutes. Place in an ice bath to cool. Once both mixtures have cooled completely, combine them and whisk together. Pass through a fine chinois and keep cold until ready to use.

SERVES 8

A great summer lunch dessert: flavorful, chilled, refreshing, and just the right size. All these components should be prepared one day in advance.

CHEF'S NOTE

When you are preparing the lemongrass sauce, make sure that the lemon juice infusion and the lemongrass milk are cold before whisking them together. If they are not cold, the sauce will curdle and separate.

CRISP ORANGE MERINGUES

¹/₂ cup / 118 ml sliced, blanched almonds

¹/₂ cup / 118 ml granulated sugar

1 teaspoon / 5 ml grated orange rind

¹/₄ cup / 59 ml confectioners' sugar

2 egg whites

Preheat the oven to 250 degrees.

Combine the almonds, ¹/₄ cup of the granulated sugar, the grated rind, and confectioners' sugar in a food processor and puree until smooth. In an electric mixer bowl, whisk the egg whites until soft peaks are formed. Add the remaining ¹/₄ cup sugar and continue to whisk until firm peaks are formed. Whisk for an additional minute and remove from the machine. Fold the dry ingredients into the egg whites.

On a parchment-lined sheet tray, using a stencil (page 252) that you have created (1 inch wide by 3 inches in length), spread the meringue over the stencil. Bake until light golden brown in color, approximately 30 minutes. Remove from the oven and allow to cool. Store in airtight container.

ASSEMBLY

Frozen Orange Mousse

Watermelon Sorbet

Cantaloupe Sorbet

Diced fresh watermelon

Diced fresh cantaloupe

Crisp Orange Meringues

Honey Tuiles (page 247)

Sugar Garnish (page 253)

Lemongrass Sauce

Remove the mousse glasses from the freezer and place two small scoops of watermelon sorbet on top of each mousse. Place a scoop of cantaloupe sorbet on top of the watermelon sorbet. Place the fresh watermelon and cantaloupe dice around the base of the sorbet. Lean a crisp orange meringue against the cantaloupe sorbet. Follow with a honey tuile. Decorate with a sugar garnish and carefully pour the lemongrass sauce over the melon dice.

Three-Layer Chocolate Malted with Ice Cream Bar

CHOCOLATE MALTED IN A GLASS

Dark Chocolate Malted Mousse

$^1/_2$ cup / 55 g milk

$^1/_4$ cup / 55 g unsalted butter

1 cup / 256 ml extra-bitter chocolate

$^1/_2$ cup / 118 ml malt syrup

4 egg yolks

1 cup / 236 ml crème fraîche

1 cup / 236 ml heavy cream

Milk Chocolate Malted Mousse

$^1/_2$ cup / 55 g milk

$^1/_4$ cup / 115 g unsalted butter

$^1/_2$ cup / 118 ml milk chocolate

$1^1/_2$ cups / 354 ml malt syrup

4 egg yolks

1 cup / 236 ml crème fraîche

1 cup / 236 ml heavy cream

Whipped Cream

2 cups / 473 ml heavy cream

$^1/_2$ cup / 118 ml granulated sugar

Place milk, butter, and chocolate for dark chocolate mousse in a double boiler over hot water and stir until melted. In an electric mixer bowl, combine syrup and egg yolks. Whisk for 5 to 6 minutes until pale and fluffy, then fold into melted chocolate. Whip the crème fraîche and cream together until soft peaks are formed, then whisk into the chocolate mixture.

Place mixture in a piping bag. Carefully pipe into eight iced-tea or other tall, thin glasses to fill one-fourth of each glass, about $1^1/_2$ inches of mousse. Place in refrigerator to set firm.

Combine milk, butter, and milk chocolate for milk chocolate mousse in double boiler over hot water until melted. In an electric mixer bowl, combine syrup and egg yolks, whisking 5 to 6 minutes until pale and fluffy. Fold into the chocolate mixture. In another mixer bowl, combine crème fraîche and heavy cream, whisking until soft peaks are formed; whisk into the chocolate mixture.

Place mixture in a piping bag. Carefully pipe the mixture into the glasses with dark chocolate mousse, filling halfway. Place in the refrigerator to set.

In an electric mixer bowl, combine cream and sugar for whipped cream, whisking until stiff. Place cream in a piping bag. Carefully pipe a layer into the glasses over the mousse layers until glasses are three-fourths full. Keep refrigerated.

SERVES 8

A fun party dessert. This one can be prepared in advance, with no last-minute worries.

CHEF'S NOTE

Plastic ice cream bar molds for the sour cream ice cream can be found in super-markets and inexpensive variety stores. They are usually for sale in the summer and are sometimes found in the children's section.

ICE CREAM BARS

Nougat

3/4 cup / 177 ml granulated sugar

6 tablespoons / 85 g unsalted butter

Pinch of salt

Place the sugar for nougat in a heavy pot and cook over medium heat until sugar begins to melt. Stir and cook the sugar until it becomes deep amber. Add the butter and salt and continue to stir, cooking for 1 to 2 minutes. Pour the mixture onto an oiled sheet pan and allow to cool. Once cooled, crush and chop with a knife. Set aside.

Sour Cream Ice Cream

4 cups / 946 ml heavy cream

1 1/2 cups / 354 ml granulated sugar

12 egg yolks

2 cups / 473 ml sour cream

Combine the cream and sugar for ice cream in a saucepan and bring to a boil. Place the yolks in a large bowl. In one motion, pour and whisk the hot cream into the yolks. Stir in the sour cream. Pass the mixture through a fine sieve. Process in an ice cream machine according to the manufacturer's instructions.

While the ice cream is still soft, fold the nougat into the ice cream and place in a pastry bag. Carefully pipe the ice cream into eight ice cream bar molds and place in freezer until half-firm. Insert sticks into ice cream bar. Put back in freezer, and freeze overnight.

Chocolate Coating for Ice Cream Bar

2 cups / 472 ml extra-bitter chocolate

1/2 cup / 118 ml cocoa butter or vegetable oil

1/2 cup / 118 ml dry chocolate cake crumbs

Remove ice cream bar molds from freezer and quickly dip into hot water. Hold the molds in the hot water for 5 seconds, then remove from the water and gently pull the bars out of the molds by the sticks. Place the bars on a new sheet tray and place back in freezer to chill 1 hour.

Chop the chocolate and cocoa butter and combine in a double boiler over hot water, whisking until melted. Pour into a thin, tall cup. One at a time, carefully dip the ice cream bars into the melted chocolate, giving them a coat of chocolate. Lightly sprinkle each ice cream bar with cake crumbs and place back in the freezer on a sheet tray. Keep frozen.

ASSEMBLY

Chocolate Malted in a Glass

Chocolate Cigarettes (page 245)

Ice Cream Bars

Chocolate Tuiles (page 247)

Place each chocolate malted on a plate lined with a paper doily or folded napkin. Place a chocolate cigarette in the chocolate malted. Set an ice cream bar next to the glass. Decorate the plates with the chocolate tuiles.

Lemon-Mango Coupe with Lemongrass Sauce

LEMON-MANGO COUPE

Lemon Custard Base

1 cup / 236 ml lemon juice

1/2 cup / 118 ml granulated sugar

4 whole eggs

2 egg yolks

1/2 cup / 118 ml crème fraîche

Zest of 1 lemon

Mango Filling

2 fresh mangoes, peeled and diced

2 cups / 473 ml crème fraîche

1/2 cup / 118 ml granulated sugar

Preheat oven to 300 degrees.

Combine lemon juice, sugar, whole eggs, and egg yolks in a bowl, whisking until smooth. Pass through a fine sieve. Add the crème fraîche and lemon zest, incorporating well.

Line the inside of a round cake pan 8 inches wide by 2 inches high with plastic wrap. The plastic wrap should be tight on the cake pan. Fill the pan with the custard until 1/2 inch deep. Place the cake pan in a water bath and bake until the custard is set, 30 minutes. Allow to cool, then place in refrigerator.

Cut the custard using eight metal tubes that measure 1 1/2 inches in diameter and 2 inches in height. The custard should remain in the tubes. Place the tubes on a sheet tray.

Lightly sprinkle the diced mango with sugar and gently toss. Place the mango in the tubes on top of the custard. Fill tubes to within 1/2 inch of tops.

In an electric mixer bowl, combine the crème fraîche and sugar for filling and whisk until stiff peaks are formed. Place the mixture in a piping bag. Carefully pipe the crème fraîche into the tubes, filling the remaining 1/2 inch. Smooth the tops. Place the tubes in the refrigerator until ready for use.

MANGO SORBET

4 cups / 946 ml diced fresh mango

1 1/2 cups / 354 ml water

2 cups / 473 ml granulated sugar

Juice of 1/2 lemon

Combine the ingredients in a saucepan and bring to a simmer. Cook for 5 to 10 minutes, remove from the heat, and puree until smooth. Pass through a chinois. Place in an ice bath to cool. Process in an ice cream machine according to the manufacturer's instructions. Keep frozen.

MANGO CHIPS

1 pureed mango

1/4 cup / 59 ml granulated sugar

Preheat oven to 200 degrees.

Create a stencil (page 252). On a nonstick silicone sheet tray, spread the mango puree over the stencil. Sprinkle the puree lightly with the sugar. Bake until

SERVES 8

On their own, fresh mangoes are very flavorful. Still, they can benefit from the acidic touch of lemon and bits of grapefruit. All these components can be prepared one to two days in advance, but leave the fruit preparation until the day you serve it.

dry and crisp, approximately 45 minutes. Remove from the oven and store in an airtight container.

SPRING ROLL TUBES

Vegetable oil, for deep-frying

8 large spring roll wrappers

1/4 cup / 59 ml clarified butter

1/4 cup / 59 ml egg whites

Heat the oil to 325 degrees.

Cut the spring roll wrappers into strips 3 inches wide by 5 inches long. Butter the strips using a brush, leaving 1 inch unbuttered. Using 16 metal tubes 1 inch in diameter by 4 inches in length, roll the wrappers around the tubes. Brush the 1-inch unbuttered portion of the wrappers with egg white and overlap a small portion of wrapper, sealing it. Deep-fry the wrappers until golden brown, 5 minutes, putting metal tubes in the deep-fryer as well. Remove from the fryer and allow to cool slightly. Slide the wrappers off of the metal tubes. Set aside. Store in an airtight container.

SOUR LEMON MERINGUES

1 cup / 236 ml sliced, blanched almonds

1 cup / 236 ml granulated sugar

Zest of 1 lemon

1 tablespoon / 15 ml citric acid

1/4 teaspoon / 1 ml turmeric

1/2 cup / 118 ml confectioners' sugar

5 egg whites

Preheat oven to 250 degrees.

Combine the almonds, 1/2 cup of the granulated sugar, the lemon zest, citric acid, turmeric, and confectioners' sugar in a food processor and puree until smooth. In an electric mixer bowl, whisk the egg whites until soft peaks are formed. Add the remaining 1/2 cup sugar and continue to whisk until firm peaks are formed. Whisk for an additional minute and remove from the machine. Fold all of the dried pureed ingredients into the egg whites.

On a parchment-lined sheet tray, using a small stencil (page 252) that you have created, spread the meringue over the stencil, creating eight disks. Bake until light golden brown, 20 to 30 minutes. Remove from the oven and allow to cool. Store in an airtight container.

LEMONGRASS SAUCE

2 cups / 473 ml milk

1 cup / 236 ml granulated sugar

2 1/2 stalks lemongrass

3/4 cup / 85 g lemon juice

In a small saucepan, combine milk, 1/2 cup of the sugar, and two stalks of lemongrass, finely chopped. Place the saucepan on medium heat and bring to a simmer. Remove from heat and steep for 20 minutes. Place in an ice bath to cool. In a separate saucepan, combine lemon juice, remaining 1/2 cup sugar, and remaining chopped 1/2 stalk of lemongrass. Bring to a

simmer, remove from the heat, and let steep for 15 to 20 minutes. Place in an ice bath and allow to cool completely. Whisk mixtures together and pass through a chinois. Keep the sauce refrigerated until ready to use.

ASSEMBLY

Mango Sorbet

Spring Roll Tubes

Sour Lemon Meringues

Lemon Mango Coupe

Diced fresh mango

Fresh grapefruit pulp

Lemongrass Sauce

Mango Chips

Sugar Garnish (page 253)

Place the mango sorbet in a pastry bag and pipe it into the spring roll tubes. Place two tubes side by side in the center of each of eight dessert plates. Set a lemon meringue on top of the tubes. Unmold the coupes onto the meringues. Sprinkle diced mango and grapefruit pulp around the base of each plate. Pour the lemongrass sauce around the plates. Decorate with mango chips and sugar garnish.

Chocolate-Espresso Cube with Chocolate Sorbet

CHOCOLATE-ESPRESSO CUBES

¹/₂ cup / 118 ml white chocolate, tempered (page 245)

3 cups / 709 ml extra-bitter chocolate, tempered (page 245)

¹/₄ cup / 59 ml milk

¹/₂ cup /118 ml milk chocolate, finely chopped

¹/₂ cup /118 ml extra-bitter chocolate, finely chopped

¹/₄ cup / 55 g unsalted butter, chopped

Grated zest of 1 orange

¹/₄ cup / 59 ml espresso extract

3 egg yolks

³/₄ cup / 177 ml granulated sugar

1¹/₂ cups / 340 g crème fraîche

³/₄ cup / 170 g heavy cream

3 cups / 709 ml diced chocolate cake

For the chocolate cubes, you'll need eight plastic boxes measuring 4 inches in height and 2¹/₂ inches in width. With a small paintbrush, paint a few strokes of the white chocolate on the inside of each box. Allow the white chocolate to solidify. With a slightly bigger paintbrush, carefully paint the entire inside of the chocolate box with the extra-bitter chocolate, covering the white chocolate. Shake out any excess chocolate and allow the chocolate to solidify. Place boxes in refrigerator and keep cool.

In a double boiler, combine the milk, milk chocolate, extra-bitter chocolate, butter, orange zest, and espresso extract. Set over hot water and allow to melt.

In an electric mixer bowl, combine the egg yolks and ¹/₄ cup of the sugar. Whisk for 4 to 5 minutes, until pale and fluffy. Fold into the melted chocolate. In a separate mixing bowl, combine the crème fraîche, cream, and remaining ¹/₂ cup sugar and whisk until soft peaks are formed. Pour the chocolate mixture into the whipped cream and whisk together until blended. Carefully fold in the chocolate cake dice.

Place the mousse in a pastry bag with a large opening and pipe into the chocolate cubes, filling completely. Smooth tops of the cubes and place in refrigerator to set overnight. Refrigerate and leave in molds until ready to serve.

CHOCOLATE-ESPRESSO SORBET

2 cups / 473 ml water

¹/₂ cup / 118 ml espresso beans, crushed

¹/₂ cup / 118 ml granulated sugar

1¹/₂ cups / 354 ml extra-bitter chocolate, chopped

Combine the water, espresso beans, and sugar in a saucepan and bring to a boil. Pour over the chopped chocolate and whisk until smooth. Pass through a chinois to strain. Place in an ice bath to cool. Process in an ice cream machine according to the manufacturer's instructions. Keep frozen.

SERVES 8

The trick to this dessert is to brush on the chocolate to obtain the thinnest shell possible. An extremely thin shell gives the dessert a delicate feel and allows the guests to eat it with minimum effort. All the components should be prepared one to two days in advance for best results.

CHEF'S NOTE

The plastic box for the chocolate-espresso cubes is nothing more than a large chocolate mold. The same rule applies for all chocolate molds: make sure that the molds are dry, polished, and clean of dirt and grease before applying the chocolate. This will help with a clean release.

CHOCOLATE MERINGUES

¹/₂ cup / 118 ml sliced, blanched almonds

¹/₂ cup / 118 ml granulated sugar

2 tablespoons / 29 ml cocoa powder

¹/₄ cup / 59 ml confectioners' sugar

2 each egg whites

Preheat oven to 250 degrees.

Combine the almonds, ¹/₄ cup of the sugar, the cocoa powder, and confectioners' sugar in a food processor and process until smooth. In an electric mixer bowl, whisk egg whites until soft peaks are formed. Add the remaining ¹/₄ cup sugar and continue to whisk until firm peaks are formed. Whisk for an additional minute and remove from the machine. Fold the dry ingredients into the egg whites.

Place the mixture in a pastry bag with a medium-size, round tip. Pipe a small amount of the mixture (about 2 inches in length) onto a parchment-lined sheet tray. Bake for 30 to 45 minutes, until dry. Remove from the oven and allow to cool. Store in an airtight container.

ASSEMBLY

2 cups Chocolate Sauce (page 246)

2 cups Espresso Sabayon Sauce (page 250)

Chocolate-Espresso Cubes

Chocolate-Espresso Sorbet

Chocolate Meringues

Chocolate Tuiles (page 247)

Pipe a zigzag formation of chocolate sauce on each of eight dessert plates. Place dots of sabayon sauce around the borders. Unmold the chocolate cubes off center on the plates. Place an oval scoop of the sorbet on top of each meringue, then place the meringues next to the cubes. Decorate with the chocolate tuiles.

Warm Blueberries in a Strudel Shell with Chamomile Sauce

SERVES 8

The smell of fresh chamomile is terrific. Infusing the flavor captures its aroma without overwhelming the warm blueberries. The sorbet, sauce, and garnishes can be prepared one to two days ahead. The other components should be made the day they are served.

CHEF'S NOTE

If you cannot find fresh chamomile for the chamomile sauce, substitute ½ cup chamomile tea.

BLUEBERRY CAKE

1 cup / 236 ml semolina flour

1 cup / 236 ml all-purpose flour

1 cup / 236 ml granulated sugar

1¼ tablespoons / 18 ml baking powder

½ teaspoon / 2 ml salt

½ cup / 118 ml egg whites

1 cup / 236 ml

Grated zest of 1 lemon

¼ cup / 115 g unsalted butter, melted

2 cups / 473 ml fresh blueberries, lightly dusted with flour

Preheat the oven to 300 degrees. Butter four 3-inch metal rings.

In an electric mixer bowl, combine all the ingredients except the butter and blueberries. Mix until smooth. Add the butter and continue to mix only until incorporated. Carefully fold in the blueberries by hand.

Pour the batter into 3-inch metal rings and bake until firm and light golden in color, 20 to 30 minutes. Allow to cool. Unmold the cakes and carefully slice off and trim the ends. Slice each cake into two ½-inch-thick disks. Set aside and cover.

STRUDEL TUBES

4 sheets strudel dough

½ cup / 118 ml clarified butter

Preheat oven to 350 degrees.

Carefully spread a sheet of strudel dough on a flat surface. Lightly brush with butter and place another sheet of strudel dough on top. Repeat these steps until all four sheets of dough have been used. Cut into eight 2-inch-wide strips. Roll the strudel dough around metal rings 2 inches wide by 3 inches in length. Bake until golden brown in color, 15 minutes. Allow to cool, then slide the tubes off of the rings. Set aside. Store in airtight container.

CHAMOMILE SAUCE

2 cups / 473 ml milk

¾ cup / 177 ml granulated sugar

1 cup / 236 ml chopped fresh chamomile

¾ cup / 85 g lemon juice

In a small saucepan, combine the milk, ½ cup of the sugar, and the chamomile. Bring to a quick simmer, remove from the heat, and steep for 20 minutes. Place the pot in an ice bath to cool.

In a separate small saucepan, place the lemon juice and remaining ¼ cup sugar. Bring to a quick simmer, remove from the heat. Place in an ice bath to cool.

Spray and prepare metal tubes.

Carefully spread and butter a layer of strudel dough.

Place a second layer of strudel dough on top of the first and butter the surface.

Trim the edges of the strudel dough.

Using a ruler or straightedge, cut strips of dough. Use the metal ring as a guide for the width.

Continue to measure and cut strips of strudel dough.

Place a metal tube at the end of the dough closest to you.

Start to roll, moving it away from you. Make sure the edges are aligned as you roll.

Continue to roll the entire strip of dough.

Bake the tubes standing upright on a parchment-lined sheet tray until golden brown. Allow to cool slightly, and slide the strudel tubes off the metal.

Once both mixtures are cooled, whisk together. Pass through a fine chinois, then store in refrigerator until ready to use.

BLUEBERRY PUREE

2 cups / 473 ml fresh blueberries

1/2 cup / 118 ml granulated sugar

Combine blueberries and sugar in a small pan and bring to a quick simmer. Cook until the blueberries are soft, 5 minutes. Puree in blender, pass through a chinois, and place in a squeeze bottle.

BLUEBERRY SORBET

3 cups / 709 ml fresh blueberries

1 1/2 cups / 354 ml granulated sugar

2 cups / 473 ml water

Juice of 1 lemon

Combine ingredients in a small saucepan and bring to a quick boil. Remove from the heat and steep for 10 minutes. Puree until smooth, pass through a chinois, and process in an ice cream machine according to the manufacturer's instructions. Keep frozen.

ASSEMBLY

Blueberry Cake

Strudel Tubes

Vanilla Ice Cream (page 254)

Fresh blueberries

Whipped crème fraîche

Sugar Garnish (page 253)

Blueberry Sorbet

Honey Tuiles (page 247)

Chamomile Sauce

Blueberry Puree

Place a slice of the blueberry cake in the center of each of eight dessert plates. Place a strudel tube on top. Place a scoop of the vanilla ice cream inside each strudel tube. Fill the tubes the rest of the way with fresh blueberries. Pipe a small amount of whipped crème fraîche on top of the blueberries. Place a sugar garnish on top of the tubes. Scoop a small amount of the blueberry sorbet and place it on the sugar garnish. Place a honey tuile on top of the blueberry sorbet. In a small saucepan, heat the fresh blueberries and chamomile sauce until blueberries are warm, then pour around the border of the plate. Decorate the plates with dots of blueberry puree.

Caramelized Banana-Mango Disks with Tamarind Sauce

BANANA-MANGO DISKS

6 bananas

1 mango, peeled, pitted, and diced small

2 tablespoons / 29 ml Tamarind Sauce ▪

Juice of ¹/₂ lime

Peel the bananas and slice lengthwise ¹/₄ inch thick. Lay the banana slices flat and right next to each other, creating a banana sheet. Using eight metal rings 2¹/₂ inches in diameter and 1¹/₂ inches high, cut into the banana sheet. Transfer the banana rings to a sheet pan. Cut the banana scraps into small dice.

Mix equal parts of the mango and the banana dice in a bowl with the sauce and juice. Fill the remainder of each ring with the mixture. Refrigerate.

SERVES 8

Tamarind has a unique, sharp, sour taste. When purchasing, buy tamarind paste that has no salt or use the fresh pods. This dessert may look complex but is actually very simple. It is basically great fresh fruit with accents of tartness. There is no dairy and very little fat. The sauces, chips, meringue, and sorbet can be prepared one to two days in advance, but the fruit preparation should be done the same day you serve it.

▪ **Tamarind Sauce**

1 cup / 236 ml tamarind paste, unsalted

1¹/₂ cups / 354 ml water

³/₄ cup / 177 ml granulated sugar

Combine ingredients in a saucepan and bring to a simmer, then cook until the paste is soft. Puree until smooth. Pass through a fine chinois. Cool in an ice bath. Store in a squeeze bottle until ready to use.

MERINGUE DISKS

¹/₂ cup / 118 ml sliced, blanched almonds

¹/₂ cup / 118 ml granulated sugar

¹/₄ cup / 59 ml confectioners' sugar

2 egg whites

Preheat oven to 250 degrees.

Combine the almonds, ¹/₄ cup of the sugar, and the confectioners' sugar in a food processor and puree until smooth. In an electric mixer bowl, whisk the egg whites until soft peaks are formed. Add the remaining ¹/₄ cup sugar and continue to whisk until firm peaks are formed. Whisk for an additional minute, then fold dry ingredients into egg whites.

On a parchment-lined sheet tray, using a small round stencil (page 252) that you have created, spread the meringue to make 16 disks. Bake until light golden brown in color, 30 minutes. Remove from the oven and allow to cool. Store in an airtight container.

MERINGUE-CRUSTED BANANAS

8 bananas

¹/₂ cup / 118 ml milk

2 cups / 473 ml Meringue Crumbs (page 248)

Peel and cut the bananas into 2¹/₂-inch lengths. Dip the cut bananas into the milk, coating slightly. Bread in the meringue crumbs. (These bananas should be coated just before serving.)

MANGO SAUCE

½ mango, peeled and pitted

¼ cup / 59 ml granulated sugar

Puree the mango and sugar in a blender until smooth. Place in a squeeze bottle until ready to use.

ASSEMBLY

Meringue-Crusted Bananas

Meringue Disks

Mango Sorbet (page 219)

Sugar Garnish (page 253)

Banana-Mango Disks

1 cup Brûlée Sugar (page 244)

Mango Chips (page 219)

Tamarind Sauce

Mango Sauce

Place the crusted bananas side by side in the middle of each of eight dessert plates. Place a meringue disk on top of the bananas. Place a scoop of mango sorbet on top of each disk. Set another meringue disk on top of the sorbet, creating a sandwich. Place a sugar garnish on top of the sandwich. Turn the banana mango rings over so that the sliced bananas appear on top. Sprinkle with brûlée sugar and glaze with a blowtorch. Remove rings and carefully place the disks on top of the sugar garnish. Decorate the plates with mango chips. Squeeze dots of tamarind sauce and mango sauce around the plates.

Glazed Mascarpone and Goat Cheese Custard with Fresh Berries and Toasted Brioche Sticks

MASCARPONE AND GOAT CHEESE CUSTARDS

³/₄ cup / 177 ml mascarpone cheese

³/₄ cup / 177 ml ricotta cheese

³/₄ cup / 177 ml fresh goat cheese

¹/₂ cup / 118 ml granulated sugar

¹/₂ vanilla bean, split in half

Zest of ¹/₂ orange

2 whole eggs

1 egg white

³/₄ cup / 170 g heavy cream

8 disks Sucre Dough (page 253), 3¹/₂ inches in diameter

Preheat oven to 300 degrees.

In a mixing bowl, combine the cheeses, sugar, vanilla, and orange zest. Mix until smooth. Add the whole eggs, egg white, and cream, mixing until smooth. Pass through a sieve.

Place the pastry disks on a parchment-lined sheet tray. Gently indent a 3-inch metal ring into each disk—make sure that the ring does not cut through the disk. Bake the disks with the rings until light golden brown in color, 20 minutes. Remove from the oven and allow to cool slightly. Lower oven to 225 degrees.

Fill rings three-fourths with the cheese mixture. Return to the oven and bake until the cheese is set, 30 minutes. Let cool, then carefully trim around the edges of the metal rings. Remove the rings and set aside. Cover and store in a cool place.

BRIOCHE STICKS

¹/₄ cup / 59 ml milk

2 tablespoons fresh yeast or 1 tablespoon active dry yeast

2¹/₄ cups / 531 ml all-purpose flour

4 whole eggs

1 cup plus 2 tablespoons / 266 ml granulated sugar

1 teaspoon / 5 ml salt

1 cup / 225 g unsalted butter, at room temperature

1 cup / 236 ml fresh raspberries

1 cup / 236 ml diced fresh strawberries

Juice of ¹/₂ lemon

¹/₂ vanilla bean split in half and seeds scraped

In a small saucepan, warm the milk. Add the yeast and ¹/₄ cup of the flour. Whisk until smooth and cover with plastic wrap. Allow to rise in a warm place until doubled in size, about 10 minutes.

Transfer yeast mixture to a large mixing bowl. Add the eggs, remaining 2 cups of flour, 2 tablespoons of the sugar, and the salt. Using a dough hook attachment, mix ingredients until smooth and elastic, approximately 10 minutes. On medium speed, add the butter a little at a time, allowing it to incorporate well each time, then continue to mix ingredients for 1 to 2 minutes. Remove from the machine and cover the dough with a damp towel to rise until doubled in size, 20–30 minutes. Punch dough down and refrigerate for 4 to 6 hours.

Roll dough into a ball and press into an 8-inch round

SERVES 8

Glazing the custard warms the cheese slightly, giving it a soft texture with a crisp sugar coating. The toasted brioche is a perfect accompaniment and the berries add a sweet sharp accent. You can bake the brioche a day in advance, but the other components should be prepared the same day you serve them.

cake pan that is 3 inches high. Cover and allow dough to rise in a warm place for 20–30 minutes.

Preheat oven to 325 degrees. Cover dough with a sheet of parchment paper and lay a flat sheet pan on top. Place in oven and bake until golden brown, about 30 minutes.

Let brioche cool, then remove it from the pan. Cut into ¼-inch-thick layers. You will need 6 layers.

In a small, heavy saucepan, combine the raspberries, strawberries, lemon juice, remaining 1 cup sugar, and vanilla seeds. Cook over a low heat, stirring, until the mixture becomes thick. Allow to cool, then spread a thin layer of berry jam on one layer of brioche, and place a second layer of brioche on top of the layer of jam, creating a sandwich. Repeat three times. Place each sandwich in a toaster oven and allow to toast until golden brown. Allow to cool. Cut each sandwich into sticks 4 inches long and 1 inch wide. Set aside.

MACERATED BERRIES

1 cup / 236 ml fresh raspberries

1½ cups / 354 ml diced fresh strawberries

1 cup / 236 ml fresh blackberries

¼ cup / 59 ml granulated sugar

Juice of 1 lemon

Juice of 1 orange

Combine ingredients in a bowl and gently toss to coat. Allow to sit for 20 minutes before using.

ASSEMBLY

Mascarpone and Goat Cheese Custards

Brûlée Sugar (page 244)

Macerated Berries

Honey Tuiles (page 247)

Brioche Sticks

Sugar Garnish (page 253)

Lightly sprinkle the custards with brûlée sugar and glaze with a blowtorch. Place one in the center of each of eight dessert plates. Place the macerated berries and their juice around the custards. Place a honey tuile on top of the glazed custards. Lean the brioche sticks against the berries and custards. Decorate with a sugar garnish.

Blueberry-Lemon Tartlets

12 disks Sucre Dough (page 253), 2 inches in diameter

1 cup / 236 ml Lemon Curd (page 248)

2 cups / 473 ml fresh blueberries

Confectioners' sugar, for dusting

Preheat oven to 300 degrees.

Line metal tartlet shells with the pastry disks and blind bake until golden brown, about 20 minutes. Remove from the oven and allow to cool completely. Remove from metal shells.

Place the lemon curd in a pastry bag and pipe a small amount into each tartlet shell, filling halfway. Arrange the blueberries on top, stacking them as high as possible. Dust lightly with sugar and serve.

YIELDS 12 TARTLETS

A small taste of sweet summer blueberries and creamy lemon curd rest on a delicate shell. Prepare the dough and lemon curd one day in advance, but bake the shells and assemble the tarts one to two hours before serving.

Lemon Panna Cotta with Peaches

2 cups / 473 ml diced peaches

1 cup / 236 ml granulated sugar

Juice of $\frac{1}{2}$ lemon

1 cup / 236 ml milk

1 cup / 236 ml heavy cream

Zest of 1 lemon

2 sheets gelatin or 2 teaspoons powdered gelatin bloomed in 2 tablespoons water

In a small saucepan, combine the peaches, $\frac{1}{2}$ cup of the sugar, and the lemon juice. Bring to a simmer and cook until soft and thick, 8 minutes. Remove from the heat and allow to cool.

Place a small amount of peach puree in the bottom of eight small ceramic or glass cups 1 inch in diameter, filling halfway. Place in refrigerator.

In a small saucepan, combine the milk, cream, remaining $\frac{1}{2}$ cup sugar, and lemon zest. Bring to a quick boil and remove from the heat. Allow to steep for 15 to 20 minutes.

Soften or bloom the gelatin in cold water and add to the milk mixture. Pass the mixture through a chinois. Allow to cool slightly.

Carefully pour the milk mixture into the cups on top of the peaches. Return to the refrigerator and allow to set.

YIELDS 16

A small creamy layer of panna cotta sits above the intense peach puree. Serve these with a small demitasse spoon so that guests can fully capture both flavors. The peach filling can be prepared, set in the glasses, and refrigerated a day in advance, but the panna cotta should be assembled two to three hours before serving.

CLOCKWISE FROM TOP LEFT: *Roasted Apple Tartlets with Fennel Salad, Milk Chocolate-Dipped Ice Cream Pops, Glazed Beignets with Warm Plum Sauce, and Candied Grapefruit Rinds*

Milk Chocolate-Dipped Ice Cream Pops

2 cups / 473 ml Vanilla Ice Cream (page 254)

2 cups / 473 ml melted milk chocolate

2 tablespoons / 29 ml melted white chocolate

Allow ice cream to soften slightly, then place in a pastry bag. Carefully pipe the ice cream into 1-inch round molds. Place in the freezer. While the ice cream is semi-hard, remove from the freezer and insert 4-inch lollipop sticks. Return to freezer and allow to freeze overnight.

Carefully dip the molds into hot water and remove the ice cream pops. Return to the freezer.

Place melted milk chocolate in a small container. Put melted white chocolate into a piping bag. Remove the ice cream pops one at a time from the freezer and quickly dip into the milk chocolate. Shake off the excess. Before the chocolate hardens, quickly pipe lines of the white chocolate onto the pop over the milk chocolate. Return to the freezer immediately. Keep frozen until ready to serve.

YIELDS 12 BARS

These small fun pops are a great way to sneak something cold into your petit fours selection. These can be prepared in advance, but cover or store in the freezer.

Candied Grapefruit Rinds

2 cups / 473 ml grapefruit rinds cut into large batons

2 cups / 473 ml granulated sugar

1 cup / 236 ml water

Juice of 1/2 lemon

1/2 cup / 118 ml corn syrup

2 cups granulated sugar, for dredging

Place the rinds in a saucepan and cover with water. Bring to a boil and drain. Repeat the process once more. Combine with the sugar, water, and lemon juice in a saucepan. Bring to a boil and add the corn syrup. Continue to boil and cook until the temperature reaches 240 degrees. Remove from the heat and pour the rinds into a strainer to drain.

Spread rinds out on a parchment-lined sheet tray. Allow the rinds to cool an additional 20 to 30 minutes. Dredge in sugar.

YIELDS 15 TO 20 PIECES

I make these year-round. Grapefruit is my favorite citrus to candy. It's meaty, juicy, and not too tart. The rinds can be cooked and stored in an airtight container, undredged. Just dredge them when you need them.

Roasted Apple Tartlets with Fennel Salad (photograph on page 236)

YIELDS 12 TARTLETS

The fennel, lime, and mint add a fresh accent to the smooth, rich apple puree. Prepare the dough and apple puree one day in advance, but bake the shells and assemble the salad and tarts one to two hours before serving.

Roasted Apple Puree

3 Granny Smith apples

1/4 cup / 59 ml granulated sugar

Fennel Salad

1 cup / 236 ml peeled and sliced fennel

Juice of 3 limes

1/4 cup / 59 ml water

1/4 cup / 59 ml granulated sugar

4 mint leaves, minced

Tartlet Shells

12 disks Sucre Dough (page 253), 2 inches in diameter

Preheat oven to 275 degrees.

Peel, core, and quarter the apples. Place on a parchment-lined sheet tray and sprinkle with sugar. Roast until the apples are soft and light brown, approximately 1 hour. Remove from oven and allow to cool. Place apples in a food processor and puree until smooth. Place the puree in a pastry bag. Refrigerate.

Place the fennel in a small bowl or container. Combine the lime juice, water, sugar, and mint and pour over fennel. Allow to sit for at least 1 hour.

Preheat oven to 300 degrees.

Place a pastry disk in each of 12 metal tartlet shells and blind bake until light golden brown, 20 minutes. Remove from the oven and allow to cool.

Carefully pipe the apple puree into the center of each tartlet shell, filling halfway. Drain some of the fennel from the liquid and place a small pile of fennel salad on top of the apple puree. Serve.

Glazed Beignets with Warm Plum Sauce *(photograph on page 236)*

2 tablespoons fresh yeast or 1
tablespoon active dry yeast

2 tablespoons / 30 g milk

1 egg

2 cups / 500 ml all-purpose flour

³/₄ cup / 177 ml granulated sugar

³/₄ teaspoon / 3 ml salt

¹/₂ cup / 118 ml water

2 tablespoons / 30 g unsalted butter

Vegetable oil, for deep-frying

1 cup / 236 ml Brûlée Sugar (page 244)

1 cup / 236 ml diced plums

¹/₂ teaspoon / 2 ml lemon juice

Confectioners' sugar, for dusting

Combine the yeast and milk in a mixing bowl and whisk until the yeast is dissolved. Add the egg, flour, ¹/₄ cup of the sugar, and the salt. In a small saucepan, combine the water and butter and heat until melted. Add to yeast mixture, and mix until incorporated. Refrigerate, allowing to rest for at least 2 hours.

Heat oil to 325 degrees. Roll the dough out on a floured surface until ¹/₂ inch thick. Cut out beignets with a 1-inch round cutter and set on a floured sheet tray. Deep-fry until golden brown, 5 minutes. Remove from the fryer and immediately coat with the brûlée sugar while still hot.

In a small saucepan, combine the plums, remaining ¹/₂ cup sugar, and the lemon juice. Bring to a simmer and cook the plums until soft, 8 minutes. Puree until smooth.

Place beignets on serving dishes. Dust with confectioners' sugar and pipe a small pool of the plum puree next to the beignets. Serve.

YIELDS 12 BEIGNETS

These are small, warm, sugar-crusted beignets with a touch of tart plum sauce for dipping. The dough and puree can be prepared early in the day; fry the beignets and warm the sauce when served.

Strawberry Mascarpone Tartlets

YIELDS 12 TARTLETS

It's hard to beat great strawberries and cream. Placing these elements on an almond snap cookie shell adds another texture. The almond snap cookie shells can be prepared one to two days ahead and stored in an airtight container. Just assemble them one hour before serving.

Almond Snap Cookies

9 tablespoons / 130 g unsalted butter

¼ cup / 59 ml granulated sugar

¼ cup / 55 g corn syrup

½ cup / 115 g honey

¼ cup / 55 ml all-purpose flour

¼ teaspoon / 1 ml lemon juice

1 cup / 236 ml sliced, blanched, and finely chopped almonds

Mascarpone Filling

½ cup / 118 ml mascarpone cheese

¼ cup / 59 ml heavy cream

3 tablespoons / 45 ml granulated sugar

½ vanilla bean, split in half and seeds scraped

8 to 10 fresh strawberries, thinly sliced

In a double boiler, combine the butter, sugar, corn syrup, and honey. Place over hot water to melt. Whisk in the flour, lemon juice, and almonds. Place in a container and allow to cool at least 2 hours in the refrigerator.

Preheat oven to 300 degrees. Create a round stencil (page 252) 2 inches in diameter. Spread the batter over the stencil onto a silicone sheet tray. Bake until golden brown, 20 minutes. Remove while still warm and place into metal tartlet shells to bend into curved tartlet shapes. Remove when cool and store in an airtight container.

In an electric mixer bowl, combine the cheese, cream, sugar, and vanilla seeds. Whisk until stiff peaks are formed. Place the mixture in a piping bag.

Place the cookies on a sheet tray and gently pipe in the filling halfway. Carefully arrange the sliced strawberries on top and serve.

Peach and Vanilla Ice Cream Sandwiches

Linzer Biscuits

1 cup / 236 ml granulated sugar

1½ cups / 354 ml hazelnuts, toasted

1½ cups / 340 g unsalted butter

2 whole eggs

2½ cups / 590 ml cake flour

1 tablespoon / 15 ml ground cinnamon

2 teaspoons / 10 ml baking powder

2 egg whites, lightly beaten

½ cup / 118 ml Brûlée Sugar (page 244)

Candied Peaches

2 medium peaches

1½ cups / 354 ml granulated sugar

1 cup / 236 ml water

Juice of ½ lemon

20 small scoops Vanilla Ice Cream (page 254)

Preheat oven to 300 degrees.

In a food processor, puree the sugar and hazelnuts until smooth. Transfer to an electric mixer bowl and add the butter. Cream until smooth. Add the eggs, flour, cinnamon, and baking powder and blend well.

Roll out the dough until it is ⅛ inch thick. Cut into 1-inch squares. Brush each square with beaten egg white and sprinkle with brûlée sugar. Bake until light golden brown, 20 minutes. Allow to cool completely, then place the biscuits in the freezer.

Cut the peaches in half and remove the pits. Cut the halves into medium dice. In a saucepan, combine the peaches, sugar, water, and lemon juice and bring to a boil. Cook until the temperature reaches 230 degrees. Drain and allow to cool. Refrigerate until ready for use.

Remove the biscuits from the freezer and place a small ball of the vanilla ice cream on one of the biscuits. Place a small mound of candied peaches on top of the ice cream and cover with another biscuit. Press down slightly. Repeat. After making all the cookies, store in freezer until ready to serve.

YIELDS 24 SANDWICHES

Ice cream and cookies are always a winning combination. Add a touch of fruit and it becomes special. You can prepare the ice cream and cookies one to two days ahead. Just assemble two to three hours before serving.

BASIC RECIPES

Almond Cookies

¹/₂ cup plus 1 tablespoon / 100 g unsalted butter

⁷/₈ cup / 207 ml granulated sugar

1³/₄ cups / 414 ml almonds, finely ground

¹/₂ cup / 118 ml all-purpose flour

³/₈ cup / 85 g water

¹/₈ cup / 30 ml almond flour

1 egg white

Preheat oven to 325 degrees.

Combine the butter, sugar, and ground almonds in an electric mixer bowl and cream until smooth. Add the remaining ingredients and mix until blended.

Using a stencil (page 252) that you have created, spread the batter over the stencil and bake until golden brown, 20 minutes. Store in an airtight container.

YIELDS 4 CUPS BATTER, ENOUGH FOR 15–25 3-INCH TO 4-INCH COOKIES

Apple Stock

4 cups / 946 ml diced unpeeled apples

3 cups / 709 ml water

¹/₂ cup / 118 ml granulated sugar

Juice of ¹/₂ lemon

¹/₂ cinnamon stick

Place ingredients in a saucepan and bring to a simmer. Simmer for 10 minutes, then remove from heat and allow to steep for 10 to 20 minutes. Strain through a cloth. Cool in an ice bath. Refrigerate until ready to use.

YIELDS 4 CUPS

Brûlée Sugar

YIELDS 4 CUPS

2 cups / 473 ml granulated sugar

2 cups / 473 ml light brown sugar

Preheat oven to 250 degrees.

Mix the sugars and spread out on a parchment-lined sheet tray. Bake for 15 minutes, remove from the oven, stir and chop the sugar, and return to oven and bake for an additional 20 minutes. Allow to cool, then place in a food processor and puree until smooth. Place in shakers for later use. Store in an airtight container for long-term storage.

Candied Rinds

YIELDS 2 CUPS

2 cups / 473 ml citrus rinds, sliced or diced

2 cups / 473 ml granulated sugar

1 cup / 236 ml water

Juice of ½ lemon

½ cup / 118 ml corn syrup

2 cups granulated sugar, for dredging

Place the rinds in a saucepan and cover with cold water. Bring to a quick boil and drain. Repeat the process. Drain. Add the sugar, 1 cup water, and lemon juice to the rinds, bring to a boil, and add the corn syrup. Boil until the mixture reaches a temperature of 240 degrees. Pour the mixture into a sieve and allow to drain and cool. Spread rinds on a sheet tray to cool further, 20 to 30 minutes. Dredge the rinds in sugar, if desired. Store at room temperature. Store undredged rinds in an airtight container.

Chocolate Garnishes

Tempered Chocolate

4 cups high-quality chocolate couverture, chopped fine

2 to 3 pieces large chunks of chocolate, roughly 2 by 2 inches

Heat saucepan of water to a simmer. Shut off the heat. Place chopped chocolate couverture in a bowl on top of the pan. Melt slowly. Using a thermometer, heat the chocolate until it reaches 110 degrees. Remove the bowl from the pan. Add the large chunks of chocolate to the melted chocolate couverture and stir with a rubber spatula until the chocolate combination cools to 86 to 88 degrees. Remove the large chunks. The chocolate is now ready to use for a variety of purposes, from painting and coating plastic molds to making chocolate garnishes.

Striped Chocolate Cigarettes

Spread a thin amount of tempered dark chocolate on a marble slab. Drag a cake decorator's comb through the chocolate to create lines. Allow the dark chocolate to set slightly, then cover with a thin layer of tempered white chocolate. Allow to set until firm but still pliable. Use a stiff metal spatula or bench scraper to push the chocolate at a 45-degree angle, rolling and curling into "cigarettes." Store in an airtight container in a cool place.

Solid or Striped Chocolate Shapes

Spread a thin layer of tempered white chocolate on top of a clean plastic sheet (acetate) or a thick sheet of foil. Drag a cake decorator's comb to create lines, or simply pipe lines of white chocolate onto the surface. Allow the white chocolate to set slightly, and cover with a thin layer of tempered dark chocolate. Allow to set, then cut into shapes by scoring with a paring knife. For solid chocolate shapes, do the same, but use only one kind of chocolate. Refrigerate and pull the plastic or foil off. Store in an airtight container in a cool place.

Chocolate Sauce

1 pound / 455 g extra-bitter chocolate, finely chopped

¾ cup / 178 ml corn syrup

1½ cups / 354 ml heavy cream

2 tablespoons / 29 ml granulated sugar

¼ cup / 59 ml vegetable oil

½ cup / 118 ml milk

Place the chopped chocolate in a double boiler to melt over hot water.

In a small saucepan, combine the corn syrup, ½ cup of the cream, the sugar, and vegetable oil. Bring to a simmer, then whisk the hot liquid into the chocolate. Whisk in the milk and remaining 1 cup cream. Pour the sauce into a bowl and refrigerate.

When chocolate sauce is needed, allow to come to room temperature or warm in a water bath.

Clear Caramel Sauce

2 cups / 473 ml granulated sugar

1 cup / 236 ml water

Juice of ½ lemon

½ cup / 118 ml corn syrup

1½ cups / 354 ml hot water

In a small, heavy saucepan, combine the sugar, 1 cup water, and lemon juice and bring to a boil. Add the corn syrup and cook until sugar turns deep amber. Carefully add the 1½ cups hot water and bring the syrup back to a boil. Cook until the temperature reaches 230 degrees. Pour into a clean container and cover with plastic wrap. Allow the sauce to cool overnight.

Creamy Caramel Sauce

1 cup / 236 ml granulated sugar

1 cup / 236 ml water

2 cups / 473 ml heavy cream

In a heavy saucepan, combine the sugar and water and bring to a boil. Cook until the sugar is deep amber. Add the cream and whisk together. Bring the sauce back to a boil. Pass through a chinois. Cool the sauce in an ice bath. Refrigerate until ready to use.

The following caramel sauces can be made by adding the desired ingredient to the basic caramel sauce.

Banana Caramel: 1 banana, pureed, added with the cream.

Coconut Caramel: Replace the 2 cups (473 ml) of cream with 1 cup (236 ml) coconut puree and 1 cup (236 ml) cream. Strain the sauce through a chinois. Add ½ cup (118 ml) unsweetened coconut.

Crepes

For crepe ingredients, see specific recipes

Place an 8-inch nonstick sauté pan over medium heat until hot. Lightly butter the pan with clarified butter, then pour 2 to 3 tablespoons of crepe batter into the pan. Tilt and rotate the pan so the batter moves in a circular motion, covering the surface evenly. Cook for about 30 seconds on the first side. Flip the crepe over and cook for only 10 seconds on the second side. Gently remove crepe from the pan; stack crepes with parchment paper separating them to prevent sticking. Cover the stack with a slightly damp cloth until ready for use.

Honey Tuiles

¾ cup / 170 g unsalted butter

⅜ cup / 89 ml honey

1½ cups / 355 ml all-purpose flour

1½ cups / 355 ml confectioners' sugar

3 egg whites

In an electric mixer bowl, cream together the butter and honey. Add the remaining ingredients and mix on a slow speed, then increase speed to high and mix for 5 minutes. Pour into a clean bowl and refrigerate for 1 to 2 hours before use.

Preheat oven to 300 degrees.

Create a stencil (page 252) and spread the batter over it. Bake until light golden brown, 20 minutes. Bend the cookies into the shapes desired while they are still warm. Store in an airtight container.

Chocolate Tuiles: Replace the 1½ cups (355 ml) flour with 1⅜ cups (325 ml) flour and ⅛ cup (30 ml) cocoa powder.

YIELDS 8 CUPS BATTER, ENOUGH FOR 8 SERVINGS

Lemon Curd

1 cup / 236 ml lemon juice

6 whole eggs

6 egg yolks

1 cup / 236 ml granulated sugar

Grated zest of 1 lemon

1 pound / 455 g unsalted butter, chopped

In an electric mixer bowl, combine the lemon juice, whole eggs, egg yolks, and sugar. Whisk until smooth. Pass through a chinois into a second bowl. Add the lemon zest and place in a double boiler over hot water. Whisk and cook for 8 to 10 minutes, until pale and thick. Whisk in the butter, then pour mixture into a clean bowl, cover tightly with plastic wrap, and place in the refrigerator until cool, 1 to 2 hours. Store in refrigerator.

Meringue Crumbs

1 cup / 236 ml granulated sugar

1 cup / 236 ml sliced, blanched almonds

1 cup / 236 ml confectioners' sugar

5 egg whites

Preheat oven to 250 degrees.

In a food processor, combine ½ cup of the granulated sugar, the almonds, and confectioners' sugar and puree until smooth. In an electric mixer bowl, whisk the egg whites until soft peaks are formed. Add the remaining ½ cup sugar and whisk until firm peaks are formed. Whisk for an additional minute and fold in the dry ingredients.

On a parchment-lined sheet tray, spread the meringue evenly until ½ inch thick. Bake until light golden brown in color, 45 minutes. Allow to cool, then break meringue into smaller pieces and crush with a rolling pin. Store in an airtight container until ready to use.

Praline Sauce

½ cup / 118 ml praline paste

1½ cups / 354 ml heavy cream

2 cups / 473 ml Vanilla Sabayon Sauce (page 250)

In an electric mixer bowl, combine the praline paste and ½ cup of the cream, mixing until smooth. Fold in the sabayon sauce. Thin the sauce slightly with the remaining 1 cup cream. Pass through a chinois. Refrigerate until ready to use.

YIELDS 4 CUPS

Puff Pastry

3½ cups / 826 ml bread flour

1 cup / 236 ml cake flour

1 cup / 236 ml water

1½ teaspoons / 7 ml salt

1 tablespoon / 15 ml white wine vinegar

2 ounces / 56 g butter, melted

14 ounces / 396 g butter, cold

In a mixing bowl, combine 3¼ cups of the bread flour with the cake flour, water, salt, vinegar, and melted butter. Mix until a soft dough forms. Do not overmix. Roll the dough into a rectangle, about ½ inch thick. Cover with plastic wrap and refrigerate for 30 minutes.

In a mixing bowl, combine the remaining ¼ cup bread flour with the cold butter. Beat until soft but still cold. The butter mixture should be the same consistency and feel as the dough (above). Remove the rolled-out dough from the refrigerator, and spread the butter mixture over two thirds of the dough, leaving a ½-inch border of unbuttered dough along the edges. Fold the unbuttered third of the dough back over the center third, covering half of the butter. Fold the remaining buttered third on top. Press and seal the edges and corners. Refrigerate for 20 minutes.

Begin the folding process by turning the folded dough so the long side is closest to you. Roll out the dough into a long, wide rectangle, about ½ inch thick. Again fold the dough into thirds and refrigerate it for 20 minutes. You have now completed one set of two folds. Repeat this process until you have completed three sets of folds (six folds total). Make sure to refrigerate the dough for 20 minutes between sets of folds. Give the dough a final 20-minute rest, then roll out to ¼-inch thickness. Cut and bake as desired. Unused dough can be wrapped tightly and frozen.

YIELDS 2 POUNDS DOUGH

Sabayon Sauce

6 egg yolks

½ cup / 118 ml granulated sugar

Flavoring of choice

1 cup / 236 ml heavy cream

1 cup / 236 ml crème fraîche

Combine the yolks, sugar, and flavoring in a double boiler and place over hot water. Whisk until pale and thick, 8 to 10 minutes. Remove from the heat and allow to rest for 1 minute.

In an electric mixer bowl, combine the cream and crème fraîche, whipping until stiff peaks form. Whisk into the sabayon. Pass through a chinois. Place in a squeeze bottle, and refrigerate until ready to use. Chill sauce at least 2 hours before using.

The following flavors of sabayon sauce can be made by adding the desired ingredient to the basic recipe.

Applejack: ¼ vanilla bean, finely chopped, and 2 tablespoons (30 ml) applejack brandy added to the egg base. Fold an additional tablespoon (15 ml) liqueur into finished sauce.

Vanilla: 1 vanilla bean, finely chopped, added to the egg base.

Chocolate: 3 teaspoons (15 ml) cocoa powder, folded into finished sauce.

Espresso: 1 tablespoon (15 ml) espresso extract and 1 teaspoon (5 ml) ground espresso beans, added to the egg base.

Star Anise: 3 tablespoons (45 ml) ground star anise, added to the egg base.

Pear: 2 tablespoons (30 ml) Pear Williams liqueur, added to the egg base. Fold an additional tablespoon (15 ml) liqueur into finished sauce.

Rum: 2 tablespoons (30 ml) dark rum, added to the egg base. Fold an additional tablespoon (15 ml) rum into finished sauce.

Pineapple: ½ cup (118 ml) pineapple puree, added to the egg base.

Lemon-Thyme: 2 tablespoons (29 ml) coarsely chopped fresh lemon thyme, added to the egg base.

Rosemary: 2 tablespoons (29 ml) coarsely chopped fresh rosemary, added to the egg base.

Lemon Verbena: 3 tablespoons (45 ml) coarsely chopped fresh lemon verbena, added to the egg base.

Ginger: 2 tablespoons (29 ml) grated fresh ginger, added to the egg base.

Snap Cookies

1 cup plus 2 tablespoons / 255 g unsalted butter

½ cup / 118 ml granulated sugar

½ cup / 115 g corn syrup

1 cup / 225 g honey

½ cup / 118 ml all-purpose flour

½ teaspoon / 2 ml lemon juice

Combine the butter, sugar, corn syrup, and honey in a double boiler over hot water. Melt and stir together. Add the flour and lemon juice, and stir until blended. Pour into a bowl and place in refrigerator to cool overnight.

Preheat oven to 325 degrees.

Create a stencil (page 252) of your choosing. Spread the batter over the stencil and bake until golden brown, 20 minutes. Once cookies have cooled, store in an airtight container.

YIELDS 4 CUPS BATTER, ENOUGH FOR 40–50 3-INCH TO 4-INCH ROUND COOKIES

Sesame Snap Cookies: Add 2 cups (473 ml) sesame seeds to the batter before baking.

Spice Syrup

1 cup / 236 ml granulated sugar

1 cup / 236 ml light brown sugar

2 cups / 473 ml water

Juice of ½ lemon

1 tablespoon / 15 ml molasses

1 teaspoon / 5 ml ground cinnamon

1 cardamom pod

½ vanilla bean, split in half and seeds scraped

¼ teaspoon / 1 ml ground nutmeg

½ cup / 118 ml dark corn syrup

Place all ingredients, except the corn syrup, in a saucepan and bring to a boil. Add the corn syrup and cook until the sauce reaches 230 degrees. Pour and strain into a clean container and cover with plastic wrap. Allow to stand at room temperature. This syrup can be stored at room temperature.

YIELDS 3 CUPS

Stencils

Stencils are simply shapes cut out of a flat piece of plastic. You can be very creative. Either use stencils with the same shape cutout repeated numerous times or use different stencils to create different shapes. Evenly spread a tuile batter or meringue over them onto a nonstick sheet or pan. Carefully lift and remove the stencils before baking. I can't remember ever intentionally buying plastic for stencils. I have always made them from empty plastic containers and lids. You can do the same. Simply cutout a shape with a sharp knife and trim to create a smooth stencil.

Strudel Crisps

YIELDS ENOUGH
CRISPS FOR 8
SERVINGS, DEPENDING
ON SIZE OF CRISP

8 sheets strudel dough
1 cup / 236 ml clarified butter
1 cup granulated sugar, for sprinkling

Preheat oven to 350 degrees.

Carefully spread a sheet of strudel dough on a flat surface. Lightly brush the dough with the butter. Place another sheet of dough on top. Repeat the process until all eight sheets have been used. Cut the dough into the desired shape. Lightly sprinkle sugar on a parchment-lined sheet tray. Place the dough shapes on the sugar and lightly sprinkle the dough with more sugar. Place a second sheet of parchment paper on top of the dough. Cover with another sheet tray, creating a sandwich. Bake until golden brown, 15 minutes. Allow to cool; store in an airtight container.

Sucre Dough

1 cup plus 2 tablespoons / 255 g unsalted butter

¾ cup confectioners' sugar

1 cup / 236 ml almond flour

2¼ cups / 531 ml all-purpose flour

2 eggs

In an electric mixer bowl, cream the butter, sugar, and almond flour. Add the all-purpose flour and eggs and mix until blended. Do not overmix. Chill for at least 2 hours.

Roll out dough to ⅛-inch thickness. Baking instructions are given for each recipe in which sucre dough is used.

YIELDS 2 POUNDS DOUGH

Sugar Garnishes

2 cups / 473 g granulated sugar

1 cup / 236 ml water

1 cup / 236 ml glucose

In a small, heavy saucepan or a copper pot, combine the sugar and water. Place on high heat and bring to a rapid boil. Add the glucose and cook until the sugar becomes light amber. Remove from the heat and dip only the bottom of the pot in an ice bath for 5 to 10 seconds. Cool at room temperature. The sugar should now have a thick, honeylike consistency. If the sugar becomes too cool, place back over low heat to maintain the proper consistency. Store all sugar garnishes in an airtight container in a cool place.

To make desired shapes, see photos on page 254.

To make spun sugar: Cook and cool the sugar in the same manner as above. Hold two or three forks in your hand. Dip all the forks into the sugar and let the excess drain off. Then gently toss and throw the sugar across a large pot or bowl. Gather the sugar that is hanging over the pot or bowl and form a shape with your hands. Store spun sugar in an airtight container.

YIELDS 3 CUPS

Boil the sugar until light amber in color, 310 degrees.

Allow to cool slightly. Dip a wooden dowel into the sugar. The sugar is ready when it flows off in an even, honeylike consistency.

Dip the dowel in the sugar and draw sugar lines on a lightly oiled marble surface. Allow the sugar to flow off the dowel and form straight lines.

Once the sugar lines have cooled, trim and cut with a sharp-edged spatula.

Allow the sugar to flow off the dowel and draw a waved or zigzag pattern of lines.

Redip the dowel to draw enough lines to cover the marble surface.

Once the sugar has cooled, cut the lines into desired lengths.

Allow the sugar to flow off the dowel, forming small circles.

Trim the excess off the circles and, while they are still warm and pliable, carefully bend and shape them into balls.

Continue to bend and shape all of the circles before they cool.

Vanilla Ice Cream

YIELDS 2 ½ QUARTS

4 cups / 946 ml heavy cream

2 cups / 473 ml milk

1½ cups / 354 ml granulated sugar

3 vanilla beans, split and finely chopped

12 egg yolks

In a large saucepan, combine the cream, milk, sugar, and vanilla beans. Bring to a simmer, remove from heat, and allow to steep for 20 minutes. Place back on the heat and bring to a second boil. In one motion, pour and whisk the hot cream into the egg yolks. Pass the mixture through a fine sieve. Allow to cool. Process in an ice cream machine according to the manufacturer's instructions. Keep frozen.

GLOSSARY
of Equipment, Ingredients, and Terms and Techniques

baking parchment Available in precut sheets and in rolls, baking parchment, which may be silicone-treated or not, is used to make any baking sheet or pan virtually nonstick. It is especially useful for delicate cakes and cookies, such as meringues. It makes cleanup a snap, and it can often be reused. Triangles of parchment can be formed into small cones to make disposable pastry bags for piping icings and similar tasks.

blowtorch A household propane blowtorch, available at any hardware store, is the tool of choice for caramelizing the sugar topping on crème brûlée; it is far easier to use and more efficient than a broiler. Smaller blowtorches are available at some specialty housewares shops, but they use butane instead of propane and seem to leave an aftertaste in the sugar; they also don't get as hot as the less expensive hardware-store type.

brûlée dishes Shallow ceramic oval baking dishes especially designed for crème brûlée result in the perfect ratio of crackly sugar topping to creamy custard; ramekins of the same volume can be substituted, but there will be less surface area available for brûléeing, and the baking time will be longer.

cake pans Good-quality heavy-gauge cake pans give the best results, because they conduct heat more evenly than flimsier pans, and they are more durable as well. Pans with sides that are 2 inches high, rather than the more common 1½ inches, are the most versatile and practical. It's handy to have two or three round pans each in several sizes; the recipes in this book use 8-inch and 10-inch round cake pans. Heavy nonstick cake pans are now available; the nonstick finish may result in a darker crust on certain baked goods.

candy thermometer An accurate candy thermometer is essential for many recipes. A good-quality combination candy/deep-fry thermometer is the most practical type; choose one that can be clipped to the side of the saucepan or pot. Many candy thermometers have handy markings indicating the different stages (from thread to hard crack) of sugar, as well as temperatures from 100 to 400 degrees Fahrenheit.

chocolate molds Chocolate molds are available in a variety of shapes and sizes. When using these molds, make sure that they are impeccably clean, free of grease, and dry before applying the chocolate; this will help ensure that the chocolate shapes are cleanly released from the molds.

cutters Metal pastry cutters come in a variety of shapes and sizes and may be plain or fluted. Round cutters are the most versatile; some of the recipes in this book also call for oval cutters. Although individual cutters are available, nested sets of cutters in graduated sizes are the most practical.

dome molds Spherical dome molds, used in recipes in this book for frozen soufflés and ice cream, are available in plastic and metal. The dome pans resemble a muffin tin with six rounded cups.

flan rings Flan rings, sometimes called tart rings, are ¾-inch-high metal rings with rolled edges that are used for baking tart shells. Stainless steel rings are the most practical, since tinned steel rusts easily. The rings come in a range of sizes, from 4 inches to almost 14 inches; there are also scalloped rings available, and some that are not rings at all, but rectangular in shape. Note that flan rings differ from cake rings, which are taller and do not have turned-over edges.

ice cream bar molds Plastic ice cream bar molds can be found in larger supermarkets and at variety stores; a seasonal item, they are usually sold in the summer.

lollipop sticks Used for several of the recipes in this book, these are available in some supermarkets and variety stores, as well as from baking and confectionery suppliers.

mandolin, or mandoline The hand-operated slicer known as a mandolin is one of the most versatile tools in the kitchen. Fitted with one or more adjustable blades, it can be used to make both paper-thin and thicker slices of fruits and vegetables, julienne strips, and waffle cuts. The classic heavy-duty professional model is made of stainless steel, but less-expensive plastic versions, particularly the razor-sharp Japanese slicer called a Benriner, are perfect for most tasks.

metal pipes and tubes Many of the recipes in this book use specially cut lengths of metal pipes or tubing for molding desserts. Larger plumbing supply stores and some hardware stores should be able to cut these for you. Metal cannoli tubes, which are 1 inch in diameter and about 5½ inches long, can be substituted in certain of the recipes as appropriate; they are available in kitchenware and specialty shops.

nonstick silicone baking sheets Until recently, these baking sheets, also called baking liners or mats, were available only to professionals, but now they are sold in many gourmet shops and through mail-order. The Silpat brand is the most widely available; it is made of flexible glass fibers and silicone and comes in several sizes, to fit most baking sheets. These liners make any baking sheet nonstick, no matter how delicate (e.g., macaroons) or sticky (e.g.,

caramel) the food baked on it; they withstand temperatures up to 500 degrees, and they can be used thousands of times. Thin nonstick fiberglass or Teflon liners are also available; some of these come in rounds and squares as well as rectangles, and although not quite as durable as the silicone liners, can be used dozens of times.

pastry bag and tips A pastry bag with a set of assorted tips has many uses, from shaping cookies or confections to decorating cakes and pastries. A pastry bag without any tip at all, or with a large plain tip, makes it easy to pipe out fillings as well as many batters and doughs. Heavy plastic-lined canvas bags are the easiest to clean, but unlined canvas bags are somewhat more flexible and may be preferable for certain jobs; lighter, easy-to-clean nylon bags are also available, and there are even packages of disposable clear plastic pastry bags, which can be cut to size as necessary. Pastry bags come in sizes from 7 to 24 inches long; the 14- to 16-inch lengths are the most practical, but it's handy to have a smaller bag or two in addition. Metal pastry tips, or tubes, come in an array of sizes and shapes; they are available individually and in sets.

ramekins These individual ceramic molds look like miniature soufflé dishes. They are used for custards, both sweet and savory, and other desserts, many of which are baked in a water bath. Ramekins come in sizes ranging from 3 to 7 ounces in volume and from 3 to about 4 inches in diameter.

ring molds Sometimes called entremet molds, ring molds are the smaller relatives of cake rings (see *flan rings,* above). Used for assembling a variety of desserts, these smooth stainless steel bands come in a wide range of diameters Most are about 1½ inches high, though special 2⅜-inch-high rings are also available.

small savarin molds These smaller versions of the ring-shaped mold used for the sweet yeast cake known as a savarin can be used for individual-sized cakes such as financiers, among others.

sheet pans Heavy-gauge sheet pans, or baking sheets, that conduct heat evenly and will not warp are the best choice. The sheet pans used in professional kitchens come in two sizes; the so-called half-sheet pans, which are 12½ by 17½ inches and 1 inch deep, the size of a large jelly-roll pan, are practical in home kitchens as well. (Strictly speaking, baking sheets are rimmed pans with four sides, while cookie sheets have only one or two sides or lips; many pastry chefs use sheet pans for everything.)

squeeze bottles Plastic squeeze bottles can be used to create decorative designs and garnishes with sauces and syrups. They are available in many drugstores and cosmetics departments, as well as housewares shops.

strainers Sieves and strainers are essential for smooth sauces and purées. A chinois, or China cap, is a conical strainer that may be made of perforated metal, usually stainless steel, or of wire mesh that can range from ultrafine to medium-coarse; fine ones are used for straining ice cream bases, purees for fruit sorbets, and gelatin-based mixtures, among others. Most of these long-handled sieves have a bracket attached so that they can be set over a deep bowl or other container for ease of use. A drum sieve, or tamis, is a flat round sieve with either a metal or wooden frame; it is useful for such tasks as removing skin and seeds from fruit purees.

tart and tartlet pans Tart and tartlet pans, or tins, come in a wide variety of shapes, sizes, and finishes; in the recipes in this book, the smaller versions are referred to as tartlet shells. Round tart pans range in diameter from 4 to $12\frac{1}{2}$ inches; rectangular and square tart pans are manufactured in several different sizes. Tartlet shells, or petit four molds, range from about 1 inch to $3\frac{1}{2}$ inches in diameter. Tart pans with removable bottoms are the most useful; tartlet pans are made as one-piece shells. Most professionals prefer black steel (sometimes called blued steel) tart pans, which produce a well-browned crust; tinned steel and nonstick steel pans are also available.

terrine molds and loaf pans Although terrine molds are generally longer and thinner than loaf pans, the two names are often used interchangeably. The most common sizes of loaf pans are 9 by 5 by 3 inches and $8\frac{1}{2}$ by $4\frac{1}{4}$ by $2\frac{1}{2}$ inches, but mini pans and other sizes are available too. The classic terrine mold is about 4 by $12\frac{1}{2}$ inches, but terrines are manufactured in many sizes—and shapes, including a long U-shaped mold. Loaf pans are made of various metals and from heatproof glass; terrine molds were originally made of earthenware, but metal, including enameled cast-iron, ceramic, and glass terrines are also widely available.

timbale molds Timbale molds, also referred to as dariole or baba au rhum molds, look like tin cups with slightly flared sides. They are made of tinned steel or stainless steel and come in several sizes, ranging from 2 to 4 ounces in volume and from 2 to $2\frac{3}{4}$ inches high.

INGREDIENTS

almond flour See *nut flours*, below.

almond paste A mixture of finely ground blanched almonds, confectioners' sugar, and glucose or corn syrup, almond paste is available in many supermarkets as well as gourmet shops. It is similar to marzipan, but slightly grainier and less sweet. Once opened, it should be tightly wrapped in plastic wrap and stored in the refrigerator, where it will keep for up to 6 months.

cake crumbs Several of the recipes in this book call for chocolate cake crumbs. They are easy to make from reserved cake trimmings: Spread them out on a sheet pan and let them dry overnight in a 200-degree oven. Then process until finely ground in a food processor; store, tightly covered, at room temperature until ready to use.

chocolate The recipes in this book use a variety of different chocolates: extra-bitter, bitter, semisweet, milk, and white. All chocolate except white chocolate is made from chocolate liquor, the bitter paste made by blending and processing cocoa beans, and, usually, sugar and other ingredients. Unsweetened chocolate, sometimes called baker's chocolate, contains only chocolate liquor. Bitter and semisweet chocolates, both of which are considered dark chocolates, also contain varying amounts of sugar, additional cocoa butter, vanilla (or the artificial flavoring vanillin), and, usually, a minute amount of lecithin, an emulsifier, for smoothness. Milk chocolate is sweet chocolate with the addition of milk solids. White chocolate doesn't contain any chocolate liquor (and, according to the USDA, cannot legally be called chocolate). The best "white chocolates" are made from cocoa butter, sugar, milk solids, and vanilla; inferior brands don't contain any cocoa butter and are essentially sweetened vegetable fat—these are sometimes labeled confectionery coating or summer coating.

The amount of chocolate liquor in a specific type of chocolate determines how "chocolaty" and deeply flavored it is. Although the USDA regulates the minimum amount of chocolate liquor each type must contain, it does not require manufacturers to list this percentage, or the amount of cocoa butter, on their packaging. Most European chocolatiers do label their packages this way, and some American chocolatiers have begun to adopt the practice. Unsweetened chocolate, as mentioned above, is 100 percent chocolate liquor; bittersweet and semisweet chocolates must be at least 35 percent chocolate liquor. Milk chocolate must have at least 10 percent chocolate liquor. Many good-quality chocolates contain much more chocolate liquor—up to 70 percent or more, in some cases—than the minimum required, as well as added cocoa butter. Try different brands to see which you prefer. High-quality chocolates are now available in some supermarkets as well as gourmet shops and through mail-order.

Store chocolate, well wrapped, in a cool, dry place (not the refrigerator), away from any foods with strong odors. Bittersweet and semisweet chocolates can be kept for up to a year; milk and white chocolate are more perishable, and shouldn't be stored for more than 6 months.

citric acid Citric acid is a flavoring agent derived from citrus juices, among other sources. It is available at some drugstores and from specialty suppliers. In some recipes, lemon juice (to taste) can be substituted for a similar effect.

cocoa butter Cocoa butter is the vegetable fat contained in cocoa beans. It is available from specialty suppliers and through mail-order.

cocoa powder Cocoa powder is made from chocolate liquor (see *chocolate*, above) that has had most of its cocoa butter removed. Dutch-processed cocoa powder has had an alkali added (unsweetened cocoa powder is mildly acidic), which darkens its color, mellows its flavor, and makes it dissolve more easily. Most European cocoa powder is Dutch-processed. Some of the recipes in this book use black cocoa, a very dark, rich cocoa powder; it is available from some baking suppliers and through mail-order.

coconut, unsweetened Unsweetened coconut is available at some health food stores and through mail-order.

eggs The recipes in this book call for U.S. Grade A large eggs. Always use eggs that are as fresh as possible. When buying eggs, avoid any with cracked or dirty shells; store them in the coldest part of the refrigerator. Because there is a very slight possiblity of the salmonella bacteria in some eggs (the yolks are more likely to carry the bacteria than the whites), desserts and other dishes made with raw eggs should not be served to older people, infants, pregnant women, or anyone who has a compromised immune system. Salmonella bacteria are killed by heat, so bringing eggs to a temperature of 160 degrees, or holding them at 140 degrees for at least 3 minutes, renders them safe. Another alternative is to use pasteurized eggs and egg products. Pasteurized liquid eggs and egg whites and dried egg white powder are increasingly available at supermarkets, as well as through specialty suppliers and mail-order sources.

To separate eggs: Eggs are most easily separated when they are cold, but egg whites whip to the greatest volume when at room temperature. For recipes that call for separated eggs, separate the refrigerator-cold eggs, then let the whites stand at room temperature for 10 to 15 minutes before whipping them.

extracts Use only pure vanilla, almond, and other extracts. Espresso and coffee extracts, as well as other more unusual extracts, are available from baking suppliers and through mail-order.

flour The recipes in this book use all-purpose, cake, bread, and semolina flours, as well as various nut flours (see *nut flours*, below). All-purpose and cake flours differ in their gluten, or protein, contents: All-purpose flour is a blend of high-gluten hard-wheat and low-gluten soft-wheat flours, with a relatively high protein content (10 to 13 grams per cup; better-quality all-purpose flours tend to be higher in protein than most supermarket brands). Cake flour is made from low-gluten soft wheat and has a much lower protein content (about 8 grams per cup); it is also finer than all-purpose flour. All-purpose and cake flour cannot be used interchangeably, but if necessary, you can substitute 1 cup less 2 tablespoons unsifted all-purpose flour for each 1 cup sifted cake flour in a recipe. Bread flour is made almost entirely from high-gluten hard wheat (with a protein content of about 14 grams per cup). Semolina flour is ground from high-gluten durum wheat; do not confuse fine semolina flour with the coarser semolina used for polenta.

gelatin A thickening agent, gelatin is available both in granular, or powder, and sheet form; the sheets are preferred by many pastry chefs. Powdered gelatin must be softened (or "bloomed") in cold water before using and then dissolved in a hot liquid; sheet gelatin is simply softened in cold water, drained, and squeezed dry before using. Powdered gelatin is available in any supermarket; gelatin sheets can be found in specialty markets and through mail-order sources.

glucose Glucose is a liquid sugar that is about half as sweet as granulated sugar. Because it doesn't crystallize nearly as readily as regular sugar does, it is used in sorbets, icings, and many other sweets, as well as in the Sugar Garnishes used in these recipes.

kaffir (kafir) lime leaves These unusual-looking double-lobed, shiny leaves, from a small Southeast Asian citrus tree (they are sometimes called wild lime leaves), are intensely aromatic. The fresh leaves are occasionally available in Asian markets, or look for them in small packages in the freezer section. Avoid the dried leaves, which have little flavor.

kataifi dough Kataifi, also called kadair, is shredded phyllo dough, used both as a component in some desserts and as a garnish. It is available from mail-order sources.

licorice root powder The ground dried root of the licorice plant, licorice root powder can be found in health food stores.

malt syrup Malt syrup, also called malt extract, is a natural sweetener made from corn and barley; it is slightly less sweet than honey. Malt syrup is available in health food stores and some supermarkets.

nut flours Almond, pistachio, and other nut flours are made from very finely ground nuts. Natural almond flour, called for in some of these recipes, is made from unblanched (natural) almonds. Nut flours are available from specialty suppliers and at some gourmet markets and health food stores.

nut oils Walnut, pistachio, and other nut oils are available at specialty markets and some supermarkets, and through mail-order. Because nut oils are highly perishable, they are best purchased in small quantities and used as soon as possible.

pistachio flour See *nut flours*, above.

pistachio oil See *nut oils*, above.

pistachio paste Pistachio paste, like praline paste (see below) is a mixture of finely ground nuts and sugar. It is available from baking suppliers and through mail-order.

praline paste A sweet mixture of ground hazelnuts, or sometimes hazelnuts and almonds, and caramelized sugar, used in many pastries and other sweets. It is available at some gourmet shops as well as from baking suppliers and mail-order sources.

strudel dough Strudel dough is available in Hungarian and other central European markets and from some baking suppliers. If necessary, phyllo dough, which can be found, refrigerated or frozen, in many supermarkets, can be substituted.

tamarind paste Tamarind paste comes from the pulp of an Asian fruit tree; it has a unique sweet-sour taste. Available in ethnic and specialty markets, it must be dissolved in liquid before using. Be sure to buy unsalted tamarind paste.

verjus Made from the juice of unripe green grapes, white verjus is an ancient flavoring that has recently been rediscovered. It is available at some gourmet markets and from specialty suppliers. In some recipes, muscato or plum wine can be substituted for verjus.

vanilla beans Vanilla beans are the intensely fragrant pods of an orchid native to Latin America, Tahiti, Madagascar, and Mexico. Tahitian vanilla beans, the type used for the recipes in this book, are especially aromatic. Vanilla beans are perishable and should be stored, tightly wrapped, in the refrigerator or freezer.

For most recipes, vanilla beans are split before they are used. The split bean can then be used as is, or the tiny dark seeds, which look like a paste more than individual seeds, scraped out and both the pod and seeds, or just the seeds, added to a liquid to be flavored or to other ingredients.

yeast Either fresh or active dry yeast can be used in the recipes in this book. Fresh yeast, also called compressed fresh yeast, comes in small crumbly cakes; it is available in the refrigerator section of some supermarkets as well as from baking suppliers. It is highly perishable and should be stored in the refrigerator for no more than a week or two or frozen. Active dry yeast comes in small envelopes and jars; it is less perishable than the fresh, but it should also be refrigerated.

zest Zest is the colored part of the rind of a citrus fruit; the underlying white pith is bitter and should be avoided. Zest can be removed with a grater, a vegetable peeler, or a sharp paring knife, or the special tool known as a zester (which removes the zest in thin strips), depending on the use. For grated zest, the new rasp-type graters are especially handy.

TERMS AND TECHNIQUES

blind bake To blind bake means to prebake—partially or entirely—a tart shell or piecrust before filling it. Most tart and tartlet shells are blind baked. To blind bake a tart or pie shell, roll out the dough, fit it into the tart or pie pan, and chill it for at least 30 minutes. Preheat the oven to the specified temperature, line the shell with parchment or foil, and fill with dried beans or rice, or pie weights. Bake for 10 to 15 minutes (or the time specified in the recipe), until the dough is set, then remove the liner and weights and continue baking until the shell is just baked through or until golden brown, depending on the recipe. Small tartlet shells do not usually need to be lined and weighted before baking. Cool any baked shells on a wire rack before proceeding with the recipe.

clarified butter Clarifying butter removes the milk solids, which brown and burn at high temperatures, from butter. Clarified butter has many uses. Brushing strudel dough with clarified butter rather than whole butter prevents dark specks from appearing on the baked dough; clarified butter can also be used for sautéing at a higher temperature than whole butter.

When clarifying butter, it is best to start with at least ½

pound (although you can clarify smaller amounts if you are careful). Cut the butter into chunks and melt it in a heavy saucepan over low heat; the milk solids will separate and drop to the bottom of the pan. Skim the foam from the top, and carefully pour the clear liquid through a fine strainer, leaving the milk solids behind (or simply pour the liquid, without skimming it first, through a strainer lined with cheesecloths, which will catch the milk solids and other residues). One pound of butter will yield about 12 ounces clarified. Clarified butter keeps for weeks in the refrigerator, and it can be frozen for several months.

deglaze Deglaze means to add a liquid, such as wine, stock, or even water, to a pan in which food has been cooked and stirring the liquid over heat to release the caramelized brown bits left on the bottom of the pan. The deglazing liquid is then used to add flavor to the recipe, often serving as the base of a sauce.

ice bath An ice bath, a mixture of ice cubes and water, is used to cool a hot food or ingredient quickly, preventing further cooking. Ice cream bases, for example, and other custard mixtures, are usually cooled in an ice bath to prevent the eggs in the base from overcooking and curdling. Fresh herbs that have been blanched are cooled in an ice bath both to prevent overcooking and to preserve their green color. See also *shock*, below.

quenelle Classically, the French word *quenelle* referred to delicate oval-shaped seafood, chicken, or meat dumplings that were poached in stock; today, the term is used to refer to any mixture or ingredient shaped into an oval. The traditional quenelle was formed using two spoons and was roughly triangular in shape, but those in the recipes in this book, and in most contemporary restaurant kitchens, are formed using only one spoon, resulting in a smooth, sleek appearance.

Quenelles may be shaped using a soupspoon, tablespoon, or demitasse spoon, depending on the desired size. Dip the spoon in hot water, then place the edge of the spoon into the food—such as ice cream or a whipped cream mixture—and pull it down and through the food in a smooth motion (sort of as if you were using an ice cream scoop) to create a smooth oval, and release it onto the serving plate.

shock In culinary terms, to shock means to quickly cool an ingredient that has been blanched or cooked in order to stop the cooking, and, often, to set its color. Usually the ingredient is plunged into an ice bath, although occasionally just cold water will do.

stencils Many of these recipes use stencils for shaping batters, doughs, and other mixtures. For instructions on making a stencil, see page 252. To use the stencil, place it on a sheet pan and, using a spatula, preferably an offset one, spread the batter or other mixture evenly in a thin layer within the stencil. Carefully lift the stencil up, and repeat to make more shapes.

tempering Tempered chocolate has been melted and cooled to specific temperatures to stabilize the cocoa butter in the chocolate. It has a smooth and a glossy sheen, and it snaps cleanly when broken. Any chocolate you buy is already tempered, and there is no need to temper chocolate for baking or cooking; however, chocolate used for candy making and for certain decorative uses must be tempered. For instructions, see page 245, which gives directions for what is sometimes called the "quick-temper method"; it is easier than the classic multistep melting and cooling method and reliable as well.

toasting nuts and seeds Toasting nuts and seeds brings out their flavors; in addition, hazelnuts must be toasted in order to remove their skins.

To toast nuts, spread them on a baking sheet and toast in a 350-degree oven for 10 to 15 minutes, or until fragrant and lightly golden, stirring once or twice.

To skin hazelnuts, toast as directed above. Wrap the hot nuts in a kitchen towel and rub briskly to remove as much of the brown skins as possible, or place the hot nuts in a sieve and rub them against the wire mesh to remove the skins.

To toast seeds, or a small amount of nuts, place in small dry skillet over low heat and heat, stirring or tossing constantly, until fragrant and lightly colored—a few minutes for seeds, slightly longer for nuts. Transfer to a plate (so they will not continue to cook in the hot skillet) and let cool.

using a blowtorch A blowtorch is the best way to caramelize and glaze the sugar topping on crème brûlée. Sprinkle an even layer of brûlée sugar (page 244) on the surface of the custard. Hold the blowtorch at an angle several inches above the top of the custard and melt and caramelize a portion of the sugar at a time, moving the torch as necessary to prevent scorching or burning. Sprinkle another even layer of brûlée sugar on top of the custard, and repeat the process until the custard is nicely caramelized.

water bath Custards and other egg-based dishes are often baked in a water bath to protect them from the direct heat of the oven and to allow them to cook evenly. To set up a water bath, place the baking dish or dishes (e.g., crème brûlée dishes or ramekins) or baking pan in a larger baking pan or roasting pan, without crowding, and add enough very hot water to come one-third to halfway up the sides of the baking dish(es) or pan. Depending on the recipe, the baked item may be cooled in the water bath or removed from it to cool.

SOURCES

Bridge Kitchenware
214 East 52nd Street
New York, NY 10022
212-688-4220
www.bridgekitchenware.com
ring molds, flan rings, and other professional baking and kitchen equipment of all kinds

Chef's Catalogue
3215 Commercial Avenue
Northbrook, IL 60062
800-338-3232
www.chefscatalog.com
professional baking and other kitchen equipment

The Chef's Collection
10631 S.W. 146th Place
Miami, FL 33186
800-596-CHEF
professional baking and other kitchen equipment

Dairyland USA
311 Manida Street
Bronx, NY 10474
718-842-8700
chocolate, Tahitian and other vanilla beans, and other specialty ingredients

Dean & Deluca
Catalog Center
8200 East 34th Street Circle North
Building 2000
Wichita, KS 67226
www.deananddeluca.com
800-221-7714
specialty ingredients of all kinds

Fillo Factory
P.O. Box 155
Dumont NJ 07628
800-653-4556
www.fillofactory.com
kataifi

Fresh & Wild
2917 Northeast 65th Street, #1
Vancouver, WA 98663
800-222-5578
dehydrated/dried corn

Kalustyan's
123 Lexington Avenue
New York, NY 10016
212-685-3451
www.kalustyans.com
tamarind paste, extracts, and other specialty ingredients

King Arthur Flour Company
The Baker's Catalogue
P.O. Box 876
Norwich, VT 05055
800-827-6836
www.KingArthurFlour.com
specialty flours, black cocoa, unsweetened coconut, extracts, and other baking ingredients; baking equipment

La Cuisine Kitchenware
3223 Cameron Street
Alexandria, VA 22314
800-521-1176; 703-836-4435
vanilla beans, extracts, and other specialty ingredients; baking and other kitchen equipment

New York Cake and Baking Distributors
56 West 22nd Street
New York, NY 10010
212-675-CAKE
candy-making and other specialty ingredients; molds and other baking equipment

Penzeys Spices
P.O. Box 933
Muskego, WI 53150
800-741-7787; 414-679-7207
www.penzeys.com
vanilla beans, extracts, and spices of all kinds

J. B. Prince
36 East 31st Street
New York, NY 10016
800-473-0577
www.jbprince.com
molds, cutters, Silpats, and other professional baking and kitchen equipment

G. B. Ratto & Company
International Grocers, Inc.
821 Washington Street
Oakland, CA 94607
800-325-3483
specialty ingredients

Sur La Table
Catalogue Division
410 Terry Avenue North
Seattle. WA 98109
800-243-0852
www.surlatable.com
baking liners, molds, and other baking and kitchen equipment

Sweet Celebrations
7009 Washington Avenue South
Edina, MN 55439
800-328-6722
www.sweetc.com
chocolate and other molds, other candy-making and baking equipment

Albert Uster
8211 Gaither Road
Gaithersburg, MD 20877
800-231-8154
www.auiswiss.com
pistachio and almond paste, other specialty ingedients

Williams-Sonoma
P.O. Box 7456
San Francisco, CA 94120
800-541-2235
www.williamssonoma.com
chocolate, cocoa, and other specialty ingredients; baking and kitchen equipment

Wilton Industries
2240 West 75th Street
Woodridge, IL 60517
630-963-7100
www.wilton.com
specialty baking ingredients; lollipop sticks, molds, cake pans, and other baking equipment

INDEX